sexual issues in marriage

Sexual Behavior—*edited by Leonard Gross*

Sexual Behavior—Current Issues:
An Interdisciplinary Perspective

Sexual Issues in Marriage
A Contemporary Perspective

sexual issues in marriage

A Contemporary Perspective

Edited by LEONARD GROSS
with foreword by CARLFRED B. BRODERICK

 S P Books Division of

SPECTRUM PUBLICATIONS, INC.
New York

Distributed by Halsted Press
A Division of John Wiley & Sons

New York   Toronto   London   Sydney

Articles reprinted from Sexual Behavior® April, May, June,
July, August, September, October, November (1971); January, February,
March, April, May, July, August, September, October (1972);
© 1971, 1972, Interpersonal Publications, Inc.

Published by SPECTRUM PUBLICATIONS, INC.
            86-19 Sancho Street, Holliswood, N.Y. 11423

Distributed solely by the Halsted Press Division of
John Wiley & Sons, Inc., New York.

Library of Congress Cataloging in Publication Data

Gross, Leonard, comp.
    Sexual issues in marriage.

    (Sexual behavior)
    "Articles reprinted from Sexual behavior."
    CONTENTS: Cuber, J.F. Sex in five types of marriage.
— Bernard, J. [et al.] How to make marital sex more excit-
ing. — Sex conflicts in young marrieds — discussion moder-
ated by J.L. Schimel. [etc.]
    1. Sex in marriage.   2.   Marriage — United States.
I. Title.
HQ21.G688 1975   301.41'76'45   75-1345
ISBN 0-470-32811-8
ISBN 0-470-32814-4 pbk.

Foreword

Of all the contexts in which sexual activities may occur marriage is among the least frequently studied. A survey of both historic and contemporary sexual research reveals a clear bias in favor of more exotic settings. For Krafft-Ebing it was the prison and the asylum, for Freud the nursery, for Masters and Johnson the laboratory and for others still the college campus, the bordello, or the gay pad. Perhaps this should not surprise anyone since, after all, in marriage sex is not only *permitted,* it is *required.* Thus, the fact that the vast majority of all human copulation takes place between husbands and their wives becomes a negative incentive for study. What anthropologist with the whole world before him would choose to study his own neighborhood?

I remember taking part in a symposium some years ago at a professional meeting on the topic of sex. The subject matter had been systematically divided among the three participants. One was to review the literature on premarital sex, one the material on extramarital sex and one the state of our knowledge on just plain marital sex. You may imagine which topic went to the one who drew the short straw and how hard he had to work to find enough material to fill his allotted thirty minutes. (Thank heaven for Terman and Kinsey who, though more intrigued by other matters, conscientiously collected and reported relevant data.) During the extended discussion period following the formal presentation every question was directed to the other two panelists.

In view of all this, the editor is bold indeed to bring out a volume dealing with sexuality in contemporary marriage. It is perhaps self evident why the emphasis is on the "contemporary" rather than on the "marriage." One wishes to avoid the implication that this is one of those books that a well meaning aunt might give us as a wedding present. Thus, after the opening chapters on how sex functions in different types of marriages, the remainder of the volume is devoted primarily to discussion of extramarital affairs, swinging, multilateral arrangements and liberated marriages. The editor is to be congratulated on the even handed way in which he insured that a wide variety of value positions were presented in discussing these ongoing issues. Irrespective of the reader's own point of view he will find wisdom here (and foolishness, for one man's wisdom is another's foolishness).

If I have one reservation growing out of my own value system it is that perhaps an undue number of the contributors to this volume make the assumption that a monogamous relationship is intrinsically dull and stultifying. Even those who defend the institution tend to argue that it need not be quite so bad if you work at it. Nowhere did I see represented the concept that well founded relationships may mellow and grow out of their own internal richness. Nowhere did I see security, possessiveness, familiarity, and exclusivity evaluated as positive rather than as negative qualities of a sexual relationship. Yet many experience them as such.

In any case, reader, you have a feast before you. Eat, enjoy!

Carlfred B. Broderick
Los Angeles

January 1975

Preface

When I proposed to the publisher that we issue a book dealing with sex in marriage, he replied "Terrific! We'll save a lot of money printing a book of blank pages!" This reminded me of the old cliché that the way to get a woman to stop desiring intercourse is to marry her! (Today it might more aptly be applied to men.)

In this so-called liberated age there is a growing feeling that marriage, rather than being the basis for sexual relations and relationships, is the very antithesis. Indeed, there is a tendency to view marriage itself as a dying institution. This happens not to be true, but it is a sentiment fostered by some of the sexual trends.

Of considerable weight is the increased tendency to engage in sex relations before marriage (a large majority of unmarried women and almost all men do so) and to live with someone of the opposite sex while in college (about a quarter of all students, according to two recent studies). More significant than engaging in premarital sex, which has been fairly common in this society since World War I, is today's phenomenon of making no secret about doing so. Until the present generation the stated (though frequently violated) credo was that sex was reserved for marriage, and was the dangling grape certain to make the enamored male leap into matrimony. Mothers warned daughters "he'll never buy what he can get free." Now that so many daughters are "giving it away" — eagerly! — the tempting but untrue syllogism is that:

    a) People marry in order to have sex relations

    b) Sex is now available without marriage

    c) Marriage will disappear.

Another consideration which for many indicates the demise of marriage as a way of life is the extent of marital strife and the consequent high divorce rate, which has doubled in each of the past two 30-year periods. However, the latter indice is deceptive in that it reflects discontent with a particular marriage rather than with the marital life style, since most divorced persons remarry. Regarding marital unhappiness, it no doubt has risen as expectations of rewards from marriage, including sexual satisfaction, have risen. Just as creature comforts generally have been pursued avidly in recent decades, the marital institution too has been suffused if not burdened with the hedonistic spirit, which includes pop psychology goals for "self-fulfillment." Hence, couples who manage to maintain a home, raise and educate children, and get along reasonably well and lovingly may now not be satisfied and experience unrest over new ambitions symbolized if not inculcated by *Joy of Sex* as well as the consciousness-raising movement. I mention this not out of a lack of sympathy for the individual with little tangible to complain about who is nonetheless stricken with malaise and the fear of having made a poor set of choices with his/her one shot at life. However, from a historic standpoint, such people are lacking what can only be considered mind-boggling luxuries, and may be demanding more of marriage to another human being than that human can hope to provide. Yet, they cannot be blamed because American mythology (women's magazines, advertising) indeed has promised them a rose garden.

The secularization of modern society also fosters the seeking of sociosexual happiness, within and without marriage, and makes easier the disruption of marriage in the course of this quest. In fact, some theorists believe that we are in a state of anomie at present, in which the traditional social program of romance-courtship-marriage is gradually being replaced by an extended format which includes cohabitation before marriage and marriage being followed by divorce and remarriage. (One envisions the marital vow "till *divorce* do us part.") They have termed this pattern "serial monogamy."

The Women's Liberation Movement, in just a few years, has had significant impact on consciousness of sex roles in relation to marriage. For many people, the women's movement has had the unfortunate effect of denigrating the home-making role for women, and thus, instilling or rationalizing moral outrage for existing discontent. The solution I would prefer to abandonment of that role or scorn for it is that advocated by Eleanor Maccoby, among others — genuine respect for the role of mother and homemaker. This would seem preferable, in terms of the merits of the position and in the effects of preserving marriages and families intact — avoiding the host of demonstrable difficulties, ranging from poverty to delinquency to poor school performance to which single-parent children seem more prone (see "The origins of alienation" by Urie Bronfenbrenner, *Scientific American*, August 1974 and "The Invisible American Father", Chapter 21 in this volume). Hopefully, the parents and children would be happier too. Those women who pursue jobs, if not careers, which includes almost half of all *mothers* today, do so under considerable strains, which include home responsibilities, poor opportunities for advancement, and role conflict. Necessity, desire, and the perfect right to be there place women in the job market, yet they are simultaneously punished for their presence there.

Clearly, people today are at a crossroads. Obeying primordial urges as well as the social program to mate (and copulate), they are, in modern society, confronted with many dilemmas. The romantic fable on which we have been reared depicts us as simple souls looking for *True Love*. Once love is found, we wed and live happily ever after. At no time in the past were we prepared for the host of obstacles to wedded bliss discussed in the chapters of this volume — not that these problems didn't exist so much as that we thought it immoral to discuss or anticipate them. Today's kids, exposed to more realistic outlooks, including TV "soap operas" and TV generally, as well as divorces of relatives and neighbors, probably will have a more tempered optimism in love-matrimony matters than generations before them.

Some social scientists, such as Slater *(The Pursuit of Loneliness,* 1970) and Friedenberg ("Current patterns of generational conflict," *J. Soc. Issues,* 1969) suggest the need in our postindustrial age for new values rather than adhering to traditions appropriate for more stable eras and environments, which were essentially agricultural, and organized around the extended family network. Generational conflict is inevitable in a society where higher education, mobility, and affluence tend to separate generations. The authoritarian father and the rules of behavior he represented have lost potency. Hence, traditional sexual proscriptions are questioned if not flouted, whether these refer to premarital sex, fidelity to one's mate, or assumption of sex roles within marriage. Individual personality needs are now recognized (if not revered) so that *a priori* rules that husbands do this and wives do that are being critically reexamined in millions of psyches and households. In the absence of firm guides for behavior there are severe contests of wills in many marriages.

In this urbanized, depersonalized and bureaucratized society, it is exceedingly difficult for the individual to gain a sense of efficacy — to feel *important*. Unable to influence so many vital forces, we are in a sense infantalized and deprived of adult status. Among the common reactions are rebelliousness and overinvolvement with the singular person we can affect, usually the spouse. The marriage relationship becomes the repository for multiple needs and hopes. When more is asked of another than that person can provide, there is frustration and conflict — a prevalent situation in marriage today. One considerable source of frustration is the glorification of sexual pleasure which tends to make many feel unhappily confined with their own sexual relationship.

It will be fascinating to observe what will occur over the next decade as the battle against Victorianism is called to an end and the dust settles. By then, ideologies will have been tested and new standards possibly adopted, though there is always the possibility that individualism and a chaotic pluralism will prevail. Interestingly, *Time* magazine recently (Nov. 25, 1974) cited several indications that sexual *avant garde*-ism is retreating. These include less interest in "swinging" (see Chapter 17) and decreased sales of pornography. Gilbert Bartell is quoted as saying, ". . . these are unsettled times. There's a more somber feeling among people, a retreat from sexual frivolity."

At any rate, people have always sought sexual happiness, have bonded or become "as one" (Robinson Jeffers, in a poem to his dead wife, writes, "Do I miss you? / No, I don't miss you. / I am mutilated. / For you were part of me."), and have always irked each other in the process (T.S. Eliot, in a poem, called his wife "My consistent critic."). These are human endeavors with the potential for the greatest human happiness and drama, and therefore worth documenting.

Leonard Gross
New York

January 1975

Contributors

Helene S. Arnstein, author of YOUR GROWING CHILD AND SEX (Avon) and Vice President of the Child Study Association of America.

Jessie Bernard, Ph.D., Professional Women's Caucus, Washington, D.C., and Department of Sociology, Pennsylvania State University.

Irving Bieber, M.D., Department of Psychiatry, New York Medical College, New York City.

Henry Biller, Ph.D., Department of Psychology, University of Rhode Island, Kingston.

Sharon Price Bonham, Ph.D., Department of Sociology, University of Tulsa, Oklahoma.

Israel W. Charny, Ph.D., Clinical Psychologist, Israel, author MARITAL LOVE AND HATE (Macmillan).

Gordon Clanton, Ph.D., Department of Religion, Rutgers University, New Brunswick, New Jersey.

Sylvia Clavan, Ph.D., Department of Sociology, Saint Joseph's College, Philadelphia, Pennsylvania.

Yehudi A. Cohen, Ph.D., Department of Anthropology, Livingston College, Rutgers University, New Brunswick, New Jersey.

Richard Connelly, Ph.D., Family Life Department, Oregon State University, Corvallis.

Joan M. Constantine, Family Therapist, Center for Family Change, Acton, Massachusetts.

Larry L. Constantine, School of Medicine, Tufts University, Medford, Massachusetts.

John F. Cuber, Ph.D., Department of Sociology, Ohio State University, Columbus.

Leo Davids, Ph.D., Department of Sociology, York University, Downsview, Ontario, Canada.

James E. DeBurger, Ph.D., Department of Sociology, University of Louisville, Kentucky.

Duane Denfeld, Ph.D., Department of Sociology, University of Connecticut, Storrs.

Max Deutscher, Ph.D., Department of Psychiatry, Roosevelt Hospital; William Alanson White Institute of Psychiatry, Psychoanalysis, and Psychology, New York City.

Jan Ehrenwald, M.D., Department of Psychiatry, The Roosevelt Hospital, New York City.

Albert Ellis, Ph.D., Institute for Advanced Study in Rational Psychotherapy, New York City.

O. Spurgeon English, M.D., Department of Psychiatry, Temple University School of Medicine, Philadelphia, Pennsylvania.

Warren Farrell, Department of Sociology, Brooklyn College of the City University of New York; author of THE LIBERATED MAN (Random House).

James L. Framo, Ph.D., Department of Psychology, Temple University, Philadelphia, Pennsylvania.

Janet Zollinger Giele, Ph.D., Sociologist and Fellow, Radcliffe Institute, Cambridge, Massachusetts.

Ruby H. Gingles, M.S., Department of Human Development and the Family, University of Nebraska, Lincoln.

Martin Goldberg, M.D., Department of Psychiatry, Family Study Division, University of Pennsylvania School of Medicine, Philadelphia.

Steven G. Goldstein, Ph.D., Departments of Psychology and Psychiatry, University of Vermont, Burlington.

Ralph G. Greenson, M.D., Department of Psychiatry, University of California School of Medicine, Los Angeles and Foundation for Research in Psychoanalysis, Beverly Hills.

James L. Hawkins, Ph.D., Department of Sociology, Indiana University-Purdue University at Indianapolis.

Melvin S. Heller, M.D., Department of Psychiatry, Temple University School of Medicine, Philadelphia, Pennsylvania.

Harold Hiatt, M.D., Department of Psychiatry, University of Cincinnati School of Medicine, Ohio.

Warren L. Jones, M.D., Southern California Psychoanalytic Institute, Los Angeles.

William M. Kephart, Ph.D., Department of Sociology, University of Pennsylvania, Philadelphia.

Reese Danley Kilgo, Ph.D., Department of Education and Sociology, University of Alabama, Huntsville.

Judith Long Laws, Ph.D., Departments of Sociology and Psychology, Cornell University, Ithaca, New York.

Rev. Hunter Leggitt, Council on Population and Environment, Chicago, Illinois.

Rebecca Liswood, M.D., Marriage Counselor and Department of Physical Education and Health, Adelphi University, Garden City, New York.

David R. Mace, Ph.D., Department of Family Sociology, Behavioral Sciences Center, Bowman Gray School of Medicine of Wake Forest University, Winston-Salem, North Carolina.

Thomas C. McGinnis, Ed.D., Department of Health Education, Graduate School, New York University, New York City.

Lonny Myers, M.D., Department of Medical Education, Midwest Population Center, Chicago, Illinois.

Herbert A. Otto, Ph.D., National Center for the Exploration of Human Potential, San Diego, California.

Margaret M. Paloma, Ph.D., Department of Sociology, University of Akron, Ohio.

James A. Peterson, Ph.D., Department of Sociology, University of Southern California, Los Angeles.

Eric Pfeiffer, M.D., Department of Psychiatry, Duke University Medical School, Durham, North Carolina.

Dorothy Riddle, Clinical Psychologist and Department of Social Sciences, Richmond College, City University of New York, Staten Island.

Robert Rimmer, author of THE HARRAD
EXPERIMENT (Bantam) and PROP-
OSITION 31, (Signet).

Leon Salzman, M.D., Department of
Psychiatry, Albert Einstein College of
Medicine and Bronx State Hospital,
New York City.

John Scanzoni, Ph.D., Department of
Sociology, Indiana University,
Bloomington.

John L. Schimel, M.D., William Alanson
White Institute of Psychiatry,
Psychoanalysis and Psychology, and
Department of Psychiatry, New York
University School of Medicine, New
York City.

John J. Schwab, M.D., Departments of
Psychiatry and Medicine, University
of Florida, Gainesville.

David E. Smith, M.D., Haight-Ashbury
Free Medical Clinic, San Francisco,
California.

James R. Smith, M.A., Department of
Political Science, University of
California, Berkeley.

Lynn G. Smith, M.A., Graduate Student,
Department of Psychology, University of California, Berkeley.

Jetse Sprey, Ph.D., Department of Sociology, Case Western Reserve University, Cleveland, Ohio.

Calvert Stein, M.D., Department of
Psychiatry, Graduate School, Spring-
field College, Massachusetts.

Marijean Suelzle, Ph.D., Candidate, Department of Sociology, University of
California, Berkeley.

Carolyn Symonds, M.A., Marriage Counselor, San Bernardino, California.

Clark E. Vincent, Ph.D., Behavioral Sci-
ences Center, The Bowman Gray
School of Medicine of Wake Forest
University, Winston-Salem, North
Carolina.

Silas Warner, M.D., Psychiatric Consultant, Swarthmore College and Department of Psychiatry, University of
Pennsylvania School of Medicine,
Philadelphia.

Robert N. Whitehurst, Ph.D., Department
of Sociology, University of Windsor,
Ontario, Canada.

CONTENTS

Preface
Foreword by Carlfred B. Broderick, Ph.D.

PART III
EXTRAMARITAL SEX

PART IV
NEW MARITAL
LIFE STYLES

Articles reprinted from Sexual Behavior® April, May, June, July, August, September, October, November (1971); January, February, March, April, May, July, August, September, October (1972); © 1971, 1972 Interpersonal Publications, Inc.

sexual issues
in marriage

PART I

Sexual Relationships in Marriage

1. Sex in Five Types of Marriage

JOHN F. CUBER

There is increasing agreement among both specialists and know-ledgeable laymen that sexual behavior is highly variable as to fre-quency, form, and importance in total life style.

Not quite so well known is the growing recognition that these various sexual styles may all be not only workable but gratifying to the people who practice them. It may, however, not be enough merely to know that various sexual styles exist and work, the important point is that they do not exist and work in a vacuum. Rather, they exist and work within a more total life fabric for each individual or pair. Nor are these patterns totally random; they fall into types which are repeated over and over again by persons and couples of similar overall marital life styles.

In a recent study we were able to identify five marital configura-tions, all of which occurred with marked frequency, all of which were the expressions of successful marriages in the sense that they were enduring and there appeared no particular likelihood that they would break up. The sexual sides of these couples' lives, while varying greatly from type to type, each fulfilled in its own unique way the sexual needs of the couple and in most instances contributed in one way or another to the total viability of the marriages.

Conflict-habituated

Probably the most dramatic of the five types is the *conflict-habituated* marital mode. As the phrase suggests, these couples

3

encompass in their lives a high amount and intensity of conflict, mostly but not exclusively verbal. As one man put it, "You know, it's funny; we have fought from the time we were in high school together . . . It's like a running guerrilla fight with intermediate periods . . . of pretty good fun and some damn good sex . . . It's hard to know what it is we fight about most of the time. You name it and we'll fight about it."

Practically everybody knows at least a couple or two who more or less fit this picture. Commonly the erroneous assumption is made that these couples are on the brink of divorce or at least estrangement, and the notion that these people may have a somewhat gratifying sexual fulfillment borders on incredibility. This is understandable for persons who operate from a conception of love, and that affection, tenderness, kindness, and similar sentiments are the more normal expression of love and an integral part of the sexual experience. Obviously for some people this is an accurate model of the interrelationship of sentiment, personal interaction, and outward behavior, but for the conflict-habituated life is organized quite differently and the role of sex is different too.

First of all, the conflict-habituated pair are not necessarily lacking in a sense of relationship which can accurately be called love. They simply express their concern and even admiration for each other in unconventional ways. A classic hyperbole of this pattern is to be found in Edward Albee's *Who's Afraid of Virginia Woolf?* The verbal combat of Martha and George can hardly be matched in vigor, vulgarity, or color. Yet, one sees from time to time in the interaction depicted in this play evidences of concern for each other, and even occasional gentleness and tenderness.

Not only is there no necessary incongruity between conflict and love, nor need there be between the two of these and sexual expression. Quite generally it is recognized that "making up after a fight" is, for many people, a highly gratifying and fulfilling sequel to what was earlier a nasty verbal encounter. The conflict-habituated apparently do not make the more conventional connections which popular stereotypes embrace among love, congenial interaction, and sexual gratification.

Passive-congenial

A second and far more prevalent type we have called the *passive-congenial*. These are relatively quiet, orderly couples who for the most part do the things they are supposed to do, like raising children, attending to their jobs and community responsibilities. Psychologically, they tend to be low on affect, high on sense of responsibility, and place considerable emphasis upon being reasonable and fair and on reputation and conventional expectations. As far as sex is concerned, they are not all alike by any means. One prevalent subtype appreciates the sexual aspect of life but holds it in close check, because sex is a dangerous emotion which gets people, especially young people, into a lot of trouble. It is logical, therefore, to avoid sexual excess either in frequency, intensity, or creativity. As a consequence, sex tends to be not only minimized, but routinized, and the well adjusted passive-congenial is for the most part quite content with this.

A passive relationship is sufficient to express the sexuality of two people who have never cared about each other deeply, or whose interests and creativity are directed elsewhere than toward the male-female relationship—careers, children, or community activities. A rather typical passive-congenial husband describes marriage as "the proper way to live. It's convenient, orderly, and solves a lot of problems. But . . . I spent nearly ten years preparing for the practice of my profession. The biggest thing to me is the practice of that profession." He sees sex as a natural need, and marriage as the natural and safe place in which to express sexuality and fulfill any felt need.

Many women, too, are content with "stable, meaningful things like home and children" and learn to accept "a life of quite modest fulfillments so far as spousal intimacy is concerned." Some feel that sex is simply not important in the total scheme of their lives and are happy with husbands who are "not too demanding."

So the passive congenials range from a "sensible view of sex—after all, life is more than one big bedroom," to those who could be called apathetic rather than just sensible. As they describe themselves, they "can take it or leave it." And beyond the apathetic are those who for one reason or another seem to be *anti* sex. This presents no particular problem if the spouses happen to agree, but such is not always the case. As one woman complained, "How are you supposed to have decent sex with a man who sees nothing really good or fun about it? He 'performs' . . . in a routine, unimaginative way . . . Whenever he talks about sex, his resentment gets through more than anything else . . ." For some of these people sex is almost a scapegoat for what's wrong with the world—especially among the young. If they favor sex education at all, and some do, it is for the purpose of instructing young people about the dangers of pregnancy, venereal disease, etc.

One should not infer from these brief descriptions that the passive-congenial couple cannot have a satisfactory sex life. Even though sex is somewhat apathetic, and tends to be regarded as a necessary concession to man's carnal nature or as a duty to a spouse, many couples are quite compatible and satisfied with these views. Such persons often seriously lament the current openness of sexual conversation and its portrayal in artistic and entertainment media. They sometimes act as if sex is a kind of ridiculous curse which has been visited on the human race, except, of course, for reproduction. The evidence leads me strongly to the view that so long as marriages combine men and women for whom these conceptions seem to be appropriate guidelines for life, their sex can be satisfying and fulfilling (even though when viewed from a more aggrandizing perspective, they seem to be missing a great deal and to have sublimated one of life's finest potentials).

Devitalized

The next type, the *devitalized*, appear to be very much like passive-congenials in their present circumstances and many of their attitudes toward sex, but there is one important difference. The devitalized marriages were once otherwise. Sex was once an important life experience. There was *joie de vivre.* But for familiar reasons this happy state of affairs did not last for long. A growing number of studies document the fact that for many of these couples the big change came with the first pregnancy or at least after the birth of the first child. Presumably this is due not merely to the necessary demands of an infant and the necessary changes in life style but from the preoccupation of the wife, and possibly the husband too, with parenthood rather than spousehood. I strongly suspect that for many women, who may be ambivalent about a vigorous sex life but have in the past enjoyed it, the convenient excuse of having to be responsible to the children provides a rationale for de-escalating the earlier sexual vigor.

Devitalization, of course, is not only due to children. Many couples would not have been able to sustain the vitality in any case. And certainly there are childless couples who find themselves, after a few years of marriage, in a devitalized relationship.

One of the interesting and sometimes saddening aspects of the devitalized sex life is the sequence of crescendoes and diminuendoes in sex which dots their personal landscape. Because they have known better days and may from time to time yearn for them, they make efforts to recapture the earlier ecstasy—vacations without the kids, anniversary celebrations with extra effort, contrived coziness with a self-conscious awareness of the sexual purpose. Because they have emerged from an earlier sexually aggrandizing experience, the devitalized show more unevenness in their sex patterns than do the passive-congenials. And sometimes, without necessarily working at it, there are occasional moments when the old *joie* seems to be there again. An evening with old friends, a visit to an important place, or a particular musical or recreational experience almost spontaneously tosses them back to the earlier fulfillment. But then the mood or the opportunity passes and the malaise returns.

Sometimes improvisations work very well and are momentarily rewarding, at other times they are dismal failures: "It was worth less than nothing." In my own counseling experience I have known numerous cases in which divorces occurred because one of the couple was willing to acquiesce to the devitalized mode, accepting it as an appropriate pattern in this later stage of marriage, and the other was unwilling or unable to settle for the sexual atrophy.

One woman who accepted the devitalized style of her life said, "Judging by the way it was when we were first married . . . things are pretty matter-of-fact now—even dull . . . We take each other for granted. We laugh at the same things sometimes, but we don't really laugh together—the way we used to. But, as he said to me the other night—with one or two under the belt—'You know, you're still a little fun now and then!' . . . Now I don't say this to complain, not in the least. There's a cycle to life . . ."

But a husband in a similar type of marriage explained his feeling as follows. "I know it makes me sound immature or like I didn't respect my age (53) but all of a sudden . . . I began to yearn for the kind of life I had briefly in the early years . . . The balance was tipped when I got to know Jean. That really reminded me of what I had stamped out of my life over the years . . . Anyway, we tried it as an affair for a while and the nearer we got to playing husband and wife, the more I wanted it for real. I paid pretty dearly . . . As the world sees prices . . . but it's the best investment I ever made. If there's anything I'm bitter about, it's those long wasted years . . ."

The devitalized marriages, then, are peopled by those who really believe it to be an appropriate mode for the middle years, those who accept the condition somewhat grudgingly because "there is still occasionally something there," and those who chafe at their sexual circumstance whether or not they overtly do something about it. Doing something about it may involve a series of more or less enduring extramarital affairs, occasional sexual flings with or without the knowledge of the spouse, or a total reorganization of one's sexual life with a new marriage—which is vital, for a time at least.

✓ital

In sharp contrast to all of the foregoing is the relationship which we have called the *vital* marriage. Couples in the vital marriage are deeply involved psychologically in each other and in the aspirations and values which the mate holds. The marriage is intrinsic; it is not utilitarian in its context of values. It is the most important and sustaining fundamental fulfillment of life.

As one couple said, "The things we do together aren't fun in themselves—the ecstasy comes from being together in the doing." The presence of the mate is indispensable to the feelings of satisfaction which the activity provides, and they find their central satisfaction in the life they live with and through each other. Sex, for these men and women, is usually highly important and their comments demonstrate it. "It's not only important; it's fun." "It seems to be getting better all the time."

Not only does sex tend to be solid pleasure for them, it is generally pleasure *at home*. Most of them are monogamous; when they are not there is an openness and honesty between the pair. Some are simply emancipated, almost bohemian. "After all, we're broadminded." "We're certainly not Victorian in these days, and as long as we're honest with each other whose business is it anyway?" To some of them sexual aggrandizement is an accepted fact of life. Frequently infidelity is condoned by the partner—some even say it is *not* infidelity since the behavior is known and accepted by the spouse. And in some instances the so-called infidelity even provides an indirect (through empathy) kind of gratification. The act is not construed as disloyalty or as a threat to continuity, but rather as a kind of basic human right which the loved one ought to be permitted to have—and which the other perhaps wants also for himself.

If a cross section of today's "swingers" could be studied according to relationship type, I strongly suspect that the vitals would constitute a large number of them, closely followed by the *de*vitalized. The motives, of course, would be different. The devitalized would be seeking to restore the *joie* of the marital relationship or to compensate for the lack thereof. The vital pairs would simply see swinging as an honest way of permitting and participating in a sexually aggrandizing experience.

Total

The fifth marital type which we studied we called the *total* relationship. This is much like the vital except that the vitality extends to virtually all important life foci. There is no pretense between them, no areas of tension; "It is as if neither has, or has had, a truly private existence." This kind of relationship is, of course, very rare, but it does exist. In its sexual aspects it differs from the vital in one important way, that is that they are not only monogamous but fiercely so. "You can't draw the line between being in bed together and just being alive together. You touch tenderly when you pass; you wait for the intimate touch in the morning . . ." "I don't understand these references to the sex *side* of life. It *is* life . . ."

Outsiders often see the total relationship as oppressively close and the partners as "too psychologically dependent on each other." Certainly the criteria and the demands of such a relationship are high and must be sought and cherished by the mates equally. Infidelity in any sense is a serious breach and extends beyond the sexual realm, as the testimony of one man indicates.

"It's not the great thing it once was if her interests take her away from *me*. If she'd rather spend even a few evenings looking for culture somewhere else then something has gone wrong with *us*. And it's not enough that she still loves me and that sex is as good as ever. There's a little break in the dike and I know it."

Certainly, many in other types of marriages wouldn't even notice, let alone care about, separate interests in nonsexual matters, but the essence of the total relationship is precisely that—the *totality* of the life sharings within the pair. For those who can be so remarkably mated that their oneness sustains them both, their sexuality pervades their lives with an added richness of which they are both constantly aware.

Because of the close linkage of a rich sex life and a vital or total relationship, it is sometimes assumed that the marriages are vital or total *because* sex is good. This may possibly be the case, but my own analysis puts the causality the other way. Obviously, of course, persons with sexual disabilities will not necessarily find them dissipated because they have found a vital relationship in other life dimensions. But granted a somewhat normal even if not yet fully awakened sexuality, a man or woman in a vital interpersonal relationship is likely to come to enjoy rich sexual fulfillments as a consequence.

It should be remembered that the marriages which formed the basis for this typology had endured a minimum of ten years and the spouses were of middle age. A substantial number had been married previously, and reported overwhelmingly that the advantages of the

Note: Quotes are from the study reported in THE SIGNIFICANT AMERICANS: A STUDY OF SEXUAL BEHAVIOR AMONG THE AFFLUENT, John F. Cuber and Peggy B. Harroff. Appleton Century, New York, 1965. Also published as SEX AND THE SIGNIFICANT AMERICANS, Penguin Books, 1966.

current marriages of whatever type over previous ones was that they were now mated with persons similar to themselves in these respects. I am sure that in a random sample of new marriages, one would not find nearly as much agreement between the spouses as to what marital type and sexual life style they find satisfying and fulfilling. In a broad sense, many if not most divorces are the result of persons who disengage themselves from one marriage to become involved in another which they think will be more compatible to their sexual-psychological wants and needs.

Comment by:
Dorothy I. Riddle
Dr. Cuber makes a point of emphasizing that "sexual styles . . . exist and work within a total life fabric" but gives us little insight as to what that more global relationship would look like. The criterion used in selecting the marriages to be described equates success with endurance, as though it were the number of days spent together that mattered rather than the quality of the interaction on those days.

Also, Dr. Cuber never defines what is meant by sex and is never explicit about exactly what behaviors characterize any given group; let me suggest that he is really describing two related but somewhat independent dimensions: (1) how couples express affection (i.e., sexuality very broadly defined); and (2) how intensely they are involved with each other.

If Dr. Cuber is actually saying that there are several styles for "good marriages," then he should be committed to feeling that couples can be equally affectionate but express it traditionally or nontraditionally; and he should also be committed to feeling, for example, that couples can relate to each other both possessively and nonpossessively while still having a "healthy" relationship.

Dr. Cuber began by calling all of these five marriage styles successful, which would seem to imply that they are all equally viable and valid. But he has managed to describe them in such a way that value judgments peek through. Look, for example, at the titles he has chosen: Conflict-habituated, Passive-congenial, Devitalized, Vitalized, and Total. Now would anyone say that these are equally interesting groups to belong to? It is hard to imagine anyone identifying himself or herself with the "Devitalized" group with pride, or to say with pleasure, "Congratulations on being a Passive-congenial couple." Dr. Cuber may be describing five successful marriage patterns, but his labels make it pretty clear that he has his favorites, and that any marriage counseling would probably reflect that.

Not only do his labels reflect biases, but the points he elaborates on as salient, or neglects to mention as important, also reflect biases. Let me point out in summary fashion value traps into which Dr. Cuber has fallen:

In failing to define sex and sexuality, he has implicity neglected the tactile (e.g., stroking, caressing, snuggling) and nonverbal (e.g., intimate eye contact, a sensing of another's needs and desires), in favor of explicit sexual activity.

His male bias in favor of heterosexual penile intercourse ultimately leads to an endless search for the perfect orgasm as the best expression of sexuality. Since many women are not so genitally fixated and get little orgasmic pleasure from simple penile insertion, they become by definition reactionary or conservative regarding sex. In actuality, the "feminine" emphasis on a more total definition of sexuality, which he puts down as being "ambivalent about a vigorous sex life," is a fuller expression of that total life fabric with which he is concerned.

He has failed to comment on how these "successful" (only, I might point out in terms of endurance) marriages compare with "unsuccessful" marriages. The same pattern may even occur in both groups.

In discussing the Conflict-habituated couple as an example of a loving relationship, it has not been indicated that couples may stay together out of fear of being alone, but may tear each other apart in the process—with occasional tenderness which may actually be a compassionate grieving for the pain inflicted and the damage done.

The Passive-congenial couple has been described as "two people who have never cared about each other deeply . . ." But the very love relationships we exalt the most (i.e., those involving religious or "brotherly" love) can be very deep without being explicitly sexual.

In discussing the Devitalized couple, the fact has been passed over that unrealistic and inappropriate societal standards for behavior can engender dissatisfaction (e.g., viewing oneself as "not sexy" if one doesn't perform x number of times or know 37 positions) and thus can undermine a real day-to-day sharing which in fact is the durable fabric of love and affection.

In discussing the Vital and Total couples, Dr. Cuber has failed to comment on the symbiotic nature of such relationships—a characteristic which we view as neurotic, if not psychotic, in other contexts.

In short, Dr. Cuber has simply reorganized and relabeled old prejudices which serve to bolster a fast-collapsing concept of marriage as the most appropriate life style. Much light remains to be shed on how sexual needs and desires can become a well-integrated part of the lives of adults who wish to relate to another person or persons while still retaining their own integrity and identity. I would submit that we all have the same need for love and affection, which we try to fulfill in one way or another—sex being only one way.

Comment by
Margaret M. Poloma

One of the most intriguing questions Dr. Cuber's paper raises is the potential difference in husbands' and wives' perceptions of the same marriages.

It brings to mind a recent study of young women by University of Michigan psychologist Judith Bardwick who found that the majority of her subjects did not report enjoying sex for sex's sake. When asked why they made love, Bardwick notes that "very very few answer because it is a pleasure for *them.*" They usually responded with comments like "It makes us feel close" or "It is an expression of our love" or even with "It is expected." These were supposedly well-adjusted women indicating their candid reactions to the sex act. I would speculate that many of the husbands are unaware of their wives' attitudes on sex; if so this raises the issue of whether a wife should fake orgasm and enjoyment of the sex act or whether she should admit finding little or no physical pleasures in sex. Bardwick contends that sex may mean different things to men and to women, concluding that for her subjects, "female eroticism is primarily psychological, primarily a function of wanting to love and to secure love."

I would also speculate that marriage as well as sex have different meanings for men and women in our society. Women have been socialized to make marriage and the family their prime goal. Even when married women have careers outside the family, it appears that the career ranks in importance only after being a wife and mother. While men, too, undoubtedly have been socialized to marry, their career obligations frequently comprise a good part of their family responsibilities. Since women have been socialized to make marriage paramount in their lives, I would contend that their expectations of marriage and their perceptions of marriage may be quite different from men's—mostly in the direction of greater expectations of so-called marital bliss.

Cuber gives several examples of how a husband and wife may view their marriage differently. A husband may be quite satisfied with the passive-congenial relationship while the wife may view it nostalgically as being devitalized (when in fact, the relationship may never have been a vital one). Or, as we found in a study of the dual-profession family coresearched with T. Neal Garland, while few husbands helped their wives extensively with domestic tasks, many wives were ready to describe their limited help in glowing terms. We see here a situation where spouses are able to perceive what they want to perceive, and there is no guarantee that husbands' and wives' perceptions are congruent. The same may hold for other aspects of marital relationship. If both spouses always were able to construct similar perceptions of reality, how could you ever have the situation where one spouse is happy and very satisfied with the marriage at a time when the other spouse unexpectedly requests a divorce?

While isolating five types of marital adjustment is an excellent means for demonstrating the fact that sexual behavior occurs within a total life style, it is unlikely that the quality of the couples' sex lives is perfectly correlated with this typology. One may encounter cases of great sexual compatibility but little compatibility in other areas of marital life. Likewise, it is not impossible to comprehend a vital or even a total relationship where sex is not a salient interest for the couple. Sexual relations are but one ingredient, although a most important one, that may be used to characterize a marriage.

Comment by:
Ralph R. Greenson
Dr. Cuber describes five sexual patterns which he found "were the expression of successful marriages, in the sense that they were enduring and there appeared no particular likelihood that they would break up." I must pause here because I cannot accept Dr. Cuber's hypothesis that a marriage which endures is necessarily a successful one. It has been my experience that many enduring marriages are unsatisfactory, and only endure because they are a lesser evil. Most people remain more or less unhappily married because they are terrified of being alone. They dread change, they are childishly dependent on one another, or they cling to the financial or social security that the marital status conveys upon them.

Endurance is not a reliable indicator of a successful marriage. Divorce after 20 or 30 years of marriage is no longer a rare occurrence in our society. The concept of "viable" marriages does not discriminate between people who share boarding house arrangements sanctified by a marriage certificate from others who are truly emotionally involved with one another. I believe you can only assess the success of a marriage if you examine the quality of the personal relationship in terms of the capacity for intimate communication, sexual interest, mutual friendship and respect. It is clear that my approach to the dynamics of marriage is basically very different from Dr. Cuber's.

The "conflict-habituated" type of marriage Dr. Cuber describes looks to me like an arrangement of couples who have accepted one another's sadomasochistic character traits. It is certainly possible to have a good marriage when the neuroses of the two partners dovetail with one another. However, there must, in addition, be a good deal of mature development in each partner to make such a marriage a good one. Martha and George in Albee's *Who's Afraid of Virginia Woolf?*, quoted by Cuber, would not be a good example in my opinion. These people are too loaded with hate, loathing and contempt for each other and themselves to have a decent marriage. *Occasional* evidences of concern or gentleness do not make for a good marriage. They may have passionate sexual relations with orgasm, from time to time, but these are only thinly disguised brutality phantasies being acted out in the sexual situation.

Dr. Cuber's second group, the "passive-congenial" couples seem to me to represent those marriages in which the individuals involved were afraid to risk loving. He states they never cared deeply about each other, their interests were directed toward careers, children or community activities. I do not believe such people are content; they are *resigned* to their marital status. They have settled for the safety of physical proximity because they are terrified of the vulnerability that loving brings with it. Dr. Cuber says they are compatible and satisfied with little or no sex. I would guess they would rather be safely undead than dangerously alive.

The "devitalized" group once had a lively sexual life and then abandoned it, often after the birth of a child. My clinical experience indicates that there are people who dare not allow themselves to feel sexual urges toward anyone who is a mother or father. Sex was permissible for them as long as there were no children, but when one's wife becomes the mother of a child, the fact that she is a mother stirs up unconscious memories of one's own mother and sexuality is repressed. Such devitalized couples usually start calling each other "mother" and "dad," a sign they have identified with their children and sexual intercourse has become incestuous and taboo.

Dr. Cuber confirms this when he describes the 53-year-old man who, after a lengthy asexual marriage, fell in love with Jean. Then he realized what he had "stamped out of his life over the years" and he wanted a new wife. "I paid pretty dearly . . . as the world sees prices . . . but it is the best investment I ever made." Yes, I agree, but I fear if his new wife has a baby by him his sexual desire for Jean will also be "stamped out."

The "vital" marriage group refers to couples who are deeply involved psychologically in each other and their relationship is the most important and sustaining element in their lives. Sex for them is highly important and extremely enjoyable. Yet, often unfaithful to one another but this is condoned by the partner; in fact, the infidelity may even be enjoyed vicariously by the other partner. I have the impression that there is more here than meets the eye. It is possible that these people have reached a "state of broadmindedness" which is beyond the scope of my own experience. I suspect, however, that the acceptance of *open* infidelity is possible because it affords the satisfaction of unconscious homosexual and voyeuristic needs in the faithful partner. I have never seen *contented* marital partners of this type professionally. After all, they would have no reason to consult me. The unhappy ones, however, did reveal many important unresolved conflicts in regard to voyeurism, exhibitionism, and homosexuality.

The fifth marital type Dr. Cuber describes is the "total relationship." "It is as if neither has, or has had, a truly private existence." They are not only fiercely monogamous but react as if a difference in interest were an act of infidelity. To me this smacks of a symbiotic relationship, not a marriage of adults. These people have to possess each other, not just love each other. I do agree, however, that if two such individuals find each other they can have a good and enduring marriage—a benign symbiosis might be a more accurate term.

In summary, I have the impression that Dr. Cuber uses the terms "successful, enduring and viable marriages" very differently from me. I believe our standard and criteria for a good and vital marriage are remarkably discordant. For me a good marriage must contain intimate communication, passion, friendship, and respect. Endurance, in our society, is usually based on infantile dependency, social and financial insecurity, and above all, on the fear of being alone.

Dr. Cuber Replies to the Comments . . .

It is more than a little ironic to me that a consistent criticism of our study runs to the effect that a marriage which is conflict-habituated, devitalized, or passive-congenial can be regarded as "successful." Some critics have apparently overlooked the fact that the term "successful marriages" was *defined* as "in the sense that they were enduring." Quite obviously there are other ways to define success for other purposes—for example, clinically. Moreover, the marriages were "successful" in that the participants in the main regarded their marriages as totally viable even though sometimes acknowledging that sexually they left much to be desired. Quite obviously, these are not my professional, much less personal, criteria for ideally fulfilling relationships from an optimal mental health point of view!

One of the main thrusts of my book *The Significant Americans* is that enduring marriages among these highly educated and accomplished people very often are deficient in the quantity, and especially quality, of sexual fulfillment, but that they endure for reasons *other than* providing sexual or relational fulfillment. In brutally pragmatic terms, then, there are two quite opposite but both quite logical meanings of "successful"—one that the marriage is psychologically (including sexually) satisfying, and second that the marriages which provide some other rewards for their partners can also be, on balance, successful if the partners so identify them.

A classic case-type is the marriage which is fraught with tensions (sexual and otherwise) but is maintained "for the sake of the children," to avoid public embarrassment, etc., etc., this tenuous style being maintained with the skilled help of a psychiatrist or two, an encounter group, or a trusted clergyman. That a mental-health oriented outsider or one who places a high priority a sexual fulfillment should regard such a state of affairs as manifestly unsuccessful is both understandable and commendable. It is also my almost unqualified personal stance. What we regretfully learned from our study is that many people are so committed to such goals as "stability in marriage," "sacrifice to children," "public reputation," and "sanctity of marriage" that they are willing and often also able to manage what many professionals rightly, I think, consider a substandard emotional and sexual life in order to attain other widely held societal and religious goals.

It is one of the consequent hard facts of modern life that many people, therefore, use marriage to attain ends which are in themselves legitimate but are quite independent of either a close man-woman relationship or a vital sex life. For many people sexual behavior and fulfillment is something subordinate, even if some believe otherwise and act or advise accordingly.

2. How To Make Marital Sex More Exciting—5 Views

JESSIE BERNARD, CLARK E. VINCENT,
JAMES L. HAWKINS, JOHN F. CUBER,
THOMAS C. McGINNIS

Jessie Bernard

For the man or woman to whom the excitement of sex is really the excitement of the chase and conquest there is, almost by definition, no way to keep marital sex from becoming boring. No way. We are reminded of the Italian movie several years ago in which a man kept marital sex from becoming boring by going to his wife on the outside ledge of the building rather than directly through the door. For him this dangerous approach made sex more exciting. Some couples find that fighting enhances the excitement of sex. Some resort to "swinging." Some achieve variety by so-called group marriage. Some try new positions, new settings, new angles. Some women try to follow the Sensuous Woman's advice to be always seductive, using different costumes, perfumes, hairdos, to reactivate excitement. (Women of the Liberation Movement totally reject the implication that the responsibility for keeping sex exciting is theirs alone.)

The secret of overcoming boredom does not lie in new body tricks; it lies in the spirit and mind. It is the mind that makes and keeps it exciting. Seductive externals are a poor substitute for self-development. Not every woman can be like Cleopatra of whom Shakespeare said that time could not wither nor custom stale her infinite variety. But almost any woman can try to keep alive. Women

17

who achieve autonomy, a good self-concept, with interests of their own, who are not colorlessly passive, dependent, or lacking in self-feeling, are not boring. Sex can continue to be exciting for both them and their partners. The man who merely uses his wife's body for sexual purposes will be a boring partner and be bored himself.

Still, making a career of keeping sex exciting can itself become a bore. And there are kinds of sex that are worse than boring—cruel, destructive, punitive, rejecting sex. Some people might wish their sex lives were, in fact, boring. It would be better than what they have. The wife whose husband comes home drunk and roughs her up would appreciate a little sexual boredom, as would also the man whose wife can find no better time to remind him of her grievances and his deficiencies.

We might think of boring sex as a zero or neutral point. Sex can vary in either direction. It can be worse as well as better than boring. There are few people who are at peak performance in anything all the time. Even champions. I once asked a group of ministers and professors what proportion of the time they thought they were good at the podium. Most felt if they could be good three times out of five, that was great. Some had even lower aspirations. Expecting sexual relations to be super-duper every time is like asking for Wagner all the time. Bach is nice too.

Clark E. Vincent

When a society attempts to bring into the open what has been previously closeted as a taboo subject, there is a tendency to overemphasize that subject as a distinct, separate area of life necessitating special approaches, different learning processes, and unique techniques. This use of "special" approaches to sexual problems may be a necessary phase in bringing any formerly taboo problem area into the open (as in the case of the early days of mental illness); but it means that we tend to ignore some fairly simple, obvious approaches in resolving sexual problems and in maintaining sexual health.

Marital sex can be kept from becoming boring in much the same way that marital eating or marital recreation can be kept from becoming dull. Few wives would prepare the same foods in exactly the same way over a period of five years or even one month. Few husbands in taking their wives out to dinner would frequent only one and the same restaurant over a period of months or years. The couple who enjoy golf would soon find it boring if they always played only one course.

Marital sex is not different from marital meals in needing stimuli for the senses, variations in content, timing, and location, and changes even in how one is dressed and in the accompanying conversation. Most wives are strenuous in relieving mealtime boredom. They plan meals in ways that appeal to the senses of taste, sight, smell, and occasionally sound and touch. Few couples always eat in the same room year after year, or even with the same silverware and dishes. It may be a barbecue in the backyard, a T.V. dinner in the family room, a hurried snack in the breakfast room, or a very quiet, lengthy, formal dinner by candlelight in the dining room.

How do husbands keep their work at the office or shop from becoming boring? If people approach their work (sex) only when they are exhausted and too tired to talk, always use exactly the same techniques and methods year after year in their work (sex), and never find time or creative energy for nonwork (non-sex) amenities with coworkers, it is quite probable that their work rarely turns them on and that they are regarded as dull plodders with out-dated methods.

Employers who are thoughtful and wise may suggest a few days off or a change in pace for an employee who appears excessively fatigued or bored. Wives who are primarily homemakers need time off and change in pace. Males who are very enthused about their work tend to stimulate enthusiasm among coworkers. Husbands who are passionately desirous of their wives tend to stimulate a response.

It seems so obvious as to how all this can be applied to keep marital sex from becoming boring that the question arises as to why the blind spot? In part, it may be that those who have worked so hard to uncloset sex have inadvertently communicated an impression that maintaining viable, exciting, and ever-growing marital sexual relations somehow involves a totally different process than preventing boredom in any area of life. Also, we still labor under, and pay the price for, the medieval notion that sexual happiness in marriage "just comes naturally." And there is the romantic myth that marital love and sex come spontaneously and impulsively without any of the creative thought and energy which we accept as necessary in other areas of life.

An increasing number of husbands are so satiated with having to prove themselves occupationally all day, every day, that they are reluctant to prove themselves as marital lovers at the end of the day—thus reversing the courtship process as they wait for their wives to turn them on. But the wife too may be so satiated with proving herself as a mother, working woman, homemaker, and community contributor that she has little energy left for being seductive.

Such a Mexican-standoff necessitates a reordering of priorities. If a viable and stimulating sex life is important to such a couple, they obviously need, at least periodically, to let their sexual activities have first call on their time, energy, and creative planning. Some couples do this by planning a "be kind to sex day (weekend) (month)." A few couples married 20 or 30 years still occasionally locate a "lover's lane" and try the backseat of the car for old time's sake. Other couples have a practice of christening every room in the house with sexual relations at least once a year, particularly every time they move into a new house. For some couples this includes even closets, as well as the front and back yards. All of which takes some ingenuity if there are children in the home and neighbors closeby. A number of couples frequently exercise the option of her asking, "Honey, what would you like special for dinner (sex) tonight?" And his asking, "What kind of special restaurant (sex) would you most enjoy tonight?"

Most couples are aware that not all meals are mountain-top, gourmet feasts; some are good and others are mediocre, and a few leave us wondering why we even bothered to eat. Such a range in satisfaction from eating is usually accepted as normal. Similarly, marital-sexual relations are on occasion mountain-top experiences, sometimes mystical and ethereal, on other occasions quite physical and even physically therapeutic, quite bland on other occasions, and sometimes totally unsatisfying. Such a range in both the kind and degree of sexual satisfaction is also par for the course.

James L. Hawkins

Growing sexually is as painful and as joyous as growth in any other area of marriage. To grow both partners must give up the notion that they know what the other wants, likes, and believes. One must also give up the idea that his mate can mysteriously understand his needs and wants without being told. Mind-reading is out. Assuming that the past inevitably determines the future is also out. It must be a new ball game—at least a new inning. When it becomes possible to openly and jointly explore each other, to offer and solicit "raw (unprocessed) data" on what feels good *and* bad, to state needs or wants and make requests, then new avenues of intersexual pleasure are possible.

Some of the "new" directions discovered may in fact be "old" ones. Despite the anxieties associated with much premarital sexual behavior, many couples report a wide variety of experiences that were basically pleasurable. Recapturing a memorable moment often adds a particular warmth to sexual relations, and may also suggest specific settings which once were and may again be stimulating in themselves.

Sharing fantasies can be a source of new sensual possibilities. Fantasies of sexual activities which one would never think of really doing are often stimulating in themselves. Some couples find relating fantasies during intercourse to be stimulating. Other mental pictures may prove enticing enough to actually try out.

The range of possible sexual stimuli that a couple can experience together is almost limitless including movies, books, and records with sexual content. Purchase of sexy clothing by and for both spouses is not uncommon, but one spouse should not assume that he or she knows what the other spouse will consider sexy. Black lace panties and a push-up bra are very often not the ticket.

Tuning in to one's own body as well as the spouse's is a major way of enhancing the sexual relationship. To me the term "sexual" includes much more than just the activities surrounding intercourse. Sensual is perhaps closer to it. How long has it been since you had a head massage, a back-rub, a leg slap, or a face tap? When was the last time you showered together, walked barefoot in grass, made mud pies, did a finger painting, danced naked in the living room, or explored each other's bodies tenderly before a mirror? Have you told your husband how you like your breasts caressed? Firmly grasped, softly stroked, or left entirely alone? And the nipples—should they be kissed, licked, or bitten, and does this vary from early foreplay to after intercourse? By the way, sir, have you told your wife yet just exactly how to handle your penis for maximum effect?

Devising new times, places and situations to have sex relations frequently pays real dividends. This is especially true if at the same time sexuality is tied in with other love messages. A Wednesday luncheon date can often improve Friday night sex. A telegram with a simple "I love you" can open floodgates of feeling as can, for some, the prompt completion of a household chore. A date often leads to sex, but usually at a late hour when both are tired. Why not sex first and then dinner out—sort of a celebration of a celebration?

Sharing ideas with another couple can be fruitful. In addition, many couples report increased sexual pleasure as well as a generally revitalized marriage after making new friends who switch partners sexually. More total experiences such as multilateral marriage between three or more persons are difficult to carry off and will appeal to fewer, but when successful these multiple unions appear to yield extraordinary results.

New sexual directions must be sought in a mutual spirit of positive regard, warmth, and genuine caring. The goal for both is to have more sexual fun, in more loving closeness.

John F. Cuber

At the outset it is probably best to admit that this is an unrealistic goal for many, many pairs. People vary tremendously in their capacities to appreciate sex and in their feelings as to what is exciting rather than distasteful, comfortable rather than boring.

The situational components of monotony are present in every aspect of marriage—set times, set places, set gestures. "After all, my work hours, the kids' ballet lessons, P.T.A. meetings are all scheduled—you have to fit everything in or there's chaos." Efficiency and predictability, however, can be particularly oppressive in one's sex life, because for most it was once spontaneous, exciting, and peculiarly persistent in its needs. But there *are* ways to inject novelty, if not spontaneity, which have been successful for some. One woman suddenly realized that she made every effort to vary menus and plan off-beat recreation for the family but never gave a thought to herself as a sexual partner. Sometimes, as in this case, just such an acute awareness is all that is needed to begin changing the sexual milieu.

Different people, of course, find different solutions to the problem, if indeed, they feel a problem at all. Many pairs rather graciously accept the "inevitability" of more quiescent sex as they grow older or as their marriages "mature." But some sensitive and creative people find their own ways to avoid the conventional malaise.

One woman found that changing the lighting in the bedroom, providing a tiny cocktail bar and portable radio gave her and her husband a retreat which they enjoyed, whether or not it ultimately led to sex. One ingredient for them was a snap lock on the door, perhaps reminiscent of earlier clandestine sex. At least, it "kept the kids from bursting into the bedroom at 7 A.M. on Sunday morning."

Another couple enjoys occasional motel dates, and still another returns regularly to a familiar hotel suite. Then, of course, there are the "swingers," a group (no one knows how large, but certainly not inconsequential) of relatively young marrieds, some of whom find that illicit, but not clandestine, sexual activity enlivens their married sex. From the research available on this practice one would hesitate to make any blanket recommendation (or condemnation) of it as a solution to monotonous monogamy.

The introduction of novelty cannot be risked, of course, unless the relationship is secure enough so that the one suggesting the innovation knows he will not be subjected to recrimination, however subtle or slight, or be put down because he is "crude," "insensitive," or otherwise lacking in good taste, as defined by the partner. Confident sex on a sustained basis is rarely possible where there does not exist a mutual confidence and, hopefully also, empathy. This is true even where the tastes are somewhat different and each must in some degree cater.

Likewise, the admonition to "talk things over" is not necessarily constructive. It may be risky unless the couple already has a very thoroughly established, mutual capacity to empathize.

While it is admittedly sometimes difficult to pull off, successful sexual encounters consist of an admixture of surprise and predictability. One may be stimulated by new words, new gestures, fresh sequences. But there is only confidence if one is at the same time reasonably sure that these novelties will occur within a context with which one can be comfortable.

Thomas C. McGinnis

To personalize this question, making it, "how do *you* keep marital sex from becoming boring?"—the most difficult task in framing an answer is figuring out who *you* are. Are you someone who entered marriage expecting sex to become less exciting as years passed and now want to achieve what you've been missing? Are you a disappointed person who expected marital sex to be instant ecstasy and to remain so with little conscious effort? Are you someone who is contemplating marriage yet resisting—afraid the sexual joys you anticipate will not last, afraid familiarity will breed boredom? Or are you one among many married people who, although knowledgeable about the joys of sex and uninhibited in your experimentation to achieve pleasure, still feels that something is lacking in spite of your sophistication and expertise?

After much thought I decided to respond to those in the latter category. Why? First because discussion of their efforts and progress will provide other readers with valuable initial steps to take in preventing or reducing boredom in their marital sexual relationships. Second, examination of their reasons for asking the key question —How do you keep marital sex from becoming boring?—will reveal why fact-gathering and experimenting with a variety of new activities are not, *per se*, what create a good sexual relationship or make one better.

Early in life most people begin to use products and services designed to enhance physical attractiveness—colognes, deodorants, shampoos, mouthwashes, and so forth. With the help of newspaper and magazine articles, books, friends, or perhaps a professional counselor, individuals develop self-confidence, discard distortions and misapprehensions about sex, and introduce newness into their relationships. By newness I mean that they may enjoy showering together, intercourse before dinner, taking polaroid pictures of intimate moments, even oral-genital stimulation. They have experimented and found that they bring variety, anticipation, and delight to their relationship. Yet they find themselves asking: Is something missing? Could the pleasures we now enjoy be even better? Must we constantly seek new and different means of stimulation in order to ward off boredom? Are there going to be enough kinds of newness invented to prevent boredom throughout marriage or will I have to find one or more sexual partners with whom to participate?

There is little danger that the multitude of things to buy or try will be exhausted in our lifetime. The real danger is that *you* may be exhausted long before you can try them all.

I use the term exhausted in this context to describe a *psychological* rather than a physical phenomenon. Experimentation and variety can become tiresome unless marital partners find ways that will put them in closer touch with their own and their partner's uniqueness. How can this be accomplished? I could become prescriptive at this point but in the long run it would defeat my purpose, for to make *your* sexual relationship a *qualitatively excellent* one it must be uniquely yours, developed and nurtured together with your marital partner. Each needs to "tune in" on your own and your partner's thoughts, feelings, and actions—to work at achieving and maintaining honest and open communication. The goal thus becomes experimenting, creatively, with the emotional as well as the physical.

A way to begin creative experimentation is to try the Masters and Johnson prescription of simply touching each other and exchanging information about what is most pleasing to each of you. As you discover and try new positions for intercourse or new techniques for mutual arousal, share your feelings about what is happening and make modifications to suit your individual partnership. In this way your activities will become something mutually created and mutually enjoyed. These experiences promote joy and love because they are built on and keep building trust, respect, concern, tenderness, caring. Open, honest communication is not likely to lead to boredom, but rather to the delight of growing and experiencing emotional and sexual intimacy together. The less mechanical you are and the more you make your sexual relationship a personal, individual expression of feeling, the better your sexual experiences will become. This new sensitivity to the needs and desires of the other person, as well as yourself, is not only a way of keeping marital sex from becoming boring but also can carry over and help make your whole marital relationship come alive.

In summary, the more you work to recognize and integrate the emotional, intellectual, and physical dimensions of yourself and your partner, the more satisfying your sexual experiences will become and the more flexible and rewarding your entire lives will be.

3. *Sexual Conflicts in "Young Marrieds"*

JOHN L. SCHIMEL, M.D.,
moderates a discussion by three young
married couples (Hank and Jean,
Paul and Danielle, Tom and Marlene).

Dr. Schimel: Sex is a central aspect of the marital arrangement. It is also an aspect of life in which, prior to marriage, many of us have been all-too-well groomed in using coercive techniques. Sex often becomes a focus of contention and a weapon in marital jockeying as well.

There are no set formulas. Not every wife will withhold sexual relations until she gets a new coat, and not every husband will refuse his wife's affection and sexual satisfaction if she overdraws their checking account. However, once you are familiar with a couple's sex life, you can tell a lot about the basic elements of their overall relationship.

The two examples I cited concern money, which is possibly the second, if not the first, most intimate sharing experience found in marriage. Do you have any thoughts on how money comes into play in sexual adjustments in marriage?

Paul: One of the real crutches of masculinity in our society is being the breadwinner. I think a guy is so down in the dumps if he can't provide for his family that he probably loses his sexual ambitions. He doesn't feel that his wife respects him enough to want him as a sex partner.

Hank: Well, I think that I have experience in that regard, because in the two years we have been married Jean has been the breadwinner. I have been going to school and I held off getting married because I didn't want to be supported by anyone. It was always a hangup, or a problem at least. Then, when I got married, I found out how easy it was. (Laughter)

25

Dr. Schimel: Who handles the money?

Jean: No one.

Hank: Nobody controls the finances.

Dr. Schimel: This is typical of young American couples and it is obviously untrue—that is to say somebody must decide about the car or vacation. Somebody must suggest it and somebody else must agree with it. There has to be an initiator and an agreer.

Hank: I think Jean is far more of an originator than I.

Jean: What do you mean by that? You mean a big spender? (Laughter)

Hank: I do think that you are a bigger spender than I, but, by that I meant you initiate the plans for buying things far more than I. For example, we have a dog. We would never have had one, had it been up to me alone.

Jean: That, too, was an outgrowth of our financial situation. We would not have had the dog had we been able to afford a child. She really is our child for a while.

Hank: Now I'm tremendously happy with the dog.

Dr. Schimel: She was the initiator and you the agreer. The result is harmonious. This example, like the majority of instances of marital persuasion, is free of malice. But sometimes when one person feels an attempt at control or manipulation is being made, he resents it without necessarily being opposed to what is being suggested.

Paul: We may be in a comparable position in that, both being professionals, we defy the convention of the man being occupation-minded and the woman being a housewife. We both teach in colleges and, if anything, she's more ambitious than I am. This equality in all things is sometimes a little tough to take.

Tom: I think I would feel inadequate if my wife was doing as well as I was occupationally, and was, in addition, more assertive.
Is that as emasculating as I imagine?

Danielle: Sometimes in front of others I'm sensitive to making things seem to be Paul's prerogative. Men still need to feel dominant.

Tom: Dr. Schimel mentioned something about resisting pressures even when it may be something you're really not against. I have that hangup. Maybe it's because my mother butted in on my affairs for so long. I take it out on Marlene.

Dr. Schimel: Afraid Marlene will turn you into a little boy again?

Tom: When Marlene's so decisive, I get uptight. Probably because I'm so unsure. It so happens that just recently I was out of work for a few months; I was on unemployment insurance and Marlene was working and together we were making out fine. There were times when I was afraid to make passes at her at night, because it would have wiped me out if she refused. Somehow I didn't think she wanted sex with me. I'd kind of lay awake looking for signals. Imagining rebuffs.

Marlene: Much of the time I thought you were down on me—that I wasn't giving you enough support when you most needed it. There were times I wanted to kiss Tom and have sex, but he seemed so preoccupied that I felt stupid. It seemed like offering a starving man a napkin. Exactly the last thing he needed at this point.

Paul: Dr. Schimel, what should the wife do in cases like this, if she knows that her husband is suffering?

Dr. Schimel: What the wife can do comes from her understanding of the stiuation. Often the wives are in the reverse situation. Their husbands always seem to be resorting to pep talks which generally make the women feel even more deficient. (Laughter)
   You all seem to recognize what I said. Have you had such experiences?

Marlene: Sure, when my husband was out of work, I said to him, are you crazy? Everything will be alright. What are you worrying about? What is the matter with you?
   I guess that all I could really do was be myself and be with him. Not very encouraging, but maybe more realistic. At times I felt awful for feeling so helpless. And I wish it hadn't intruded in our love life.

Tom: I certainly sensed Marlene's help. Many times, my mood during this period of unemployment was one of rejection, depression, and so on. I did feel rejected. I did feel left out of it. Sometimes I would let it out on Marlene. I was aware of a terrible anxiety most of the time.

Jean: Did it cause you to want to be more dominant, to want to order your wife around or did it cause you to want her to take a stronger role, and thus kind of eliminate any anxieties? In other words, did it make you feel more dominant toward her or more submissive?

Dr. Schimel: Before you answer that Tom, anybody with such a good question probably has an answer in mind. What do you think, Jean?

Jean: I think it would make him more dominating.

Paul: And what about sex?

Jean: That's puzzling. A tendency toward impotence doesn't seem to jibe with acting more dominant.

Paul: I think there would be some problem with sex, or at least less of it. That was Tom's case.

Hank: Well, wouldn't some guys, Dr. Schimel, try to have intercourse more and more to bolster their sense of masculinity that way?

Dr. Schimel: That's been one explanation of the Don Juan type. Some psychiatrists have attributed the promiscuity of the disadvantaged male in America to his frustrated hope of achieving social and economic status.

Hank: What about other women who carry the major part of the economic load? Do they feel uncared for or unfeminine if they have to help out to such an extent?

Danielle: Only if she were doing some drudgery. It would depend on the nature of her work. If she felt that her own best qualities were reflected in what she did, she would feel better, more a whole person. But if she had to do something just for the dollar, that had no relationship to her personality or to what she wanted to contribute, then I think that she would feel less lovable.

Dr. Schimel: Let's put the question on a more personal level. We have three attractive young women here. Are you more turned on by successful men or unsuccessful men?

Jean: Successful.

Marlene: Unsuccessful.

Danielle: I think I am most turned on when *I* am successful.

Dr. Schimel: Marlene, you gave us an interesting answer. Why did you answer the way you did? How do you define an unsuccessful man?

Marlene: Well, for the most part I have fallen in love with men who are poor. And with men who have artistic tendencies, but are not established.

Paul: I can think of two explanations. One is that you don't think you are so great yourself so you don't think you rate a fellow who is doing well, and the other is that you want to have a fellow who needs you, for whom you can do something.

Marlene: I want somebody to be inspired by me. Perhaps it would be a little clearer if I speak of a friend who we have, who keeps finding herself in romantic situations in which she is bound to suffer. She is drawn to suffering artists. She has dated a few successful artists, but they don't turn her on. They have to be suffering. They have to be mixed up. They have to be, you know, turbulent and let her in on this genius.

Jean: Sanity is very boring.

Marlene: Exactly. I don't think that misery is such a terrible thing. Tom could have turned me on most in that goofed-up period of unemployment. Too bad he didn't see it as an experiment in living and that he got so solemn. (Laughter)

Jean: One thing I resent, which has to do with this business of male and female roles, is being asked to fetch things. You know, like get me a drink, get me an ashtray. Little things like that bug me. Asking and telling are different. If he said, Jean, would you mind handing me this, it would be all right. When he says, Jean, *get* me, I want to say, get it yourself you so and so. It affects my pride and self-esteem, because it reflects his whole attitude toward me.

Paul: Early in my marriage I used to be very conscious of who was asking who to do what, and who was serving who. It was a bad habit that I was aware of. Now, we've achieved a state of ease. But who is getting the best of whom can be a real concern that's tied in with the worry about being an adequate man or silly putty. This must affect lovemaking, though I'm not sure how.

Hank: When a man's wife has turned him down over some petty thing and he is harboring a grievance I think he's reluctant to make an overture in bed. He may want to get revenge, or he may be scared of being rejected again. I would say the guy would feel bugged and he would withhold any affection.

Tom: It might be love-hate operating.

Paul: Yeah, that's just it. Everything is so relative. Given such a situation or an argument, maybe the partners might take it out in very violent sex acts—or just the opposite, complete turnoff, no contact.

Tom: Marlene knows about this thing in my past. I used to go with a girl who was mean, a real bitch. But she was beautiful. She brought out an aggression in me in sex I didn't know I had—it was extremely pleasurable, but hostile. You know, I was really doing a job on her. In this case, sadism, a mixture of sex and hostility—really became meaningful for me. I really gave it to her! (Laughter)

Hank: I have never experienced anything like that, but I feel the same way as Paul. If I were bugged or if I were in a bad mood because of something that Jean did, I just wouldn't do anything. If she made an overture, I would probably just reject her.

Jean: I will say that I have felt rejected at times because of things just like that. Although I didn't know the cause of your hostility, I sensed it. You didn't say anything; you just kept reading. Generally when we are feeling that way, we manage to get to one another. I generally burst into tears, for at least two hours.

Danielle: What happens then?

Jean: If I have felt rejected or unhappy, then I think that the tension is released in tears; when sexual frustration mounts, that also is released in tears, so that there would never be lovemaking after I cry.

Hank: I don't think that is true. I do remember making love after you cried. Two or three times.

Jean: That may be, but then I'm not sexually responsive. We always do wind up feeling close, whether it is through sexual means or not. It may take a while, but we get back to each other. Do I cry in order to get held? I don't know. Babies do. I guess I might also.

Dr. Schimel: May we turn to the subject of how you keep up careers that are very taxing, and still keep open your lines of communication? Even though you both come home tired and preoccupied with your many responsibilities, you can still achieve some kind of emotional harmony and be able to express your love for each other?

Paul: That is an extremely hard thing. Living in New York City, having a child and each of us having jobs, we find getting together emotionally to be a tremendous problem. I can't say that in any way we have solved it.

Tom: When Danielle is tired and bugged and harried, do you accept it as being from overwork or do you think it has something to do with you?

Paul: If she would give me overwork as her reason, I would take it solely as such.

Danielle: On my part, I wouldn't get too upset at the notion that Paul cares more about his job than about paying attention to me. I guess at times he does. But, on the other hand, many times I care more about my job than anything else. So I realize that I have an awful lot of "masculine" drive myself and I am very ambitious. When I have something that I consider very important, I really drop everything and just turn myself on to my work.

Hank: You don't need as much cuddling and lovey dovey as everyone else?

Danielle: Well, I think I do, but I need it when I am through doing my job.

Hank: Certainly there are problems and there are pressures that arise from all our work and careers. When I come home I let it out in discussion. I think that draws us more together. Jean discusses her work problems too—if not for advice, just to release some emotions so as not to build them up, which would inevitably affect your love.

Tom: I feel that way too. When everything has gone wrong, I always feel better when I come home and we can talk about it.

Marlene: Yes, I do too.

Paul: But there are lots of guys, and me among them, who tend to be inexpressive, to contain their troubles. I know that in my case, I get the feeling that, well, it bugs me so bad, and it's goddamn dreary, why burden somebody else with it? I would try to forget it, rather than share it.

Sometimes you can't help but be preoccupied and grumpy, so that Danielle asks what is on my mind? To me it is not worth talking about. I would like to let it evaporate, let it fade away. Sometimes she is curious about what went on in a boring phone call that went on too long, and I don't come across. It is enough that I had to endure it once. Don't make me do it twice.

Marlene: Tom used to be like that. He wouldn't say a word to me, not a word. Then I said, well you have to speak because you speak to me in other ways. Even in your silence you speak to me. So you might as well just tell it right out.

Tom: If I'm in a foul mood, I might want to engage in lovemaking to cleanse myself of the crap that is on my mind. That beats ceaseless brain picking, *ad nauseam.*

Dr. Schimel: Do you think people get their frustrations or their daily troubles out sexually, as opposed to verbally? Do you feel you can do this?

Tom: Sure I do. It is just a matter of jumping that one hurdle, to get away from dreariness and over to loveliness. Once you embark on lovemaking, you never regret it.

Jean: Well, certainly, sexual activity brings a great deal of physical and mental pleasure. But I don't think it relieves the problems that you have on your mind if you haven't discussed them. The problem is still there.

Marlene: Sex can relieve tensions, which are psychosomatic.

Tom: What did the man say?—there is nothing good or bad but thinking makes it so. It's the same with problems. A problem that's not on your mind is no problem.

Hank: Is sex a good panacea for life's frustrations? Dr. Masters talks about the futility or the great harm done by people trying to force sexual functioning when they are really not in the proper mood for it, but trying to force it for reasons such as those we are talking about.

Dr. Schimel: There are so many things that vary in lovemaking. I really would recommend to all of you that if you use sex solely for relaxation, for heaven's sake, invest a few dollars and get a sauna bath. (Laughter)

Marlene: But that gives me claustrophobia.

Dr. Schimel: Sex has that effect on some people too. (Laughter)

Hank: Danielle said before that she is very masculine in her ambitions, in her strivings, and in her application to her work.

Danielle: *I* don't consider it masculine. It is what the culture teaches. I consider it natural.

Hank: It's interesting that you can make a distinction between what you think of yourself and what others might think.

Danielle: I make that distinction.

Hank: Do career women still feel feminine and lovable after being indoctrinated with the belief that their life style is not feminine?

Danielle: It is very hard to feel . . . how shall I say . . . quite "dainty" if you are ambitious or a little bit different from the stereotype.

Marlene: Well I kind of take my femininity for granted and I get very upset when I feel Paul isn't reciprocating. I just sort of assume that I am simultaneously feminine and aggressive. Then I wait for the signal to come in naturally to confirm it.

Dr. Schimel: Traditionally women have considered themselves recipients of a man's lovemaking. A man does things to them to please them. Women got pleased too, but didn't show it too much. Now we live in an era where we have learned that women can function as well and derive as much pleasure, if not more pleasure, from lovemaking; that there is nothing unfeminine about the woman being the aggressor in lovemaking. She can initiate lovemaking and be more active generally, such as by fondling the male's genitals just as the man has always fondled hers. There is a new and growing sense of the feminine role in lovemaking.

In your experience, does the woman derive more joy by being more active? Can the man take it or is he threatened by the woman showing more lust and more eagerness than he may have himself at the moment? (Pause)

Don't all speak at once because it will be difficult to record. (Laughter)

Hank: I think that is a major question. I feel strongly that if we adopt a Women's Lib attitude, which I think we have in our relationship, we ought to adopt it in bed also. It certainly wouldn't be threatening to me.

Tom: Her being an initiator and an aggressor would not frighten you?

Hank: No, if she would, and when she is, it doesn't frighten me.

Jean: It does frighten me, if you ask me. Unlike fellows who try to force a sexual situation, whether they like a girl or not, I really do have to associate it with affection. I would never be able to have sex successfully with someone I did not know if I were not drawn to him in a very big way. I would never be able to be sexually aggressive in that respect.

Dr. Schimel: You are saying the other person has to show certain kinds of activity to make you feel you are loved?

Jean: Right. I can initiate, but if I don't get a lot of feedback then I start to feel cheap.

Hank: Dr. Schimel, could I prevail on you to give her some brief counseling on why she shouldn't feel cheap—or perhaps, she should?

Dr. Schimel: Well, I think she is entitled to feel the way she does. (Laughter)

Jean: I thank you for what you said, Dr. Schimel. That made me feel good. I was afraid that my conviction and orientation might be interpreted in terms of hangups and inhibitions.

Dr. Schimel: This is a very crucial issue. The effort you might expend to initiate or to approach sex with some male stereotype of behavior embarrasses you. It embarrasses many women, actually.

How do you see this, Hank? Do you feel embarrassed when your wife takes the lead sexually? Do you like being made love to?

Hank: I would like to be made love to at times, definitely.

Tom: I know I want Marlene to share my enthusiasm for sex. I become annoyed when I feel she is holding back, like when she doesn't share my zeal or is exercising restraint.

Hank: Well, I think that annoyance is natural.

Dr. Schimel: I think it is also not a bad description of tyranny—if you don't join in spontaneously and exactly that way I want you to, I am going to be mad at you.

Marlene: No, I think that he feels bad that she doesn't feel as he does.

Tom: Dr. Schimel, if that's tyrannical, it is the most benevolent despotism.

Dr. Schimel: Yes, I know. "It's for your own good." I never believed it from my father, and my kids never believe it from me. (Laughter)

Tom: Tyranny in the pursuit of pleasure is no tyranny.

Dr. Schimel: I find it to be a very interesting question, except that you have already decided it. What if the man feels one way, feels more excited, and the woman doesn't feel quite as excited? Of course it works the other way. The woman who makes advances, as Jean mentioned, while he is reading his damn newspaper. The level of interest often does vary and people aren't Greek choruses singing in unison.

How that issue is settled can be very interesting. If one party gets mad, that is a form of coercion. To himself it is an inner experience, but, as a communication, it is a form of coercion.

Paul: Well, sex is much easier for the female to acquiesce in than it is for the male to participate in physically without real enthusiasm.

Marlene: You are so right. When the wife isn't really interested but the husband is, should she fake excitement?

Paul: Excitement, love, and everything!

Jean: That offends me. The idea of perhaps not being excited and yet being affectionate and caressing even though you might not feel passion is acceptable to me. But I don't like the idea of saying, like a red-hot sexpot, "come and get me," when I don't feel that way.

Danielle: I think it is wrong to have intercourse when you don't want to, and really idiotic to pretend to be having orgasms, as I understand some women do.

Hank: Female prostitutes moan and groan pretending to have orgasms all over the place. They really feel contempt for their partners.

Marlene: I have some news for you all. (Laughter) You don't tell a person everything and you don't tell a person everything emotionally. Sometimes you do bluff, and sometimes, through the bluff, you begin to feel the way you are acting. Sometimes it doesn't work; but you've heard of the Stanislavsky method of acting.

Danielle: Well, I think the wife who does that is making a fool of her husband too. People who love each other don't relate to each other in such charades. Bolstering his ego that way is a really condescending type of manipulation.

Tom: A certain amount of pressuring has to go on in that largely unspoken drama of puzzling out each other's sex desires and attitudes: Do we make love now? How do we make love? What position? What act? Somebody is leading somebody else in these acts.

Danielle: I would say, from my own experience it would be the force and the passion of the counter-prevailing power. If Paul just plumped into my study, I think I would have immediately transferred all my passion to sex right on the spot. (Laughter)

Dr. Schimel: So you are suggesting that a timid lover is more likely to be told to get lost?

Danielle: Yes.

Paul: Sure. I think that if you have one very strong person, that is all it takes. That analogy is almost perfect for thermodynamics. (Laughter) If you don't have any interaction, you are going to keep one body at 100 degrees and the other at 10. I think the critical observation here is there has to be a strong mutual interaction for there to be a transfer of desire. Once that does take place, if there is nothing else wrong with the marriage at that moment it should work exactly according to the laws of physics.

Tom: To me the most interesting thing was that Danielle could be swept off her feet with a passion that was kindled by Paul's desire. In the old days a woman would dutifully concede in order to get rid of the man, getting the sex over with fast and with minimum involvement on her part.

Dr. Schimel: I would like to ask Danielle, and also the other two women . . . these times when you were *so* busy that you told your husband to get lost, in retrospect now couldn't you have spared twenty minutes or an hour during the evening?

Danielle: It is really not the time. It is really the direction of your involvement.

Tom: You don't want to be interrupted?

Danielle: If you engage in intellectual activity, you channel a lot of energy in that direction and it becomes really hard to rechannel.

Hank: I agree with her. I think it is really hard, if you are on one thing, to make love and then come back to it.

Paul: You just don't turn on for twenty minutes or a half hour and then go back. (Laughter)

Dr. Schimel: I know that intellectual passions can be rated very highly by some people. Of course, there are others who can work very hard on a problem and take an hour off for sex. There are others who can interrupt by taking a walk around the block, which is okay for some intellectuals where sex isn't.

Here we have a hierarchy of interruptions in which sex doesn't make it. Napoleon, while he was mapping the strategies of war, would keep a beautiful woman in an antechamber. Periodically he would interrupt his concentrations for lovemaking and then return to his labors.

Hank: In your analogy with Napoleon, you have pinpointed the difference between his very brief time commitment to the person with whom he had intercourse, and the fact that with your wife or husband you just don't do it and then run out. I just wouldn't jump out of bed and say, okay, now I go back to work.

Tom: Well, I would. I think if you really dig your wife sexually, you would. If you'll only do it in the semi-anonymity of darkness, in response to the body warmth, I think you really don't turn each other on. Being "absorbed" or "too busy" is just an excuse.

Dr. Schimel: What the others seem to be saying, Tom, is that sex is not a casual thing. If you really must give your whole heart and soul to sex, it can't be a twenty minute matinee break.

Paul: Sex is very different from going to the john for a few minutes to relieve yourself.

Dr. Schimel: This is really a very interesting idea—that the sex act is a sacrament. Not a gymnastic accomplishment or casual release.

Jean: That's right. I don't feel that it is primarily a biological release.

Dr. Schimel: Kinsey has pointed out that there is much more sex among the lower classes than among the educated classes, which is what this group is. Whereas a truck driver whose route goes past his home, comes home, has his lunch and sex break, and goes back on the truck. When the boys ask, "how did it go today," he says "nice matinee."

Here we are talking about an almost religious attitude toward the sexual experience—the exact circumstances, the proper attitudes of both parties, and a very high order of requirements.

Tom: This reminds me of a friend who is a symphonic composer. He was once beset by a person in advertising who said, why don't you write jingles and little melodies for our ads? My friend didn't want to put him down by pointing out the vast difference in their attitudes toward art, so he said tactfully "Well, I have to write long and involved works whose beauty develops in stages."

The ad man said, "Can't you write something that is short and beautiful?" I think this is comparable to sex. I don't know if I should be ashamed of it or not, but I'm in the short and beautiful camp.

Danielle: I don't think it is a matter of time really. It is really the attitude implied if Paul just knocked on my door and said, okay, sex break. (Laughter)

Well, he could go to hell. But if he dragged me off, I would go.

Tom: Isn't there a difference between the sexes here, in that the male responds more quickly and more easily?

Jean: The woman does have to be wooed. I can't blow hot and cold. It's corny, I suppose, but I like to feel cherished.

Tom: I think sex can be engaged in without elaborate preparation. I think you can also have an extremely intense love experience and then go back to something else. I don't see why you have to dwell in each other's arms for the next eight hours in order for it to be a glorious experience.

I do not like the analogy between having intercourse without much ado and going to the bathroom. It is an odious comparison.

Let's say that by now you are on page 80 of a book. Your eyes are getting a little bleary. Now do you want to go make a sandwich or do you see your beautiful wife there and make whoopee instead? Afterwards you feel terrific and so does she, and you go on reading the book. Nobody has been treated at all badly. Dr. Schimel, why do some people treat sex as a sacrament, as you call it?

Dr. Schimel: Speaking generally, practices that are infused with awe, fear, and lack of understanding are elevated to the status of sacrament. These criteria apply to sexuality in our culture, especially among the more educated, the middle-class.

Danielle: Dr. Schimel, are you suggesting we adopt the hit-and-run type of sex?

Dr. Schimel: A patient of mine once complained to the effect that I "freed" him from being cheap, so that now he eats in fine restaurants whereas he used to eat at Nedicks. When he had a financial reversal he asked, "What do you want me to do, go back to Nedicks?" I didn't care which restaurant he went to in the first place. Further, because he felt free enough to go to the Four Seasons to eat doesn't mean he had to hate Nedicks. (Laughter)

Tom: I would like to raise the question of abnormality. Accusations of abnormality and fears of being abnormal are sometimes used by people to control other peoples' sex life.

For example, men often want oral-genital sexual activity and the woman won't do it; maybe, because she feels it is beneath her. Maybe the man agrees it demeans her and that's why he wants it. Is there anything we can say about this?

Hank: I can see how it's good for a man's vanity to have a woman, in a sense, "prove her love" by doing something she had previously considered wrong.

Tom: It can make a man feel important. I know of cases, back in college, where guys kind of put girls down by persuading them to "go down" on them. The same could happen in marriage.

Dr. Schimel: Well, sacraments grow up around things that people fear or revere or both. So, the question of oral-genital sex relates to attitudes of dirtiness or coercion. You see, I am not convinced that this is a liberated generation. The forms have changed, but in many ways the problems continue.

So it becomes, to some people at least, not only a question of pleasing the other person, but appeasing. Which then gets into your theme of dominance. Dominance—I used the word tyranny earlier, which shook Tom up; dominance almost always breeds resentment. Where there is the sacramental attitude there are also attitudes of awe, fear, or evil. In genital activities in our culture, we still have such feelings. These feelings are usually unconscious but may be operating consciously. The woman may find it disgusting more often than the man.

There is also the whole business of fads. We live in a culture where everybody wants the best or the jazziest, and very often this is forbidden to most. For some people this may be the matter of oral-genital sex.

This is of no consequence to other cultural groups. For the middle class, the practice of oral-genital sex is almost faddish. You are not "with it" unless you do it.

Sociologists and anthropologists use a concept of "cultural lag." The man may be more up to date or stylish in his attitudes toward oral-genital sex. The woman may be lagging behind, or vice versa. The conditions are then ripe for a struggle. What fascinates me in this question is the process of decision-making. You can talk about this in terms of dominance and submissiveness, which is one way of looking at it. I am also interested in the process of decision-making.

How does a man who wants oral-genital activity, for example, make out with the wife who is not willing to do it? Sometimes there is a compromise. Perhaps she does it every fifth or ninth time around. Or she may agree to stimulate him, but not to orgasm. So, all these various intimate, personal interchanges are affected by cultural attitudes about what is good and what is fancy, and they may occasion a power struggle.

I once treated a bunch of cronies who were all married and they all had girlfriends on the side. The men were all homebodies, afraid of losing their wives, homes, careers, reputations, and so on—although in this group of people I have found that the discovery of adultery rarely if ever leads to divorce.

In each case the primary attraction was that the girlfriend would engage in oral sex with him where his wife didn't. In a couple of cases, when the issue came out into the open, the wives said, why didn't he say something? I've been interested for years and I didn't dare bring up the subject. (Laughter)

Communications are very important. A completely crazy expectation of what the woman is like can go on and on for 50 years of marriage. The man may not have the faintest idea, in certain areas, of what is acceptable or even desired by his wife, and vice versa, of course.

Hank: I have a question that relates to a man's strength, both of the body and of his will. Does a good, fulfilling sex experience wipe a guy out for the next day, in that he may feel a little depleted, a little too sated and maybe acquiescent. Perhaps he doesn't care to battle and may give in to others instead of taking a stand. Do you remember the general in Dr. Strangelove, mourning his vital fluids?

Tom: I think it's just the opposite. A good night of sex perks me up in every way. It gets your metabolism going. You feel buoyant, masterful, ready to take charge.

Dr. Schimel: This talk sounds very much like the stories about masturbation; it will cause your brain to deteriorate and hair will grow on the palms, and all sorts of other things, none of them true. It is also a folk idea that sex is physiologically good for you. There is an older folk idea that sex, for the male particularly, is depleting.

Sexual intercourse may result in a better mood for the man who feels he has done a masterful job of copulation—with his wife, his girlfriend, or the fellow who works at the next desk. (Laughter)

Some men feel depressed. Some can't stand the sight of their sexual partner after intercourse. Some men fall asleep. If anything, I think that is the closest to a physiological response to sex.

Hank: I have seen situations in which couples were having some sort of struggle. Usually the wife was being a flirt. A man's wife recently flirted with me, and I knew it had nothing to do with me but it had to do with her trying to do something to her husband. She was bugging him, really putting him on edge.

Danielle: In a couple we know, the wife always fondles the other men present. She talks to them with that intent look. She turns them on. Her husband never feels secure. I think she does it because she resents his business success, his being out there in the world. She is really too ambitious to be locked in at home.

Paul: Maybe she does it because it makes her more fascinating to her husband. He's such a consumer type. If he didn't think every guy lusted after her he'd probably get a girlfriend. This way he thinks he's got a Rolls Royce and he's in constant danger of defaulting on payments.

Marlene: I went to a party in hot pants the other weekend, and a lot of the men there didn't know I was married. A lot of them tried to date me and grab me.

Hank: You happen to have a knockout figure, and also dress to advantage. Tom, how do you feel, knowing that the guys think your wife is extremely attractive?

Tom: Sometimes I feel bugged. Marlene dresses to be attractive. That's only natural. Occasionally, and I do say only occasionally, and particularly at parties we get separated and all of a sudden I get back to her and she is surrounded by a couple of guys. Sometimes I feel jealous. That was one reason I didn't want to go to parties when I was out of work. It made me uneasy to be around those cocksure guys who were doing well.

Jean: Cocksure, indeed!

Paul: But we've already established that Marlene likes losers. (Laughter)

Tom: I imagine the same thing would hold true for her if we were separated at a party and all of a sudden I got caught in a corner with attractive gals—there might be some pang of jealousy.

Marlene: I do feel jealous of him at times. One time, when he was friendly with a girl at the office, I was really jealous. I invited her to dinner just to see what she was like.

Tom: After you found what she was like, you didn't care. (Laughter)

Marlene: I will talk to just about anybody. I don't do it to flirt. I just talk to people, but people are so grabby sometimes. It's ridiculous!

Paul: Forgive my frankness, but you wear lovely sweaters with your nipples showing and . . .

Marlene: I see nothing wrong with that.

Paul: I know, but a man would have to be a stone not to be affected by it.

Tom: To come to Marlene's defense, I don't think that she is dressing so much more outlandishly or so much more revealingly than other women.

Dr. Schimel: Women's Lib slants the issues of jealousy and fidelity in terms of the woman being the chattel of the man—call it *possessiveness.* Sociologists call this feature *exclusivity.* That is, he or she is yours and nobody else's. Some Women's Lib propagandists drum up an image of the woman slavishly and joylessly making herself available for sex, while the man fulfills his lust. Now, really, anyone who believes that a man is going to have a whale of a good time in bed with a long suffering woman is really an idiot. (Laughter)

Marlene: You know, if Tom had an affair with somebody, as long as he loved me and was nice to me—if it did him good—maybe I'd be happy about it. I don't know.

Dr. Schimel: There are two factors involved. One is the factor of exclusivity and the other of permanence. So, you are stressing the permanence factor, Marlene. You'd love exclusivity, but you would settle for permanence, especially if you felt that straying did him some good.

Jean: I'd take exclusivity. I'd take exclusivity over permanence.

Dr. Schimel: You mean you'd rather have all of him for a short time than some of him for a long time?

Jean: Right on.

4. Sex and Aging

ERIC PFEIFFER

As the life span increases, there is a corresponding increase in concern over the quality of existence in old age. Healthy older people take pride in their accomplishments, maintain vitality to pursue interests, and dread the inert existence of the infirm. They continue to have sexual and affectional needs, and enjoy the enhanced self-esteem that comes with being loved.

However, when it comes to the area of sex in old age, rigid taboos inhibit them. Sex may be considered inappropriate, a threat to health, or no longer possible. Until very recently, there has been very little scientific concern with the sexuality of this age group.

In fact, the taboo against sex in old age would seem to be a factor in impeding systematic studies on the subject. Investigators have found it extremely difficult to recruit aged subjects for their studies. Often, when subjects do volunteer, relatives find out and insist that they leave the study.

The taboo extends into the scientific community. Physicians are not immune to such prejudices and may sidestep counseling geriatric men who may be suffering potency difficulties or women who may be suffering from sexual frustrations. The impression is conveyed that sex is not to be part of this life phase.

In one study at Duke University, young doctors found it difficult to inquire into the sex lives, past or present, of aged women who had been single all of their lives. There were fourteen such women in the study, and in only four of these were any sexual data obtained.

Where does this taboo come from? Is it a hangover from Victorian times? To this day there are forces keeping it alive. In spite of the recent emphasis on "sex for its own sake," our society still holds reproduction to be the primary function of sex, particularly with regard to one's parents' generation. Sex among older people clearly is considered somewhat indecent.

Our entire notion of what constitutes sexual attractiveness is associated with youth, and our culture indoctrinates its members with a reaction of repugnance or distaste when considering sexual activity by the elderly. Vigorous coitus seems incongruous with the limited locomotion and unathletic bodies of older people.

The taboo is also related to the incest taboo. Children of all ages feel intense anxiety from observations or thoughts of their parents doing anything sexual. An older man who expresses sexual interest is labelled a "dirty old man."

With sexual expression so much in disfavor, not to mention fear of heart attacks and other physical damage caused by sexual activity, it is not surprising that a considerable damper is placed on the ardor of the old. They may lose sexual interest because they are expected to lose it. Other elderly persons who say that they are still sexually active are liable to be considered either perverse or engaging in wishful fantasy.

Included in the groups studied by Alfred Kinsey were 106 men and 56 women who were 60 years old and over. Some of his findings are most interesting. Kinsey found that at age 60 only 1 man in 5 was incapable of sexual intercourse. By age 80 this ratio had risen to 3 in 4. He found that married males of all ages had somewhat higher frequencies of sexual outlet, but single men and widowers had only slightly less frequent sexual activity than the married men.

Kinsey noticed a gradual slowing down in sex activity for women between the age of 20 and 60, but he felt this had to do with the aging process in the male. He saw "little evidence of any aging in the sexual capacities of the female until late in her life." Compared to men, single and widowed women had sex activity rates far below those for men in the same category.

Masters and Johnson did more research than Kinsey did on older people. They got their information from interviews and also from live participation in their laboratory. In fact, 48 pages in their famous work, *Human Sexual Response,* are devoted to the sex activity of the aged.

For men over 60 years, Masters and Johnson found a slower development of erection, a longer time to ejaculation, and fewer genital spasms during orgasm. In addition, the physical signs of sexual excitement, the "sex flush" and muscle tension, were less apparent.

Women also experienced a decrease in the signs of sexual excitement after the age of 60. On the other hand, the ability to respond the orgasm was not diminished, especially in those women who experienced sexual stimulation regularly.

Masters and Johnson state, "We must, in fact, destroy the concept that women in the 50-70 year age group not only have no interest in but also have no facility for active sexual expression. Nothing could be further from the truth than the often-expressed concept that aging women do not maintain a high level of sexual orientation."

They also learned that many men who do not understand the natural slowing-down process panic and think their ability to function sexually has disappeared, which is what they expect to happen in the later years anyhow. The slowing down of response results in a fear of performance, leading to impotence or a retreat from sexual interaction. Actually, the older man can gain confidence from the knowledge that not only can he function sexually, but he may be a more effective sexual partner than the 20- or 40-year-old man since he has considerably more control over his ejaculation.

Masters and Johnson advise that wives be aware of the physiologic changes in men, so they will not misinterpret less frequent demand and slower response to loss of capacity or to loss of love or sexual interest in them. They found that aging does not detract from the pleasure of orgasm in the man or the woman. Interestingly, of the previously potent older men whom they treated for impotence, 65% regained potency.

Masters and Johnson also found that the man who is sexually effective in old age is liable to have been sexually interested and active to a high degree all his life. They report that "certainly it is true for the male geriatric sample that those men currently interested in relatively high levels of sexual expression report similar activity levels from their formative years." Other studies have also shown that men who were very sexually active in their youth maintained that sexual interest in old age.

For older women, Masters and Johnson found, as did Kinsey, that the postmenopausal sex drive is directly related to the sexual habits of the woman during her childbearing years. But, they state that from a psychological standpoint "there is no reason why the milestone of the menopause should be expected to blunt the human female's sexual capacity, performance, or drive." Some women were aided by administration of female sex hormones, the secretion of which is usually greatly reduced following menopause. They also found that there is increased masturbation by women in these years due to their husband's demise, infirmity, or lapse in sexual relations. Another study by Christenson and Gagnon found that masturbation was practiced with some regularity among older unmarried women, regardless of whether they had been married.

Studies at Duke University

Duke University has been conducting a long-term study on old age. Part of the study has been the investigation of sex activity during this time of life. It has been found that sexual interest and activity in this age group is by no means rare. There also seems to be a marked difference in patterns of sexual interest and activity between men and women. For men, there is a gradual progression into old age: most men—4 out of 5—who retain good health are sexually interested past age 65. While 2 out of 3 men in their sixties are still sexually active, only 1 in 5 is still active in his eighties. There does not seem to be any age beyond which all men stop having sexual intercourse.

It's a different story for women. There are fewer women than men who are sexually active and interested in sex in their sixties. About 1 in 3 reports sexual interest, while only 1 in 5 is actually having sex. Women also differ from men in that their rates of interest and activity don't seem to fall off with increasing age. One possible explanation for the lower rates for women is that the clearly demarcated menopause may have a negative psychological impact; some women think that their sex life is over with menopause. It is also possible that some women have lower levels of sexual interest and activity all their lives, and therefore there is not really such a decline with age.

Men may contribute most to the cessation of intercourse on the part of women. For one, there is a higher death rate at this age for men, leaving many women widowed. This trend is exaggerated by the fact that most men marry women somewhat younger than themselves; one study found that the average 70-year-old man had a wife 66 years old, and the average 70-year-old woman had a husband 74 years old. A full 86% of the women in our own study reported that they had stopped having intercourse because their husbands had died, become ill, lost interest, or lost potency. Husbands corroborated this opinion—those living agreed that it was they who were in general responsible for termination of sex activity.

In contrast to the usual pattern of declining activity, we made the surprising observation that 13% to 15% of the aged persons, when studied over a period of years, actually showed a pattern of more sex interest and activity. Also the frequency of sexual outlet for older men seemed to be unaffected by whether they were married or not. This fact could have something to do with the double standard in our society. There is also a biological double standard: the gift of longevity to women might mean that those men who do survive find the sex ratio distinctly in their favor!

At any rate, it is time for the taboo against sex activity of old people to be dropped. It is certainly clear that the activity is physically possible, and there is no reason why sexual expression should not be an important source of emotional reward. The aged must be granted their own sexuality with accompanying dignity.

Comment by:
HAROLD HIATT
The truth of the matter is now known. When the scientific measuring stick is applied to older persons, it is found that sexual expression in aging persons does occur. Dr. Pfeiffer has studied sexual practices in the young, the middle aged, and the aged and has not only confirmed some of the previous observations of Kinsey, and Masters and Johnson, but has moved into the more exacting scientific area of statistical confirmation.

As Meerloo[1] has pointed out, the sexual taboo with older patients is similar to the resistance met by Freud in the discovery of infantile sexuality. Grotjahn[2] has said that the therapist who hopes the "old person will live beyond sin and sex, like angels, is likely not to understand one of their most important sources of conflict, guilt, and depression." With Dr. Pfeiffer's revealing studies, the medical student or physician must not deny the reality that those persons over age 60 do participate in and enjoy intimate physical relationships. The taboo is on the other foot.

As a result of cultural attitudes, the aging person subjectively has come to expect that his sexual interests will wane. It is important to counteract this negative self-fulfilling prophecy and to see more clearly some of the psychological inhibitions that are involved. I would like to add to Dr. Pfeiffer's observations two additional points which I think contribute to sexual inhibition in the aging person.

The first is the fact that many of the persons now over age 60 were at the peak of their sexual potential during the depression years of the 30s. This was the era of "economic contraception" to limit the number of children in a given family during the depression years. The inhibitions upon sexual performance because of fear of pregnancy may have contributed to a habit pattern of continence which tended to weaken the libidinal drive that many carried into the aging years.

A second point related to the aging person's self-image and the inhibition of his sexuality, may be related to the fear of physical harm. The "la petite mort" following orgasm may be symbolically connected with "la grande mort." The little death of sexual satisfaction which is a subjective physiologic and pyschologic relaxation may be connected with the greater fear of physical damage caused by sexual activities.

Does the aging person fear death? It is my observation as a physician that the large majority of persons face death realistically, but that they psychologically do not tolerate rejection by their loved ones. Sexual expression is one of the human activities which demonstrates mutual acceptance and I would hazard the guess that fear or shame of rejection or failure is perhaps greater than fear of death.

Finally, in an effort to counteract the cultural taboos and the innate rejection of the aged, it should be pointed out that in the aging process a person psychologically experiences the "Dacapo effect," or a playing through the chorus of their early life. It seems logical to me that masturbation, sexual curiosity, sexual teasing, exhibitionism, and the "cuddling" of body contact with another that is seen in childhood, would have a recrudescence in aging years.

References

1. Meerloo, J.A.M.: Transference and resistance in geriatric psychotherapy. Psychoanal. Review 42:72-82, 1955.
2. Grotjahn, M.: Analytic psychotherapy with the elderly. Psychoanal. Review 42:419-427, 1955.

Comment by:
Ruby H. Gingles
A better understanding of human sexuality throughout the life cycle is being gained through the contributions of Kinsey, Masters and Johnson, Duke University and other researchers. Dr. Pfeiffer presents a strong case for dropping the taboo against sexual activity for old people through his interpretation of relevant research findings. I concur with the need to overcome the stigma against open discussion of sex in old age. At the same time I am concerned about the effects of publicizing some of the present data. Unsophisticated readers may not realize that data are far from complete and may overgeneralize as they apply findings to themselves.

Perhaps the most important aspect of research at this time is to clarify some of the myths and fallacies surrounding sex in old age. As we bring the subject into the open and gradually eliminate the taboos, more older men and women may be willing to participate in research studies. Up to the present time, most research efforts have yielded quantitative data; i.e., percentages of older people who are sexually active, frequency of coitus, prevalence of impotency, and ability to have erections, ejaculations, and orgasms at various ages. Although this information is valuable and does help to dispel some of the existing fallacies, more research is needed regarding the qualitative nature of sex in old age.

To understand the needs, the feelings, and the satisfactions of sexual relations, the cooperation of older subjects is essential. Such understanding would be valuable in the adjustment of older couples to this aspect of married life. Also, it would contribute to a recognition of the sexual needs of the ever-increasing numbers of elderly people who have no societally approved avenues of sexual outlet.

At this time in the history of research on sex in old age, I am concerned about the possible interpretation of findings. Will a 50-year-old male, reading that he can expect a decline in his sexual capability, become overanxious about losing his youth? Will such anxiety either hasten his sexual inadequacy or lead him to unnatural increased activity "before it's too late"? Will older married women, presently content with their sexual relations pattern, become dissatisfied and feel their husbands are not helping them reach maximum sexual fulfillment? Or, hopefully, will the data be reassuring and lead to a better understanding of one's sexual nature in old age?

My concern is prompted by the pattern of reaction to initially published findings in another area of sex information, regarding the achievement of orgasm in sexual intercourse. Many wives and husbands became extremely apprehensive and felt it imperative to achieve orgasm with each sexual experience. Previously satisfied wives felt unfulfilled, and husbands felt inadequate if they were not able to bring their wives to orgasm. With time more realistic understandings have been achieved by the public. Dr. Pfeiffer's accurate and insightful interpretation of the present state of our knowledge about sex and aging is a valuable contribution to dispelling the taboos about sex in old age.

PART II

Marital Discord

5. Delinquent Sex and Marriage Counselors

DAVID R. MACE

There is no way of knowing how many people seek counseling for sexual and marital problems in the United States today. All evidence suggests, however, that the number of such persons is large and is steadily increasing. Masters and Johnson, who are not given to exaggeration, have estimated that in approximately half of all marriages there is sexual inadequacy of one kind or another. Outside marriage, as counselors know, more people than we hear about are having trouble in the area of their sex lives.

The number of marriages that end in divorce is in the region of one for every three new marriages. This is by no means the whole picture, however. As Bossard and Boll have pointed out, "When one combined the data on divorce, annulments, desertions, separations, and reported unhappiness among couples living together, the proportion of family discord is amazing. At any one moment, possibly one out of every two couples is chafing at the domestic bit." Lederer and Jackson go further. They suggest that the "stable-satisfactory marriage," representing the state of complete harmony and compatibility that many couples aim for, constitutes only from 5 to 10 percent of all marriages.

By no means do all of the unhappy people represented by these estimates seek the aid of counselors, professional or otherwise. But the trend is increasingly to do so, and it appears likely that the field of sexual and marital counseling has a big future. Already, sex and marriage may well be the major areas in which people seek counseling help. Apart from the cases dealt with by marriage counselors, investigations of the case loads of psychiatrists, psychologists, social workers, and clergymen invariably show a high incidence of problems in these areas.

Competence and integrity in the counselor

When we try to assess the quality of service available to meet this burgeoning volume of human need, we find a most confusing picture. We have no reliable information about the distribution of competence among the wide variety of therapists involved. We know that some highly responsible and very skilled persons are included, and also, unfortunately, some who are either incompetent or unscrupulous, or both. It is with the latter categories that this paper is concerned.

From time to time, publicity has been given to some of the more flagrant examples of "phonies" and "quacks" in this field. Successful action to deal with this problem has already been taken in a few states by the licensing of marriage counselors. In general, however, any attempt at effective control presents great difficulties. Abuses are not easy to expose, because the private nature of the counseling relationship makes investigation very difficult, and victims are generally reluctant to identify themselves.

The issue was raised from a somewhat new angle in the Masters and Johnson report on *Human Sexual Inadequacy*. In the final pages of this volume, the authors go out of their way to draw attention to the fact that "Foundation personnel frequently encounter during their in-depth interviews reports of tragic psychotherapeutic malpractice, that of the therapist seducing the essentially defenseless patient into mutual sexual experience . . . There are on record an unfortunately large number of reasonably documented cases to support the necessity for a plea for personal and professional integrity among those individuals counseling for sexual inadequacy."

We therefore appear to be confronted with different kinds of malpractice among sexual and marital counselors, ranging from the grossly incompetent charlatan to the highly qualified but unscrupulous professional. It would obviously be unreasonable and unfair to focus attention exclusively on only one dimension of this problem and to ignore others. All aspects of delinquency in sexual and marital counseling need to be reviewed.

We must therefore distinguish two essentials of good counseling, the absence of either of which would amount to delinquency in the practitioner concerned. The first is competence, the second integrity. It is a truism to say that the public, in seeking help to resolve marital and sexual problems, or indeed any other types of personal inadequacy, takes it for granted that anyone declaring himself to be a counselor or therapist, and practicing in what looks like a professional setting, can be assumed to be both competent and trustworthy. If this assumption were to be proved false on any scale, the result could be quite devastating.

All counselors can thus be divided into four groups. First, there are those who are both competent and scrupulous, and it is to be hoped that these represent the overwhelming majority. At the other end of the scale are those who are both incompetent and unscrupulous, and our hope is that there are very few of these. Somewhere between these extremes, there are counselors who are scrupulous but incompetent, and counselors who are competent but unscrupulous.

Phony marriage counselors

Let us begin with the outright "quacks." These are the people who prey on the ignorance and desperation of people in trouble by offering to provide remedies which they simply cannot deliver. They have undergone no recognized training, and have no recognized qualifications. They exploit the needy for personal gain—usually for money, but occasionally also for sexual and other purposes. Such persons are manifestly cheats and frauds, and in a responsible society people have the right to be protected from such exploitation.

All the traditionally recognized "helping professions" have sought to provide such protection by setting standards for competence and requiring their identified members to meet those standards. This internal self-policing of the professionals needs, however, to be reinforced by state laws requiring recognized accreditation, and stipulating penalties for offenders. Unfortunately, new professions and sub-professions take time to set up these safeguards, and during that period charlatans may flourish. This is the present state of affairs in the recently established fields of sexual and marital counseling.

Examples of the outright charlatan have been reported by the press and in magazine articles. Here are three examples.

California, before it passed a law in 1964 requiring the licensing of marriage counselors, had quite a crop of "phonies." Probably the most bizarre was a man who claimed to have a Ph.D. degree, and ran a "problem clinic" purporting to be a branch of the "National Association for Family Service." When a former Los Angeles policewoman acting as an undercover investigator went to keep an appointment with him, he greeted her in a turquoise turban and surgical smock, held her hand during the interview, and advised her to give up the thyroid pills her doctor had prescribed. She had complained of sexual difficulties in her marriage, and the counselor promised to cure her in six interviews at $10 a time. Called in for questioning later, he admitted that he had awarded himself the Ph.D. degree (his formal education ended in the tenth grade), and that he had no qualifications whatsoever for the practice of marriage counseling. The investigation was in 1962, before the licensing law had been passed, and no legal action could be taken to prevent him from continuing his practice.

In Michigan, before the licensing law was passed, the *Detroit Free Press* exposed a quack marriage counselor who claimed to hypnotize married couples and resolve their marital problems. He also injected some with a special "serum." He charged one woman client $3,000 and left her so emotionally disturbed that she had to have remedial psychiatric treatment. His Ph.D. proved to have cost him $58 from a diploma mill. He was convicted of practicing as a psychologist without appropriate qualifications, and received a suspended sentence in return for agreeing to leave the state.

Probably the most notorious case of all was that of a group of fifteen quack marriage counselors investigated in New York. All were without recognized qualifications, but through the yellow pages of the Manhattan telephone directory they fleeced unsuspecting married couples. In testimony before the New York Committee on Matrimonial and Family Laws, a "chamber of horrors was described—of women undressing for their 'therapists' to overcome inhibitions, of sexual abuses, adultery, and promiscuity." The group charged high fees, made extra money by setting up sexual assignments between clients, and arranged abortions and divorces.

No argument is likely to be raised against the taking of appropriate legal measures to protect the public from this kind of chicanery. As we have noted, however, the enactment of legislation tends to be delayed—not because of any disagreement about the principle, but because the drawing of precise lines of demarcation to divide the sheep from the goats always proves to be difficult and highly controversial.

What is incompetence?

Now let us consider the counselors who are scrupulous but incompetent. It might be argued that no one could be regarded as responsible if he offered services which he was not qualified to provide. The matter is not, however, as simple as that. Standards of competence not only vary widely, but judgment concerning what competence implies also varies. Even if we consider a sick person requiring surgery, it is possible for a faith healer to believe quite sincerely that he can offer a cure which will prove to be as effective as any operation. We may question his judgment on this point, but his integrity is not necessarily impugned.

Likewise, there are those who consider themselves quite competent to resolve marital and sexual problems by prayer and hypnosis, by invoking the magic of the earth or the mysterious influence of the stars. They may be deeply convinced that these powers are much more efficacious than the skill of a therapist who merely possesses a Ph.D. in clinical psychology or a Master's degree in social work. Moreover, there are people who would have more faith in the former procedures than the latter. A well-known marriage counselor once told me that in order to secure an evaluation of a number of marriage manuals, he gave his clients a miscellaneous selection of these books to read and asked for their opinions. To his consternation, the book which the clients ranked as the best proved to be the one which the counselor himself judged to be the worst!

This is not to say that objective judgments cannot be made. Most of us firmly believe that a person professionally trained to deal with human problems will be better able to serve those who come to him in need than a person without such training. Yet in specific situations this is not at all easy to prove. Thorough and extensive research to check the long-term results of sexual and marital counseling has so far been conspicuous by its absence. The self-imposed standard of the Masters-Johnson team, which will not claim success till therapy has stood the test of a five-year follow-up, is without parallel in this field. Some other attempts to judge the efficacy of professional skills, such as the evaluation of psychotherapy in England by Eysenck, have not come up with very encouraging results.

The truth, then, is that while we have faith in the counselor who has received a thorough scientific and professional training, we cannot yet rule out the possibility that some persons who follow other procedures may also produce good results. Their very confidence in their methods can be highly therapeutic. Jerome Frank and others have found that the belief of the therapist in his own powers is one of the most important factors in his success.

Does this therefore mean that it is useless to try to establish standards of competence for sex and marriage counselors? Not at all. There can be no question that, as a whole, the membership of the American Association of Marriage and Family Counselors, who have undergone the discipline of gaining a thorough knowledge of the subject and of being trained under skilled supervision to use the therapeutic techniques presently available to us, will render better service to the public than the unorganized mass of other practitioners who could not meet these high standards. What remains true, however, is that this kind of accreditation cannot operate in any absolute sense, for there will always be exceptions to the rule on both sides of the dividing line. What is also true is that, in the present state of our knowledge, a marriage counselor who would be judged incompetent, even highly incompetent, by the AAMFC, is not necessarily unscrupulous.

Unscrupulous therapists

We now turn our attention to those sexual and marital counselors who would be considered competent by existing professional standards, but whose behavior would expose them to the judgment that they are also unscrupulous. The word "unscrupulous" is defined by one modern dictionary as meaning "contemptuous of what is right or honorable."

The particular misdemeanor to which Masters and Johnson have drawn attention is the sexual exploitation of the client or patient. This is not the only form of exploitation of which competent counselors may be guilty, but it is the one most often considered. According to Masters and Johnson, "On record at the Foundation are histories recording direct statements of sexual exchange between patients and therapists from every conceivable level of professional discipline involved in consultation and/or treatment of a sexually inadequate individual. Listed specifically by patients are physicians of every established discipline treating sexually inadequate men or women, behaviorists (the major disciplines), theologians (the major religions), and legal advisors. Representatives of each of these disciplines have been recorded in histories as participants in the seduction of men and women seeking their professional support or as encouraging direct personal approaches from such persons."

The question that immediately arises is, how do we know that these incidents really happened? Couldn't they be either fantasy on the part of the clients, or malicious reprisals against therapists who collect a lot of money yet fail to solve the problem? It is certainly possible that all of these accusations by clients may not necessarily be well-founded. However, according to Masters and Johnson, "suffice it to say that time and time again, year in and year out, male and female patients have reported sexual experience with their therapists (old or new, ongoing or rejected), and that the specifics of the material as reported are far and away too real for the Foundation's personnel to credit to patient fantasy in most cases. Even if only twenty-five percent of these specific reports are correct, there still is an overwhelming issue confronting those professionals serving as therapists in the field of human dysfunction." In further support of the veracity of these accounts must be adduced the existence of similar evidence from other sources. Despite all safeguards, complaints of sexual exploitation by therapists lead occasionally to legal action and are reported in the press from time to time. Further, ethics committees of the professional organizations, on some of which I have served, deal with accusations of this kind and find some of them well substantiated. In addition, on several occasions I have had to investigate such situations personally on behalf of a client, and have received an admission of complicity from the therapist concerned. The American Psychological Association has in some of its regional panels brought out this delicate issue for open discussion. The subject was also discussed at a national conference of this association held in California.

There can therefore be no doubt that indiscretions of this kind *do* occur. What cannot be established at the present time is the scale on which they occur. In the Masters-Johnson group of nearly 800 persons accepted for therapy, it appears that the proportion reporting such misdemeanors was high. How representative this is of sex and marriage counseling generally, we have no way of knowing.

Sexual delinquency in the therapist

Do sexual relations of various kinds, including intercourse, between therapist and clients necessarily represent unscrupulous behavior? Masters and Johnson think so, and traditional standards of professional ethics would emphatically agree. In a recent article entitled "The Seductive Psychotherapist," psychiatrist Judd Marmor states that the ultimate consequences of patient-therapist sexual involvement are inevitably antitherapeutic: "I have yet to see a woman who became involved in an erotic relationship with a therapist who did not end up resenting and feeling betrayed by him." He adds that such experiences have even precipitated psychotic breakdowns. A similar condemnation of such practices was issued by psychiatrist Charles Clay Dahlberg, in an article titled "Sexual Contact Between Patient and Therapist." He wrote: "The patient comes because he needs help—an admission of weakness. He is encouraged at times to be weak. This implies that the therapist is strong enough, at least, not to take advantage of his patient's weakness. Irrationality is encouraged only because the therapist is the temporary repository of rationality. Anything less is exploitation. It really isn't fair play."

Some involved therapists might, however, attempt to defend themselves. It could be argued that they were solving the client's immediate problem by providing a responsible and secure sexual outlet, or freeing the client from unfounded fears and inhibitions—that this was nothing more than an overt expression of the "transference-countertransference" relationship in which the therapist represents meaningful figures in the patient's life, to be worked through and discarded when it had fulfilled its purpose.

There is one obvious response to this kind of argument. If there are indeed valid therapeutic goals to be attained by such procedures, surely this should be openly declared and defended, not practiced furtively. We may appropriately recall here Edward Westermarck's famous dictum that "concealment of the truth is the only indecorum known to science."

In the cases that come to light, the client has manifestly *not* been helped. The particular weight of the testimony of Masters and Johnson lies in the fact that all their reports came from subjects for whom therapy proved unsuccessful; otherwise the referral to the Foundation would not have been necessary. Yet investigation cannot be complete unless we are ready to hear testimony of another kind. Where would we stand if substantial evidence *could* be adduced that therapists had brought lasting benefits to their clients by having sex relations with them?

Most of the Masters-Johnson reports concern heterosexual liaisons with female clients, initiated by, or accepted from, male therapists. Since these were nearly all marital units, it appears that the therapist, having accepted the client in order to assist her to a more satisfactory sexual relationship with her husband, proceeded by the startling route of involving her in an attempt to establish a satisfactory sexual relationship with himself! It happens that one of the findings of the Masters-Johnson study is that a woman cannot easily "transfer" a satisfactory sex relationship with one particular male from that male to another, because each relationship for her tends to be deeply individualized. The male, however, can with much greater facility make this kind of transfer. The logical conclusion would be that female therapists might with impunity claim a therapeutic basis for sexual involvement with their male patients, but not the other way round! Masters and Johnson also found cases where therapists initiated troubled patients into lesbianism and male homosexual activity.

But, of course, most of the situations we have been considering involved no claim whatever to be therapeutic, but simply represented failures in self-discipline on the part of the therapists concerned. The fact had better be faced that the counseling relationship can assume highly erotic overtones and undertones, and it is the responsibility of the counselor to understand what is going on, and to establish the appropriate controls and restraints. A college counselor has described this hazard with unusual candor. "Counseling the sexual area," he says, "can be very threatening. The problem is especially important in counseling female students. The counselor must be open to what the girl is saying. The counselor must be aware of the fact that she may be developing highly complex feelings, including sexual feelings, for him . . . Unless the counselor is capable of handling this, he will become either defensive or overinvolved in the student . . . It is not easy to sit in a closed office confronted by a sexually disturbed, occasionally promiscuous female student. Warmth and objectivity are both required."

Dr. Aaron Rutledge, a veteran marriage counselor and trainer of marriage counselors, sounds an appropriate warning. "Many a counselor," he says, "meets the challenge of his life as he tries to navigate the ship of therapy between the Charybdis of the client's surging emotional and sexual needs on the one hand, and the Scylla of his own unmet needs on the other."

Without question there is enough evidence of this kind to justify the concern of Masters and Johnson. Yet it would be tragic if women needing help about their intimate personal problems were to lose their confidence in the integrity of thousands of responsible and trustworthy counselors because a few had betrayed the trust reposed in them. Alert surveillance by professional associations is one safeguard, but in the end the issue probably rests with the sense of responsibility of the individual counselor himself, and his awareness of the serious damage that can result from indiscretion on his part—not only to his client and himself, but also to the professional colleagues whose good name he can bring into disrepute.

Guidelines for those seeking help

There are, of course, other aspects of this highly controversial subject which call for investigation, but are outside the scope of this chapter. It is to be hoped, now that the subject is being given publicity, that the appropriate professional organizations will accept their responsibility to initiate a full inquiry. Perhaps I may appropriately conclude with some words of counsel to be transmitted to any who have had the misfortune to receive poor or irresponsible service from a sexual or marital counselor, or who wonders what to do if such an eventuality should arise.

The following points should be clearly understood by all members of the public who find themselves troubled with sexual or marital difficulties which they are unable to resolve by their own unaided efforts:

1. Outside the narrow circle of completely trustworthy friends and relatives, personal sexual and marital problems should be discussed only with qualified professionals, such as pastors, doctors, lawyers, psychologists, and trained and qualified counselors.

2. Beyond such general discussion, more intensive counseling should be sought only from persons who have had *specific training in this field.* Counseling concerned with these problems is quite difficult and complex, and you are simply not likely to obtain a high level of help from counselors, however sympathetic and understanding they may be, who are professionally poorly qualified.

3. It should be recognized that discussion of sexual marital situations often stirs strong emotions, in the client and sometimes in the counselor as well. Erotic feelings may be aroused which can get in the way of the therapeutic process. A well-trained and experienced counselor understands this and knows how to handle it, both in himself and in his client. If the client temporarily "falls in love" with the counselor, this is a form of "transference" that is well understood. It doesn't bother or embarrass the therapist. He accepts it, just as he accepts the client in other respects, and takes it into consideration as he proceeds with the counseling task. The existence of these feelings may be openly discussed. But whether this happens or not, the counselor will almost certainly become aware of what is happening.

4. If a counselor makes some suggestion or advance which a client considers to be improper, it should be challenged at once. Not to do so is to risk damaging quite severely the "rapport" that is all-important to effective counseling. No client should ever be required to participate in any form of so-called "therapy" that is not ethically acceptable to him or her.

5. If the counselor persists in inappropriate behavior, or takes liberties which make the client feel uncomfortable, the counseling relationship should be terminated and the reason for doing so made quite clear to the counselor. If the counselor's behavior has been serious enough to cause harm, the client should accept the duty of reporting this to the professional association to which the counselor belongs. Even if this may be a somewhat embarrassing action to take, unscrupulous counselors cannot be restrained unless those who are harmed by their actions will cooperate by alerting the appropriate professional authorities. A counselor who behaves improperly toward one client may well do so toward others, and he may do a great deal of harm to many people unless someone takes steps to expose him.

6. In conclusion, despite the unhappy cases of delinquency quoted in this article, there is still every reason to believe that the great majority of qualified and accredited professional persons who practice sexual and marital counseling are completely responsible, dependable, and trustworthy.

References

1. Bellivieu, F., and Richter, L.: *Understanding Human Sexual Inadequacy* (New York: Bantam Books, 1970).
2. Bossard, J.H.S., and Boll, E.S.: *Why Marriages Go Wrong* (New York: Ronald Press, 1958), p. 13.
3. Dahlberg, C.C.: Sexual contact between patient and therapist. *Contemp. Psychoanal.* 6:2, Spring 1970.
4. Davidson, B.: Quack Marriage Counselors. *Saturday Evening Post*, Dec. 1962.
5. Eysenck, H.J.: *Handbook of Abnormal Psychology* (New York: Basic Books, 1961), pp. 719-720.
6. Frank, J.D.: The dynamics of the psychotherapeutic relationship. *Psychiatry* 22:17-39, 1959.
7. Kaplan, J.: Frauds Who Prey on Shaky Marriages. *Today's Health,* June 1969.
8. Lederer, W.J., and Jackson, D.D.: *The Mirages of Marriage* (New York: Norton, 1969), p. 129.
9. Marmor, J.: The seductive psychotherapist. *Psychiat. Digest* 31:10, Oct. 1970.
10. Masters, W.H., and Johnson, V.E.: *Human Sexual Inadequacy* (Boston: Little, 1970), pp. 388-389.
11. Rubenstein, R.L.: *Rabbinical Counseling* (Earl A. Grollman, ed.) (New York: Block, 1966), pp. 27-28.
12. Rutledge, A.L., in *Pastoral Psychol.,* Oct. 1962.
13. Westermarck, E.: *The History of Human Marriage* (London: Macmillan, 1925), Vol. 1, p. 25.

6.   *Sex In Troubled Marriages*

JAMES E. DeBURGER

There are two schools of thought about the significance of sexual problems revealed by persons seeking help for a disrupted marriage. One holds that sexual and affectional relations between mates are especially vulnerable to deterioration under such crisis situations as unemployment and that sexual complaints usually represent a convenient focus of personal attack on the mate's deficiencies. In other words, the sexual problem is not the primary one. The point of view I subscribe to holds that sexual problems should be recognized as central and fundamentally related to the level of happiness in marital relations. Given the emerging and critically important role of the marital relationship as possibly the last bastion of primary person-to-person relationships in a mass society, it seems that revealed marital problems (and especially sexual problems) may increasingly tend to reflect concern with the attainment of happiness in the intimate relations between mates.

One thing has become apparent to me over several years of counseling experience: among seriously troubled married persons seeking professional help, major marital problems connected with the intimate patterns of interaction between mates far outweigh other types of problems. This conclusion is supported by a research project I conducted recently.

The research and the subjects

I analyzed letters requesting help from the national office of the American Association of Marriage Counselors written by 252 husbands and 1160 wives from various parts of the United States. These letters constituted a sample from a much larger collection of over 14,000 received by the Association over a ten-year period.

Each was carefully analyzed and coded to indicate major and secondary problems revealed by the writer—a problem was considered major if it appeared to be considered by the help-seeker as the chief cause of marital unhappiness; secondary problems included any other complaints or concerns discussed in the letter.

Among the 1412 help-seekers represented in this study, the average age was 39 for husbands and 36 for wives. Most were Protestant and all were Caucasian. The average length of marrriage for all subjects was approximately 12 years.

Several kinds of major problems were revealed: Sexual, Affectional, Role Tasks, Parental-Role, Intercultural and Situations Conditions, Deviant Behavior, and Personality Conflict. Of all the findings which grew out of the entire research project,[1] my emphasis here on sexual problems was impelled both by their prominence and recurrence and by my conviction that successful sexual interaction will emerge as the expressive behavioral core of meaningful and satisfactory marital relations. In addition to analysis of its problem content, each help request was inspected and coded for various aspects of the help-seeking process itself and for the emotional tone or orientation associated with the marital difficulties.

Affectional problems are blamed by many

Sexual relations problems ranked second only to the closely related category of affectional relations. Nearly one fourth of the 1412 help-seekers saw their marital trouble as due to some form of maladjustment in sexual relations. Specific complaints reported included in order of frequency (1) serious overall dissatisfaction in sexual relations, (2) difficulties connected with orgasm dysfunction, frigidity or impotence, (3) feelings of sex deprivation or insufficient coital frequency, and (4) "unnatural" sex desires on the part of the mate. Most problems were encompassed by the first three items; the few cited under the fourth category consisted almost entirely of repugnance toward the mate's insistence on oral sex. The large proportion of those who traced their marital disruption to some sexual problem is dramatically compounded when both major and secondary problems were combined. Forty-one percent of those who had not revealed a sex-related major problem were discovered under further analysis to be complaining nevertheless of some sexual difficulty in their marriage!

It is remarkable that so few major problems involving parental role relations were disclosed by these help-seekers. Since so many of them (nearly 80%) were parents, it was expected that a fairly large proportion would indicate parental problems as a major source of difficulty for their troubled marriage. This was not borne out by the analysis. This lack of parental problems may be implicit support for the argument that the crucially determining forces at work in a seriously troubled marriage should be sought in the network of intimate (sexual and affectional) relations between mates. We cannot suggest that everything will be "just great" in a familial situation if only the intimate interaction of the married pair is satisfying. However, given the increasing significance of emotional sustenance needs and functions in the American scheme of marriage, it seems unlikely that a couple will consider their marriage satisfactory if sexual and affectional interaction does not provide these gratifications.

Husbands and wives see different problems

In accordance with prior research that pointed to sex differences in the disclosure of problems, our analysis showed that husbands and wives did indeed differ significantly in regard to the kinds of major problems, particularly sexual ones, revealed in their help-request letters.

The proportion of husbands citing a sexual relations problem as the major cause of their marital difficulties (42.1%) was more than double that of wives (20.6%). The pattern was reversed in the closely related area of affectional relations, with wives accounting for many more (31%) of the affectional relations problems than the husbands (11.5%). When we take the two kinds of problems together—sexual and affectional—it becomes clear that these two problem types constitute more than 50 percent of all major problems revealed by these help-seekers.

It could be argued, of course, that affectional and sexual components are very similar and are perhaps overlapping. In an attempt to distinguish between them problems were recorded as sexual only if there was a clear erotic element present in the description. Affectional relations problems struck two themes: a lack of affectional gestures, contact, or verbalization; and the presence or threat of lowered commitment to the marriage by the mate. Undoubtedly there may be sexual undertones in these complaints but for our purposes it seemed feasible to make a distinction between the two kinds of problems, a distinction which supports Ehrmann's conclusion that ". . . females seem more directly and overtly concerned with romanticism and males with eroticism."[2]

If, as Ehrmann has suggested, females are brought up with an affectional rather than a sexual orientation to marriage, wives probably are more sensitive than husbands to any change in their spouse's display of affection. It seems to me that the possession impulse in marriage—the need for security based on ownership—also operates more strongly among women than men. Among our subjects the need for maintaining feelings of exclusiveness in affectional relations was much stronger among wives. Speaking as a counselor, it seems that exclusiveness and the possessive attitude are very often a prelude to "taking the other for granted." This process may lead to strong male disenchantment and a vicious cycle of male behavior ("I'll show her!") calculated to maintain a sense of unique personal worth and attractiveness. At the risk of appearing chauvinistic, I must note that many husbands resort to the pursuit of extramarital sex objects as an outgrowth of their feelings of no longer being sexually desired within marriage. Predictably, in our subjects, husbands much more often than wives appeared as role-deviant due to their extramarital sexual activities.

In general, then, husbands and wives differ in their disclosure of problems perceived to be central to marital disruption. The specific complaints cited predominantly by wives are: (1) "mate is in love with another," (2) "mate wants sex too often," (3) sex relations per se are disgusting, (4) mate's "crudeness in sex behavior," (5) orgasm dysfunction, and (6) "mate's extramarital sex relations." Those cited more often by husbands are: (1) general serious dissatisfaction with quality of marital sex relations, (2) "sex frustration—inadequate frequency of coitus," (3) "affectional approach spurned by mate," (4) "mate is cold . . . unloving," and (5) worries about effect of low sex drive on marriage. Conflict and arguments with the mate showed the same sex-differentiated pattern. Most husbands reported conflicts over sexual relations while most wives reported conflicts associated with exclusive-possessive aspects of affectional relations. Overall, it appears when a marriage is in serious trouble that the wife is most likely to define the problem in affectional terms and the husband in sexual. At the risk of appearing simplistic, I must suggest that such a dichotomy (one which I believe to be widespread in marital disruptions in this society) can be resolved if our primary agencies of socialization adopt realistic procedures for education in sexuality and affectional behavior for both males and females.

Major marital problems involving sexual relations were much more frequently revealed by blue-collar than while-collar husbands. On the other hand, while more than one fifth of the white-collar husbands disclosed major problems in the affectional relations category, none of the blue-collar husbands did. We must note here that within either social class the husband-wife differences discussed earlier persisted for both problems types. When blue-collar and white-collar wives were compared, no drastic differences were seen in the extent to which sexual and affectional problems were revealed.

Analysis of those help-requests in which length of marriage had been identified (758) revealed some association between length of marriage and the disclosure of problems in the areas of sexuality and affection. Since most of the data in this study pertain to marriages of somewhat less than ten years duration, the findings on this point are quite tentative. However, two trends seem to emerge. First, for both husbands and wives problems connected with affectional relations tend to increase significantly with length of marriage. Secondly, for husbands, sexual problems show considerable decrease over time. Among wives, however, while sexual relations problems are appreciably less than for husbands, they tend to persist and even increase slightly in the later years of marriage.

Emotional factors

Negative feelings were much more frequently reported by persons experiencing sexual problems than by those who disclosed other kinds of problems. There was also some indication of sex differences. A much larger proportion of wives than husbands (20% to 8%) reported feeling that they were degraded by their mate. About the same proportionate differences between husbands and wives were found in regard to expressions of anger, resentment toward the mate, depression, nervous exhaustion, and disillusionment in marriage. This sex difference was somewhat weaker for the white-collar than for the blue-collar class. Data collected by Gurin[3] showed that women report greater stress and more problems in marriage than do husbands. There is also some evidence to suggest that women to a greater extent than men consciously experience tension and dwell on their marital problems and that more wives than husbands feel inadequate in their familial roles.

A much larger proportion of wives than husbands (50% to 25%) blamed the mate for the sexual relations problem and the consequent marital disruption. Also, more husbands than wives attribute blame to themselves. These differences were somewhat stronger in the blue-collar than in the white-collar class. This prominence in self-blaming may be related to the male's somewhat greater initiative in certain forms of deviant sexual behavior. Again, assuming a persisting tendency in this culture to portray marital failure in terms of wrongdoer and the wronged, it may be that blame would more likely be attached to the more initiatory, aggressive role of the husband than to the relatively more passive role of wife.

Among those who were seeking help for sexual relations problems, husbands more often expressed optimism and less often experienced pessimism regarding possibility of resolving the difficulties. This difference was more pronounced in the blue-collar class. One could speculate that these differences stem from integral sex-role differences which begin early in life and persist in marriage. Thus, the centrality of the wife's role in modern marriage probably ensures that she will have more immediate and persisting contact with the everyday dynamics and content of a troubled marriage. These conditions may account in part for the observed sex differences in revealed feelings of despair, depression, degradation, and disappointment.

The help-seeking process

Females are much more frequent seekers of help than males. There is almost a five-to-one ratio of wives to husbands among the persons represented in our data. This concurs with other studies of persons utilizing professional help-sources. It may be that wives are relatively more involved in and committed to their marital roles than are husbands, and therefore more highly motivated than husbands to seek professional help as a means of preserving a marriage.

For about 80 percent of all 1412 cases, the help-request letter was the first step toward contact with a formal helping agency. In this respect there was very little difference between persons with sexual relations problems and those having other kinds of problems. Among persons with sexual relations problems husbands more often than wives (33% to 12%) had sought help elsewhere.

Of those who had sought help elsewhere for sexual problems, most (66%) had talked with a physician, but were still unable to deal with their problems. The remaining third had consulted with clergymen, psychiatrists, or psychologists, and miscellaneous other persons and agencies. A social class difference was found in only one instance: more white-collar than blue-collar persons consulted psychiatrists or psychologists. Numerous complaints emerged concerning the quasi-counselor role of physicians. Many help-seekers felt that the physician ". . . was too brusque, really not concerned about my problem," or that ". . . he gave me pills but no guidance about our sexual problem."

The help-request letter was, of course, a response to information about sources of help for sexual and marital problems. But what were the sources of this information? Approximately two thirds of both husbands and wives reported magazines as their source of information. Very few, indeed less than 2 percent, had learned about the referral role of the American Association of Marriage Counselors from professionals (such as physicians and clergymen) in their local community. Miscellaneous reported sources of information included newspapers, lectures, radio or TV programs, books, and the advice of friends. In view of the increasing significance of sexuality for the conjugal family system, it seems remarkable that so few resources exist for the systematic referral, processing, and treatment of problems related to marital sexual relations.

One interesting implication of these data is that some forms of the mass media may serve significant functions in linking problems and troubled marriages with suitable sources of help. In this connection, most of the prominent women's and family magazines have in recent years frequently carried "case record" articles dealing with problems of sexuality in marriage. Such articles are sometimes accompanied by an offer to refer troubled persons to competent counselors or therapists. Articles dealing with sexual problems (especially "case histories") conceivably afford a means by which a sexually troubled marriage or a specific sexual problem may be identified. Furthermore, models of appropriate help-seeking and problem-solving behavior may be provided in such materials.

This speculation raises a rather broad but pertinent question which is not adequately treated in the literature of sex research: namely, the impact of culture on the patterns and dynamics of the help-seeking process. For the question of how Americans actually do try to solve their sex-related marital problems cannot be separated from the related question of how they *ought* to solve them in the light of relevant cultural norms. In this respect the role of mass media is probably crucial in the transmission of socially approved models of help-seeking and in providing channels of information and communication between troubled persons and the professional sources of help.

A striking characteristic of all these requests for help was their lack of mutuality and lack of urgency. Less than 19 percent of the documents revealed a joint effort in the problem-solving; few expressed desire on the part of both husband and wife to work out the sexual difficulties troubling the marriage. In spite of the massive problem content of the help-requests only about 10 percent expressed urgency or pressed for an immediate answer to their plea. One last and intriguing observation: most help-requests from husbands were written during colder weather while those from wives during warmer seasons. I leave interpretation of this phenomenon to those who wish to speculate on the effect of climate on behavior.

As for the kinds of information sought, the most frequent request was for the title of a book or manual which might help solve the sexual relations problem at hand. This kind of request, reflective perhaps of the "do-it-yourself" tendency in American culture, came from over 95 percent of both husbands and wives. There are implications here of a cookbook approach to marital problems which assumes the notion of ready-made "self-help" formulas, comparable to the phenomena of self-diagnosis and self-treatment in physical illness. Other requests were for information on sex techniques, aphrodisiacs (husbands 44%, wives 27%), and sexual anatomy and physiology (husbands 44%, wives 27%).

Conclusion

Generally speaking the patterns which are seen in the help-seeking behavior of persons experiencing sexual problems in marriage seem little different from those observed in marriages experiencing other kinds of problems. This is probably due in part to the fact that problem-solving resources for troubled marriages in this society give little special emphasis to the problems connected with sexuality per se. Marriages beset with parental role problems can often obtain help from "child guidance" centers, for example, but where does one find a sexual guidance center in this society?

These data support our original proposition that in seriously troubled marriages, the unhappiness is closely related to unsatisfactory patterns of intimate relations between mates. Rather than euphemizing—talking about "communication," "transaction," etc.—we should recognize the specifically sexual and affectional character of these intimate relations. A close look at the changes occurring in contemporary society suggests that the quality of intimate relations between mates may become crucial to criteria of marital happiness or unhappiness as the family group becomes more isolated from kin networks.

References

1. DeBurger, J.E.: Husband-Wife Differences in the Revelation of Marital Problems: A Content Analysis. Unpublished Ph.D. thesis, 1966, Indiana University.
2. Ehrmann, W.: Premarital Dating Behavior (New York: Bantam Books, 1960).
3. Gurin, G., et al.: Americans View Their Mental Health (New York: Basic Books, 1960).

Comment by:
Steven G. Goldstein
There would seem to be no question but that sexual problems are one of the major concomitants of what we call "marital difficulties." They are symptomatic of the difficulties that people have in communicating with one another; but while a person may speak easily to friends and colleagues about the fact that some difficulty is being encountered in making decisions with a spouse, the topic of sexual relations between husband and wife is not easily explored. Thus the anonymous cry for help through the mail and the hope that some expert somewhere can provide advice without demanding involvement.

It is unfortunate to note that over the past two decades the easing of social strictures dealing with sexuality has not had very much effect on the ability of two people bound together in a multi-level relationship to solve the problems that such a relationship brings forth. In fact, it would appear that it has only intensified certain difficulties because, under the guise of "doing my thing," escape is easier without resolution.

One of the other changes that has taken place has been in statistical reporting, so that we now are told about the marriages which have broken up. When compared with the incidence of dissolved marriages some 20 years ago, our present society is judged looser and more immoral (or amoral). I think that what it really shows us is that people who do not wish to live with each other anymore have found more public ways of dispensing with each other's company. Separate bedrooms and weeks of silence are no longer acceptable.

Dr. DeBurger's paper would seem to indicate that our society has come part of the way down the necessary road. We now acknowledge that there are sexual problems in marriage and, by asking for help, form the expectation that help can be provided. We have yet to come the rest of the way down the road which says that sexual problems are symptomatic of a more complete interpersonal difficulty and that they have to be dealt with, not through the mail, not anonymously, but as part of the entire growth process.

7. Violently Jealous Husbands

ROBERT N. WHITEHURST

Events of the last decade have caused us to look closer at man's inhuman and violent treatment of his fellow man. Since the early part of the century, when Freud defined sexuality and aggressiveness as basic characteristics of man's nature, interest in the problem has increased.

The recent work of anthropologist Lionel Tiger has been concerned in part with the violence of males. He notes that at the onset of puberty, males produce 20 to 30 times more testosterone than do females. Although the total amounts produced in the body are minute, he claims that the effects on aggressive male behavior cannot be ascribed solely to culturally induced differences. To understand male violence, then, we must recognize that there is some kind of biological difference that accounts for it, at least in part.

Violence between husbands and wives cannot be separated from the complexities of the marriage relationship. As such, the expression of such violence appears to the observer to be contradictory and even mixed with mutual loyalty. Anyone who has ever tried to break up a marital brawl can attest to this.

Men turn to violence in dealing with their wives because of their inability to control a specific situation to their satisfaction. They perceive the situation as threatening their need to "be in control." In fact, this inability to control or come to some sort of compromise is an essential component of marital violence. How these situations arise in such a large number of marriages, and their implications for both the society and individuals will make up the major portion of our discussion.

The struggle for equality for women is so new that we have inadequately understood the threatening nature of this change. Men of the lower socioeconomic classes are most fearful of meaningful interaction and feelings of equality in their wives. The impact of the mass media, especially television, on freedom-seeking women cannot be underestimated. We may even predict an increase in male violence against women in the future, for there appears to be no way to move in terms of women's liberation except forward to increased equality between the sexes. As husbands retreat from relationships with wives who seek more freedom, there is increasing loss of control by husbands. Increased female participation in the labor market, as well as demands for equal pay for women, adds yet another factor tending to weaken the control of husbands. Add to these the changes in society which give women increased freedom and greater mobility to roam freely, and we further complicate some husbands' problems with their wives. The second car, television, the pill, and free time granted by gadgetry in the household have created wives of a different order than those of former years. This potential equality, ever-demanding and showing itself in new ways, has had no counterpart in the history of man. Men simply have no culturally approved ways of coping with uppity women who want to be really free.

The double standard

A further problem arises for the wife who violates the sexual norms of a double-standard society. A wife can understand if she cannot forgive a husband's sexual indiscretions, for men are often felt to be "that way." Now that we have learned from such studies as Masters and Johnson's that women are as sexy as men, husbands will some day be more tolerant and less likely to become violent if their wives are unfaithful. But one should not expect too much too soon!

As of now, husbands have little choice but to become irate and often violent when wives are unfaithful since there is as yet no socially accepted alternative reaction. It is no doubt a function of male insecurity that this tradition persists. Throughout most of mankind's history on earth, man has had the force of law on his side if he killed his wife, her lover, or both, if he caught them in an act of adultery.

Violence is a male prerogative. The cult of male violence has been described by many social scientists. When all other sources of masculine identity fail, men can always rely on being "tough" as a sign of manhood. Handling wives in aggressive ways is in some respects an extension of the normal techniques by which men learn to handle a variety of problems. Some men do not differentiate the sex of their opponents. In certain ways this relates to a tendency of aggressive men to make an instantaneous assessment of a situation, define it as threatening, and respond with violence. This may be related to early habits in sizing up an enemy, then making the first move to ensure maximum impact.

The view of wives as sometimes "deserving" of physical abuse is essentially lower-class. But elements of this belief seem to be found in men of all social classes. Most men seem to believe that a woman will behave better and may even enjoy the feeling of being put in her "rightful" (subservient) place by physical punishment. Part of the male folklore has it that women really enjoy a male domination-female submissive relationship. Like so many other things in life, this is sometimes true. Our feeling as men that we need to control, plus our belief that women enjoy a little violence, makes violence more likely.

Social class differences

The idea that domestic violence is essentially a lower-class phenomenon is a vastly oversimplified view of the problem. Violence in families is found everywhere, but it is highly variable in its pattern and in its outcome. What evidence there is leads us to the tentative conclusion that nearly all families at some time or another experienced it. Middle-class families are different only in the degree of violence, its frequency, and reactions to its outcome.

Middle-class wives are less passive than lower-class wives. In part this is due to their greater verbal capabilities and their unwillingness to play a subservient role as often as the lower-class wife. This may be an important factor in middle-class violence. Husbands of the middle-class are more prone to hit or strike out at a wife only once, and then immediately to regain control. Perhaps this is because of long training in nonviolence. Once he strikes, the middle-class male is likely to reassess the situation and to see the total consequences to himself. Involvement with the law is a much greater threat to him and to his occupational status. The intrusion of other relatives, of neighbors and of friends is more of a control over his actions than in the case of the lower-class male. Once the middle-class male becomes violent, his well-trained sense of guilt and shame acts to keep the incident within the family context, rather than brought to the attention of the community, the law, and the courts.

This is why no one has an accurate idea as to the actual amount or frequency of middle-class family violence. Lower-class families, having fewer resources within the family structure, more often turn to outside agencies for help. The controls over violence are thus different for middle-class and lower-class families.

Violence is used in the lower-class subculture as a means to achieve some goals and to assert independence and masculinity. Violence thus carries with it approval in ways not at all acceptable in the middle classes. The lower-class male has been trained to quickly weigh the advantages with the disadvantages of using violence; thus his trained capacity to think in these terms is often finely honed as compared to the middle-class male, who has little training in this kind of response. Another factor is described as the "Sure Winner" syndrome. Some men low in the status hierarchy seem to use violence only when they are assured of a victory. Whether sure winners are both lower and middle-class is problematical, but the pattern is one that cannot be ignored.

Unfounded jealousy

There appears also to be a difference in the way men of different social classes talk about their violent acts. Men do not readily tell the whole story of their violent acts. Even more so, middle-class men almost never reveal to anyone their violation of the taboo against hitting a wife. Such an admission is very threatening, and is done under only the rarest conditions. It is very rare for a husband to plead guilty in a public courtroom to charges of assaulting a wife. Men in court tend to view such physical contact with their wives as benign, restraining, or otherwise nonmalicious. Wives dramatize the cruelty of the husbands and the severe damage done them. Court cases also demonstrate some of the ambivalence wives and husbands reflect when the violence comes to trial.

Take the case of Vera and Bill, who were married eight years, had one child, and were separated because of Bill's extreme jealousy.

He worked the second shift from afternoon till midnight in an auto plant, where he had the habit of calling Vera never less than two to three times in an evening to be sure she was home. He occasionally had his friends checking on her to be sure she had no one with her. No real evidence was ever submitted that in fact Vera was having affairs with anyone.

One of Vera's girl friends finally convinced her that life with Bill was becoming impossible because of his jealousy. She left him and moved in with her mother, taking the child with her. Bill had threatened her on several occasions before, so she asked for the presence of a policeman when she returned to their apartment to get her belongings.

Bill was there and an argument broke out. The policeman managed to keep some sort of uneasy peace. After leaving, Vera discovered she had left her purse in the house. On re-entering the house, Bill grabbed her arm at the wrist—a sign of either love or hostility, depending on how this gesture is performed. She wrenched free and went after her purse. Again he grabbed her, this time at the waist. He pinched her, and according to Vera made bruise marks on her body.

This final bedroom scene—interrupted by the policeman—seems to have much of the frustration and ambivalence so often found in husband-wife conflicts. Neither was able to separate the old from the new, to separate effectively the hate from the love. The obvious messages sent by Bill involve much less the intent to harm than to control. How often violent gestures can also be seen as love turned hostile is unknown. I suspect it is a more usual type of response than generally believed.

Sex and jealousy get mixed up, with highly complex results. In many cases violence is associated with the jealousy of husbands when they reached a false conclusion about their wives' unfaithfulness on the basis of little or no evidence.

Although it is usually assumed in the literature that it is mostly lower-class males who accuse their wives of having affairs on the basis of little evidence, we actually know little about these ratios or frequencies. The mild forms of paranoia that husbands and wives generate within their relationships, suspecting the other of having sexual affairs, are almost certainly one of the highly destructive aspects of modern marriage. This will only increase with time. If we do not begin now to develop some new norms of openness and trust, we may expect more violence within marriage in the future. Why do men engage in the fairly regular practice of wife-accusing? Some psychologists think the habit is probably related to the husband's fantasies about sexual adventures outside his marriage. He projects or transplants these fantasies onto his wife. In reality she may or may not be sexually involved with another man. It is necessary to understand that even though the husband may have manufactured his wife's sexual infidelity out of thin air, his sense of frustration is real. His irrational responses may be just as real to the recipient of his irrational anger—his wife.

When an extramarital affair does occur, it is common for a husband to blame his wife and be unable to see any of his own involvement. For wives, it is more common for them to blame themselves. Wives may be expected to swallow their bitterness, to internalize their hostility. This produces psychosomatic diseases, alcoholism, depression, or even in extreme cases suicide.

Swapping mates

Swinging—mate swapping with mutual consent—seems to cut across social class lines. Often, it is the husband who suggests that the pair join swinging activities in which sexual partners are traded. Wives are at first hesitant, but often join reluctantly in order to salvage a marriage relationship they feel is otherwise good. At the outset, husbands experience the same feeling as a five-year-old with a ten dollar bill in a candy store. As the novelty begins to pale, he is willing to let the swinging experience fade into history. But the wife, having a very different set of reactions at the beginning, may start to lose her inhibitions. She may find a new sense of herself sexually. The swinging scene has things to recommend it for females that does not prove equally useful for males, given the limits placed on male sexual performance.

Her pleasure and his inadequacy now may lead to a reluctance on the part of the husband. How much of this is due to jealousy is unknown. But frictions do result. When it is the husband who wants to stop the swinging relations and the wife who wants to continue, it is a very new ball game. The stage is set for hostility. In most cases known to the author, the conflict has been peacefully resolved in favor of the husband. If swinging becomes more of a national experience, one may predict an upswing of marital violence.

Difficulty of attaining a single standard

What may be a fairly typical response to husband jealousy in the new life style of young marrieds can be seen in the case of one couple. The husband and wife, both university graduates, had talked at length before marriage about handling sexual attractions to others. Their set of marital rules provided that they would each maintain some separate parts of their lives. They agreed that in the event of extramarital sexual affairs, they would not talk about them until after they were ended. They felt that this approach would lessen the threat to their marriage. The wife was the first to be involved with an outsider. When the third party moved away and the husband was told about the affair, he was shocked to find his wife sexually involved. He felt seriously wronged and responded with violent jealousy.

They had been married only a short time. His agreement about extramarital sex was projected somewhere into a dim future. He found, much to his own chagrin, that he had sexual double-standard feelings which he had previously denied. He admitted now that he was able to indulge in an affair himself, but was not ready to face the same behavior in his wife.

Although he claimed to love her, he separated from her and later obtained a divorce. He was unable to live with an arrangement he himself had encouraged. This is probably not at all uncommon these days. It is relatively easy for males, especially young ones who consider themselves "with it," to fail to recognize the problem. They find it easy to commit themselves to a single-standard relationship with a woman as long as no other males are around to seek her sexual favors. This intellectual commitment flies out the window when followed through with real emotional and sexual commitment.

Working through such problems is a part of life for many young marrieds. It is likely to become a more prevalent problem. This is because the culture provides no ready-made set of rules by which people can assimilate a sexual experience with others outside of marriage.

Perhaps emerging new life styles will inform and educate the new generation. In the meantime, there is more violence potential in the response of husbands struggling with an idea they can accommodate intellectually, but not in real life.

Ingrained readiness to violence

In the meantime, what we really know about the patterns of violence and potential violence in our society is limited. In what way do men and women respond to each other that creates the stuff of family violence? Why can't husbands work out substitute reactions for violence instead of assaulting wives? These and many more questions can only be hinted at and not answered fully.

In my own study of middle-class marriages I have found that threats of violence are frequent among husbands as a means of controlling wives. This was second only to the most frequent device used—that of controlling money. For wives, their most frequent threat was withdrawal of affection.

If a spouse were to admit an extramarital sexual situation, over half of the people interviewed claimed that they could not help being jealous and would probably respond with violence. One third of them claimed that no kind of extramarital sexual situation is worthy of serious jealousy or violence. The intellectual commitment to nonjealous reactions is fairly easy to make—so long as it is someone else's spouse involved.

In another survey some people saw positive effects in family fights. They felt that conflict could be a sign of love as well as of hostility. Over 61% felt men should be tough and not back away from a fight. These were people who are presumably trained to think and to reason. If the potential violence indicated in these middle-class responses is not atypical, perhaps we can understand how very real is the pattern of violence built into males at all stages of their life cycle. We cannot pretend, however, that violence is simply a response of insecure or inadequate males to their own psychological needs. Women tend to be interactors; they help to build up the violence-potential in husbands.

There are covertly hostile means by which the wife punishes her erring husband. A wife is sometimes willing to allow the law to be her accomplice in carrying out this punishment. One technique involves the missing of trial dates. If the husband is subpoenaed and shows up for the trial in a case of assault on the wife, the wife often does not show up. Or her lawyer will make an excuse for her absence and delay the trial. Wives seem to have the knack of expressing their own violence-potential in passively hostile ways. This is hardly unnatural behavior for one who is usually the weaker of the two physically.

Denials of sex relations

Men can become violent if they feel sexually rejected by women. An attempt at love which is thwarted by the female can create immediate frustration in the male aggressor. A lover has few ways to internalize his rejection by a woman, not his wife. He is unable to retain his feeling of being in control, and this often leads to violence.

For the male, being in control sometimes involves his wife's sexual satisfaction. One husband in his thirties, a physician, always defined his sexual prowess as superior. He felt that his wife should be more than satisfied with sex from him and should never be attracted to other men. On learning that another man had been in the apartment with his wife one day, he struck her. He then promptly felt bad, made love to her, and decided as a result of her sexual response that the incident could not possibly occur again. A few weeks later, he came home at an odd time and found his wife in bed with another man—a friend of his. He thereupon set upon both of them in a jealous rage. His own need to control and feel superior was simply too much of an emotional burden for him to handle without recourse to violence.

Dinner-table squabbling
One traditional source of family fights lies in the preparation and serving of food. Arguments often start at the table, not necessarily over the food itself. The responses of a husband to the closeness of the relations between sex and food and love are all-important.

Exactly how food and sex get mixed with love and jealousy is something of a mystery. One authority claims that male aggression is related to our failure to act out aggressive impulses through biting. He claims that if we could visualize ourselves taking bites out of someone's body, this would release certain tensions that go into violent acts. This does raise an interesting question about the closeness of food, eating, and violence between men and women.

No one knows how often husbands and wives develop a hostile relationship out of their own sexual needs. For some men violence can become a substitute orgasm. It is also common among married couples to note that sex after a battle has an increased intensity. Making up can be great fun. How much wives and husbands may subtly encourage each other in violence for sexual purposes is not known. Perhaps in some cases couples get carried away by their own game. They overreact and lose control of what was intended as a preliminary to coitus.

Only about one third of those who learn about their mate's infidelities threaten divorce if they do not stop. Divorce tends to punish the punisher a whole lot more than the supposed wrongdoer. Thus we find a range of techniques, including some violence, devised to get wayward spouses to stay in line. Verbal threats, visits to lawyers, and outbursts of emotion and violence are all parts of the regular scene in homes where we would little suspect such irrationality. No such relationship can long survive, however, without damage to one or more of the participants. It is most often the female who has fewer ways to protect herself from the effects of this emotional setting leading to violence. More of the central part of her identity is invested in the family and home. She has fewer personal contacts to help her reevaluate her own life situation.

Thus, wives most often bear the brunt of the violence in a relationship which is undesirable. But they may have little will or power to change it.

Our culture teaches men to be tough and ready to fight if necessary. To expect men to also become tender lovers and responsive husbands seems to be asking more than logic can allow. Much of the aggressive hostility vented on wives must be seen as a product of our sexually schizoid culture.

Men are not programmed to be other than aggressive. One might wonder why there is not more violence in a culture that does such strange things to people.

8. *Nagging And Sex*

JAMES A. PETERSON

Many years ago a student in a marriage class brought me a set of marriage commandments, one for men and one for women. The fourth and fifth commandments for women follow:

Thou shalt not quiz thy wedded husband. Hit him with an axe. It is more kind.

Thou shalt not nag thy husband. Shoot him with a revolver. It is more kind.

Any therapist who has watched men cower and shrivel under the onslaughts of suspicious and angry females must agree that almost any treatment is preferable to quizzing and nagging. Fortunately there are interactional processes which can eliminate these alienating behaviors without resorting to the axe or the gun. We shall mention them in due course.

The correlation between nagging and a poor sexual life is obvious to any doctor. Nagging is a weak form of aggression. It is practiced by men and women who lack the ego strength essential to honest expression of anger. Nagging is one way persons have of letting their hostility seep out. The person who is nagged is perfectly aware of the controlled hostility that it expresses. It is difficult to have tenderness or intimacy with a person who has just demonstrated a repressed form of hatred. Furthermore, nagging always carries with it an overtone of derogation. "If you loved me as you say you do, you would take me to the beach on Saturday." "If you were the man you say you are, you would give me those things I need." Even if the qualifying phrase is not used, the person nagged is made to feel inferior. He is not performing as expected. There is a further aspect to nagging. It goes on and on. It is something like the Chinese torture chamber where one drop of water falls on the victim's head over and over. The person nagged comes to live in a state of perpetual dread. He is always about to be "put down" for what he has not done. Unless one is schizoid it is almost impossible to yearn to hold the nagger in his arms, to whisper tender things, and then to give that person sexual satisfaction.

Nagging and marital satisfaction

The relationship of nagging and a poor sexual life is not unidimensional. A poor marital relationship that eventuates in a nagging partner has a profound negative influence on sexual performance. But it is also true that a poor sexual life may result in poor interactional patterns which are expressed in nagging. We shall consider both situations. We have some empirical evidence in terms of the influence of nagging on marital adjustment. In our studies of role adjustment in marriage at the University of Southern California, we have adapted a particular scale of measurement which throws considerable light on this subject. The instrument is called the Interpersonal Check List and was devised by Leary after many years of experimental use at the Kaiser Foundation in San Francisco.

In general, the poorly adjusted couples were comprised of at least one individual whose interpersonal profile was characterized by *weak hostility*. The characteristic description by the mate of individuals who fell in the weak-hostility category was that they were *suspicious, nagging* individuals. Leary described persons in one category of maladjusted marriages as being passively resistant, bitter, distrustful personalities, and those who fall in the other maladjusted category as "passive, submissive, self-punishing masochistic personalities." Persons belonging to well-adjusted-marriages described their mates as *strong* and *trusting* individuals.

It is significant that case histories of individuals who fall in maladjusted categories are full of references to their inadequate sexual lives, to their failure to work out economic agreements, and to almost constant quarrels about how to raise their children or get along with their in-laws. In these cases the specific area of conflict seems not so important as the intrapsychic deficits which they exhibit and which prohibit them from adequate communication and decision-making in marriage. It is obvious that such persons have no power in demanding that their needs be met. Their exaggerated accusations and nagging demands so alienate the mate that the initial gratifications of the marriage shrivel. This occasions further nagging and further alienation.

Case history: Mary and Bill had been married six years when they presented themselves to the clinic. They were on the brink of divorce and said the clinic represented "their last hope." Testing revealed a mildly hostile man who still clung to his mother for emotional support and who had difficulty in facing any conflict situation. His ego score was very low. His adjustment technique with his mother had been to give in and to lie.

Because he had such a low ego he was a perfectionist and demanded from his wife a rigorous schedule, a clean house, and near-gourmet meals. But he was very indirect in his requirements and she was subjected to six years of nagging, inquisitions, and at the same time reassurance that he loved her. After six years this double bind overwhelmed her and she sued for divorce.

During the therapy, Bill was able to express his deep hostility to his mother and his self-hatred for not being a strong person. After many months he became more openly assertive, honest in his emotions, and could forsake his suspicious and nagging behavior. His wife was supportive of his growth and abandoned the divorce action.

Poor sexual adjustment with resultant nagging

The second type of case is just the obverse of that cited above. In these cases the nagging and general poor marital adjustment is derived from sexual failure. While some of the same personality characteristics may be involved, the total alienation process is different. Here the sexual failure is basically instrumental in the production of such negative reactions as nagging. The following case illustrates this process:

Case history: Jack and Helen had been married for ten years and had produced a boy and a girl by the time they came for help. They had moved to California from Iowa where they had lived as children and been educated. They had met in a small Protestant church they both attended. They had moved to California because of better occupational rewards but also to avoid contact with Jack's parents who were described by both of them as narrow and rigid.

Both Jack and Helen had been very conservative in their dating patterns and held a strict control on their expressions of affection. Helen never doubted Jack's love for her and felt that once they were married he would become a more avid lover than he was during courtship. In fact, because of her own background she was grateful that Jack did not press her for sexual activities during their long engagement.

During the first year of marriage Jack proved to be inept sexually and was much embarrassed because he could not seem to help Helen have a climax. She felt that he did not have a very strong libido in the beginning and that his failure inhibited him even more. But she had a strong sexual need and became more and more impatient with Jack when he refused to visit a doctor or a counselor. He felt that he should be "man enough" to solve sexual problems himself and not depend on someone else. But he solved this problem, as well as others, by avoidant behavior and Helen began to lose respect for him as a man.

After the fifth year of their marriage she told him she would have no more children because he was not man enough to be a father . She began to nag him to see a doctor, to make love to her, to become a man, etc. All of this nagging made Jack even more inhibited so that he began to have episodes of impotence. In their seventh year Helen had a six month affair which Jack never knew about. It relieved her frustrations for that period, but when her lover had to leave town she was more frustrated than ever. She then began to nag Jack about everything from the way he treated his children to his sexual ineptness. He began to avoid coming home and it was at this juncture that they came to the clinic.

This particular combination of a woman who was richly endowed in terms of her libido and a miserably inhibited man resulted in such frustration that nagging and poor marital adjustment were inevitable. While the average couple with good sexual adjustment may not feel that their sexual lives are of paramount importance to their adjustment, the reverse is true when there is utter sexual failure. Then the couple is apt to fixate on sex and it becomes critical in terms of all other adjustments. This may be more of a factor now than twenty-five years ago because of the enormous press given to sex. Some therapists have remarked that they are having to deal with more sexual problems now than in the past, not because there are more problems but because of the focus of the mass media on sex as the pivotal aspect of the good life.

Nagging and the "new morality"
A recent case of a young nagging wife introduces a further complication for the marriage counselor. A young woman of twenty-two was seen recently with her husband because of his complaint that she was emasculating him. A review of their case revealed that this young lady had had some two dozen affairs before marriage. She had experienced greater variation in sexual response and techniques before marriage

than members of her mother's generation experienced in their whole lifetime. The young man she married probably appealed to her because he was not overly sophisticated and perhaps had more promise of economic security than did her previous sexual partners, who seemed to be hedonistic swingers not at all interested in marriage, home, or the future.

Her husband was not sophisticated, but he had an adequate ego and he was not about to allow her to be dominant in decision-making or in bed. She made several major mistakes in belittling his sexual approach and he replied in kind about her lack of dignity and culture. The process of alienation began and their sexual life degenerated while their destructive nagging increased. They separated for a time but the young wife was not satisfied to resume her promiscuous ways. She tried that pattern but her experiences only confirmed her previous judgment that her companions were not about to leave their wives, or if single, to settle down. Her husband did not make a reconciliation easier by nagging her about her "masculine" need to dominate. Nevertheless, she returned to him, but made him promise that he would visit a counselor with her.

Cases like this are interesting because they introduce the possibility that given new freedom there is every possibility that some, if not many, wives will come to the marriage bed with greater experience and greater expectations than the husbands. While society is moving toward equality of the sexes, it does not seem that the movement has gone far enough yet for men to appreciate wives who will teach them about sex. There is then the possibility for a great deal of mischief because such an imbalance can produce hostility. In cases where that hostility cannot be expressed openly and honestly it will lead to nagging and suspiciousness. In several cases like this, the young husband is adamant in his demand to know all about his wife's previous sexual experiences; if she is foolish enough to tell him, he becomes almost paranoid in his fear that she will repeat her promiscuity during marriage.

A variation on this case presented itself when a young dentist came by himself into the clinic because he had a sexual problem. He had married after thirty, after a very long and careful process of mate choice. He still believed he had married the girl he wanted for a companion and to be the mother of his children. What troubled him was that after only a year and a half of marriage he no longer found his sexual life exciting. He missed the element of conquest and the exhilaration of a new and different female.

He was most ashamed of himself, stating that he thought he had gotten the need for variety out of his system and really meant to be faithful once he was married. But he saw that his sexual training had not been for monogamy. He had developed a dependence on the stimulation accompanying a variety of sex partners and he was sorely troubled by his deep disappointment with his wife. He said that he could not reveal any of these things to her and so he had begun to complain about a great many things he should not complain about. He was intelligent enough to see that he was making his wife a scapegoat for his own ambivalence, but found he could not do anything about it so he came for help.

Nagging and sexual problems

There is a special problem for middle-aged persons in terms of marriage and sex. Most of these problems are spelled out in detail in the author's book *Married Love in the Middle Years* and can only be summarized briefly here. Every major study of marriage in America proves that time is a "corrosive" factor in sexual adjustment, that sexual frequency and pleasure decrease as the longevity of the marriage increases. It seems almost that the personality and sexual resources that couples have to share with each other are exhausted after twenty years of marriage. The result is high boredom and little zest.

Cuber, in one of the major studies of upper-middle-class men and women in our society, described the majority of these marriages as falling into three categories: *the Habitually-Conflicted, the Devitalized, and the Passive-Congenial.* The first type certainly have their share of either nagging or open hostility, the second are almost too dead to quarrel, and the third are equally dead but better accepted. Marriage for middle-aged Americans seems to lose all spontaneity and vitality. The studies indicate that concomitantly sexual activity of the middle years is sporadic, routinized, and dull. With the loss of joy and sexual rewards, irritation, nagging, and neglect grow.

After menopause there is a tendency for some females who are suddenly free of child-rearing concerns to exercise maternal dominance over their husbands. At the same time men who controlled the world about them are often content, as they grow older, to control themselves to fit into the demands of their environment. This role reversal on the part of both men and women sometimes is expressed in terms of constant irritation and nagging on the part of the wife who, paradoxically, cannot tolerate the retreat of her husband. Her growing dominance and his growing obeisance often result in the cessation of their sexual interaction.

Nagging that focuses on sex itself

One of the most devastating ways to destroy the desire for sex in the partner is to nag about sex. The frustrated male or female who reacts to real or imagined sexual deprivation by constant negative complaints only steels the partner against meeting his or her needs. Often implicit in the nagging is a judgment about the normality of the other. Just as frequently there is egocentric reference to the deep hurt the other is inflicting.

Nagging differs from real discussion of a problem because it is of the "hit and run" school of games. If one attempts to counter the nagger by asking for some specific suggestions or by inviting him to look at the total situation he retreats into further and more openly hostile denunciations. For most individuals sexual response and capacity fall in a tender area and the sure result of another's nagging is self-doubt and retreat.

In some cases encountered by the author the nagging proved to be blatant projection in which the nagger was dealing with his own sexual fears by locating them in the psyche of his mate. Thus nagging delays his own encounter with his problem while at the same time intensifies the ambivalence of his sexual partner. Because nagging effectively communicates depreciation of the other it drives the other out of the bed. In dealing with nagging husbands and wives, therefore, it is essential to discover what basic intrapsychic and interpersonal dynamics are being represented by this conduct.

Handling the nagging spouse

It simply does no good for the doctor to point out to the husband or wife that nagging is a form of punishment which does little to modify behavior, but rather raises the defenses so that the potential for change is lowered. Nagging is, after all, only a symptom of a more profound problem or series of problems. If the doctor defines nagging or suspiciousness as products of a personality that is marked by hostility and weakness, the therapeutic goal becomes obvious. The ego must be nurtured until it is strong enough to stand honest confrontation and secure enough to stick with the confrontation until some resolution of the problem is achieved. After all, a part of the hostility expressed in nagging is self-hatred because the person cannot stand his own weakness. As he becomes stronger the need to project that hatred disappears.

In the case of poor sexual adjustment the resolution lies generally in reducing inhibition and bolstering sexual identification, not in perfecting sexual techniques. Individual psychotherapy is rarely sufficient to handle these cases. Communication processes and decision-making processes have been so impaired that couple therapy is often necessary to repair the wounds to the family system that have been incurred in the alienation process. Without such conjoint sessions the growth in the ego strength of one person may only make that person a more formidable opponent in the battle. If the couple expend the time and effort to work out both their personal deficiencies and their interpersonal blocks, they may be surprised to observe that consuming nagging will be gone from their lives—not to mention the axe and the revolver they may have thought of using in desperation.

9. The Crisis of Becoming A Father

HELENE S. ARNSTEIN

Literature on maternity has long emphasized pregnancy as a time of stress and strain for the expectant mother. Descriptions are given of her physical discomforts often accompanied by psychological changes as well; increased dependency, sensitivity, sudden mood swings, irritability, odd food cravings, fear, and of course the "baby blues" or possibly post-partum depression.

But the husband and *his* problems during this time have been overlooked or just swept under the rug. He has been considered mostly in terms of how he can better "understand" his wife during her pregnancy and give her added emotional support. The humorous aspects of his predicament have been played up in jokes and cartoons: rushing out in the middle of the night to get his wife some pickles, nervously pacing the maternity corridor of the hospital when an obstetrician gives him a hearty slap on the back assuring him, "We've never lost a father yet!", and fainting when the brightly smiling nurse hands him a bundle announcing, "It's twins!"

However, the truth is that pregnancy is no joke for some fathers. The findings of a number of recent studies indicate that pregnancy and childbirth—particularly for first-time fathers—can also be a time of stress for *him*. These studies suggest that a man not only undergoes major changes in his outer life but in his inner life as well. His response to the crisis will be colored by an interplay of many forces. These include external pressures, how he faces the new and added responsibilities, his own personality makeup, and reawakening of events and feelings connected with his own parents, brothers, and sisters. Many unresolved childhood sexual conflicts and fantasies may be reawakened; fears about his masculinity, body intactness, vague memories and imaginings about the mysteries of pregnancy and child-birth, ancient parental loves and hates and jealousies may provoke many defenses and acting-out behavior. They range from sudden frenzied spurts of physical activity, malaise, bizarre physical symptoms and "sympathy pains," deviant sexual behavior, and emotional illness.

An English psychiatrist, Dr. W.H. Trethowan, recently carried out an investigation of 327 expectant fathers and discovered that 1 out of 9 suffered from minor ailments including abdominal pains, loss of appetite, indigestion, colic, nausea, vomiting, and toothache. These men apparently had been in good health—physically and mentally—and their complaints occurred only during the periods of their wives' pregnancies.

Dr. Trethowan's study is important because it is one of the largest to focus on the "normal" population of fathers-to-be. A somewhat similar but smaller scale study conducted in Washington shows that about 42 of 64 first-time fathers studied developed "pregnancy symptoms" that were almost identical to those of the British fathers. In addition, the American men had headaches, temporary weight gains, backaches, and peptic ulcers. A number of these husbands gave up smoking and began to drink milk. Some reported insomnia and restlessness, and toward the end of their wives' pregnancies a few husbands took to bed while still others became physically overactive and daring and even injured themselves in sport activities.

Many of these odd happenings were also revelaed in an earlier pioneering study conducted by Dr. James L. Curtis of Cornell University Medical College in New York City. At that time—in the mid-fifties—Dr. Curtis was Chief of Psychiatric Services at Mitchell Field Air Base. Dr. Curtis observed 55 expectant fathers, 31 of whom were expecting their first child. Seventeen of the servicemen had histories of emotional problems that were considered serious, 14 men had presented problems considered to be minor, and a control group of 24 expectant fathers never had sought or had been referred for psychiatric consultation. The psychosomatic symptoms already described were present *in all 3 groups,* particularly during the first and last months of the wives' pregnancies. But, as Dr. Curtis pointed out, "the men were seldom aware that their recent problems had any relation to their approaching parenthood."

(This lack of awareness was also borne out in Dr. Trethowan's investigations and in those of Dr. William H. Wainwright, a New York psychiatrist who worked with a group of men hospitalized for mental illness precipitated by the birth of a child. Dr. Wainwright's patients believed that stock market losses and other such factors accounted for their breakdowns.)

Some of Dr. Curtis' servicemen developed ravenous appetites. One man had to be grounded from air service because he put on 50 pounds. Greater restlessness was shown in the home lives of all 3 groups of expectant fathers, and marital tensions appeared increasingly because many of the men wanted to get out of the home in the evenings. Some began to drink excessively. One father became absorbed in expensive new hobbies that left his wife with little money for her necessary household expenses. This particular serviceman bought model planes and trains, started a coin collection, purchased a violin and began to take lessons. With an increased desire for motion and activity, several men in each group asked for transfers to other military bases. A few became accident prone and reported a series of minor cuts and sprains from automobile and other accidents. It was also believed that—as in other reports—a number of men were having sexual involvements with other women.

The comparatively mild disturbance in the sex life of some "normal" expectant fathers may be magnified in the lives of the emotionally disturbed. Dr. A. Arthur Hartman, Director of Psychology and Research at the Psychiatric Institute of the Municipal Circuit Court of Chicago and Dr. Robert C. Nicolay, Associate Professor of Psychology at Loyola University, Chicago, have indicated that arrests for sex offenses are well over twice as high among expectant fathers during their wives' first pregnancies than among other married men arrested. The researchers compared 91 expectant fathers apprehended for the first time with another group of 91 married men who were equated for age, race, and year of arrest. The sexual offenses were more apt to occur in the last 4 months of pregnancy when the likelihood of sexual deprivation increases. The nature of the expectant fathers' sexual acting out (molesting children, masturbating in public, rape, attempted rape, making obscene telephone calls, and sending obscene letters, etc.) suggests that these men had particularly weak impulse control and suffered from emotional disorders. Their regressive forms of sexual behavior, the authors state, may be viewed as immature adjustive reactions to the inner anxiety brought on by their wives' pregnancies.

How is all of this behavior explained? What makes the adjustment to pregnancy tinged with so much anxiety for some men? The interpretations of the phenomena seem to be as varied as the forms of behavior described.

"Couvade"

A number of leading psychiatrists have pointed to the connection between the "sympathy pains"—an especially close type of identification shown by some husbands with their wives during pregnancy —and the ancient ritual of "couvade." (This word is borrowed from the French "couver" which means "to brood" or "to hatch.") In the couvade ritual—known throughout the centuries and throughout the world, particularly in primitive societies—the husband would go to bed at the time of his wife's confinement and would go through all the motions of labor himself. Uttering moans and groans and threshing about, he acted as if *he* were bearing the child. When the baby was born, family and friends hovered over him, paid him homage, and brought him gifts and delicacies. The new father was put on a strict diet and made to rest for a given time, during which he was not allowed to hunt or fish.

A few anthropologists interpret couvade as the father's attempt to assert his rightful paternity and to proclaim his share in parenthood. Others feel that couvade represents a husband's desire and magic attempts to protect his wife from harm by warding off the evil spirits causing her pain and redirecting them to invade his own body instead.

Man's unconscious envy of female procreativity

Some psychiatrists, including the late Dr. Gregory Zilboorg, take a different view. They say that couvade has its roots in man's ambivalent feeling toward childbirth. Just as woman has been awed by and envious of the abilities and privileges of the male over the years, so has the male been envious of the woman. The human male, they maintain, has a deep unconscious envy of woman's ability to create a child, and this envy brings with it feelings of hostility. By identifying with the mother and her suffering in the couvade ritual, the father's feelings of guilt and hostility could be magically replaced by those of love and concern.

The theme of man's unconscious jealousy of woman's capacity to bear children appears frequently in mythology. Zeus, for example, annoyed and exasperated by his pregnant wife's wisdom, swallowed her and eventually delivered the goddess Athena through his forehead. One version of the Dionysius myth describes Zeus tearing the 6-month-old fetus from the burning body of his mortal love

Semele, sewing it up into his loins and carrying it to full term, thereby giving birth to Dionysius. And then of course there is the oldest legend of them all; Adam, who gave birth to Eve through his rib!

Drawing from more down-to-earth examples, a California psychoanalyst, Dr. Lawrence J. Friedman, observes that man's daily language is studded with expressions such as "This is *my* creation, *my* baby, I thought of it first." Or, he points out, "one can be pregnant with a new idea, give birth to, or have an abortive thought, have a brain child, etc." Dr. Friedman also tells of a writer who has a book published every time his wife gives birth to a child. Along with other psychoanalysts, Dr. Friedman tells of many male patients who have pregnancy fantasies and dreams.

Young mothers often discover that their preschool sons are as outspoken about wanting to have babies as are little girls. They may play with dolls, feed and bathe them as mother did with her babies. By and large, psychoanalysts agree that in the early preschool years a boy first identifies with his mother, then gradually makes the transition to a healthy identification with his father, consolidating his masculinity.

A good deal of evidence seems to indicate that with certain men—quite "masculine" men in fact—the event of their wives' pregnancy may temporarily reactivate some remnants of this early identification with the mother. Besides, the unborn child may unconsciously become a rival for the attention of a much loved woman, just as the expectant father's little brother or sister or his own father had once been. Added to these fantasies and fears, sometimes the prospective father actually *does* feel shut out and unloved, believing that his wife has become more interested in the unborn child than she is in him. This is particularly true if the wife withdraws some of the emotional support she has given her husband previously. As Dr. Wainwright puts it, "She may want *extra* support from him while he receives *less* in return." If a woman has held a job, the loss of her earnings may be a deprivation for them both, but more important, the wife may miss working. Dr. Wainwright adds, "Often when a woman stops working she experiences the loss of one of her main satisfactions in life. Unwittingly then, she may take out her dissatisfaction on her husband by demanding more companionship, attention, and love than before."

Unexpressed conflicting feelings

The ancient formal rituals and ceremonies of primitive people gave man a chance to make peace with his opposing and bothersome emotions. Through these ceremonies he purged himself of his hates and fears. Civilized man seems to have no such comfortable outlets for his negative and unacceptable feelings, so these feelings often remain bottled up within himself but pop out again in new forms—as physical and psychological symptoms.

Dr. Trethowan, the British researcher, explains that modern man has negative as well as loving feelings about his pregnant wife. As already shown, the expectant father may worry that the baby will usurp his place in his wife's affections. Or, he may resent other aspects of the pregnancy; being tied down, hemmed in (the carefree honeymoon stage of marriage ended, "Am I really ready to become a father? It will be harder to get out of this marriage now if I ever want to"). At the same time the husband may feel guilt and shame—after all he did make his wife pregnant and maybe he has endangered her life. According to Dr. Wainwright, "One of the real difficulties for a father-to-be in our particular culture is that he is supposed to have only positive feelings for the forthcoming event." And Dr. Trethowan concurs by saying that when unacceptable feelings occur, they are often accompanied by guilt and anxiety—even more so if a man has a strict conscience. In order to avoid the painful anxiety, the father-to-be tries to repress the thoughts and feelings but he is not usually successful. "Accordingly, and in ways which are not yet completely understood, repression is bolstered by translating the conflict into physical terms; a process known as conversion."

Sex during pregnancy

The whole matter of sexual relations during pregnancy is highly controversial and most certainly individual. It often happens that a man and wife misunderstand how the other feels about it. Furthermore the capacity to withstand some sexual frustration—when and if it is required—varies from man to man, as does his particular way of working out the situation.

Medical advice on this question also varies from doctor to doctor. Sexual intercourse during pregnancy depends, too, upon the physical condition of the mother. Some couples enjoy their sexual relationship more than ever during pregnancy, while for others sexual activity may decline.

In interviewing 117 pregnant women, Masters and Johnson reported that during the 4th, 5th and 6th month, the majority of women indicated their desire for and enjoyment of sexual intimacy substantially increased, often reaching a higher level than before the pregnancy. Nevertheless, several women expressed concern because they thought their husbands were disturbed by their changing figures and had become sexually uninterested.

And how did the husbands feel? Of 79 questioned, 31 seemed to withdraw gradually from approaching their wives sexually. (Actually, only 5 described the physical changes in their wives as an objection.) Eighteen men stated that they weren't really interested and "didn't know why." Hartman and Nicolay have said that "Pregnancy emphasizes the maternal role of the wife. This may reinforce the husband's associations of identification with a mother figure as against a wife image with a consequent disturbance of sex reactions, or a reinstatement of conflicts and inhibitions centering around the mother." Another study shows that for a few men, a pregnant wife can stimulate incestuous fantasies with consequent anxieties.

In the Masters and Johnson study a good number of husbands indicated—toward the end of the sixth month—that they were afraid of causing injury to both unborn child and wife in intercourse.

This seems to be a fairly universal fear of men (and wives too) that occurs at even earlier stages of pregnancy. In most instances these fears are medically unfounded.

Regarding abstinence (in general, a large proportion of obstetricians permit intercourse up to the very last weeks of pregnancy unless there are specific medical indications to the contrary), 77 out of 101 women in the Masters and Johnson survey were warned by their physicians to avoid intercourse during the last 3 months of pregnancy until quite some time after childbirth. Other doctors set an abstinence period from 6 weeks before childbirth until 6 weeks after birth. Eighteen of the husbands whose wives had been advised to abstain from intercourse for long periods responded by seeking extramarital sex.

While long abstinence periods may rock the marriage boat in some cases and expectant fathers so inclined may seek sexual gratification outside of the home, it is felt by many family life experts that these outlets on the part of the husband often reflect his attempts to reduce inner tensions that are as much related to the crisis of approaching fatherhood as to his sexual needs.

To ease misunderstandings and resentments—and it is always difficult for a man to accept any sexual restrictions *imposed* on him ("nobody can tell *me* . . .")—many doctors feel that expectant fathers should get to know their wife's obstetrician so that if there are any sexual restrictions for medical reasons he can understand why. Masters and Johnson state that many of the men who were interviewed did not understand the "reasons," they "weren't sure" that the doctors had said it, or they wished the doctors had explained it to them as well as to their wives. A number of men believed their wives had simply invented the period of continence in order to avoid intercourse.

Ways of reducing anxieties

All the suggestions for helping prevent or reduce the difficulties some expectant fathers may experience seem to focus on the importance of free and open communication between husband and wife. Many misunderstandings can be avoided if an expectant couple can talk things out together, share their worries and doubts in a spirit of mutual tolerance, understanding, and sympathy. By indicating her belief in her husband as a man, as a human being as well as a prospective father, the pregnant wife may be able to allay any fears he may have that he will be replaced in her love by the unborn child.

It is not unusual for an expectant father to identify to some degree with his wife and unborn child. This identification may help him respond well to their needs for his love and care. However, *extreme* sympathy pains, restlessness, total immersion in work or hobbies or other forms of "escape" described here may be largely due to a husband's unconscious attempts to rid himself of painful tensions heightened by the internal and external stresses of the pregnancy situation.

Pregnancy and childbirth may be a crucial time in a man's life, but the experience of becoming a father rather than just a son may enable him to free himself from his own childhood, from the early patterns of response to the challenges of life. In the long run the deep satisfactions of becoming a father and his increasing interest in and love for his new and enlarged family usually motivate a man to higher levels of self-awareness, maturity, and fulfillment.

Comment by:
John L. Schimel

Helene Arnstein has reviewed the anxieties fathers may experience during the course of pregnancy as well as some of the possible unfortunate consequences of such anxieties. I believe, however, that she has overstated the case, even in regard to the material she quoted. Dr. Trethowan's study, she reports, "discovered that 1 out of 9 (expectant fathers) suffered from *minor ailments* including abdominal pains, loss of appetite, indigestion, colic, nausea, vomiting, and toothache . . . only during the periods of their wives' pregnancies." I can report that wives whose husbands are addicted to weekend watching of pro football on TV suffer a distinctly higher rate of minor ailments during the football season, which is shorter than the term of pregnancy. College psychiatrists can tell you that the rate of minor (and not so minor) ailments of college students during an exam week is also distinctly higher. The foregoing is not to dispute the findings offered, but to put them into some perspective. After all, 8 out of 9 of the fathers in Dr. Trethowan's study showed *no* signs of even minor ailments during the period of pregnancy. This certainly seems healthier than the general population and could suggest that the period of pregnancy for many fathers (as it is for many mothers) is a period of unusual well-being and good health.

I wonder how many of the readers of this paper can report *any* nine month period without *any* minor physical ailment. The author is also misleading in her opening stress on the negative possibilities for the mothers.

The author, in her pursuit of things that can go wrong during pregnancy, has overlooked the fact that many positive aspects of fathering may only become apparent during pregnancy or after the birth of the child. In our culture, it is true that the birth of a child has tended to be regarded as primarily a woman's affair. In other cultures, the pride of paternity is more clearly felt and expressed than in the United States, with its emphasis on stoicism for the male. The pride and joy that many American fathers experience following the birth of a child may surprise them.

Some threats to the father occur after the birth of the child. There has been increasing pressure on fathers to show that they "love" the child by sharing in its physical care, even when the father is employed and the mother is not. Some fathers who don't feel the prescribed amount of interest, say in diapering, come to feel that they are "unnatural" parents. I would remind the reader, too, that the sometimes observed jealousy by the father of the mother's attentions to the baby need not be all that unrealistic. For some mothers, the birth of a baby signals the end of interest in the husband. She may feel overwhelmed or inadequate to the task or she may have an image of mothering as a full-time job with father as an adjutant. Some mothers see in the male child an opportunity to create the ideal male that they failed to find in the husband. *And so on.*

Comment by:
Max Deutscher
It is only somewhat useful to note that men as well as women, husbands as well as wives, and fathers as well as mothers have anxieties in the course of becoming parents. I think that what we need much more than this observation is a psychology of pregnancy that identifies pregnancy as a normal, developmental phase in the cycle of adult life and family development—that in the transition from couple to family status, which occurs through the pregnancy, a great deal has to be

learned and relearned in a very brief time. Given this necessity, anxiety may reasonably accompany such learning. But florid and bizarre symptoms will only develop when anxieties are too intense and when the person is overwhelmed by them. Thus they would reflect serious difficulties and failures, not the norm.

I attach little credence to the notion that the ultimate cause of the man's anxiety during pregnancy is based on his envy of his wife's capacity to bear children; similarly, I do not adhere to the notion that woman's pregnancy gives her the long wished-for penis and assuages her penis envy. In a marriage where there is mutual love, respect and caring and where things are going well enough so that the couple want to have a child, they're not having *her* child—she is bearing *their* child. Of course each will be having a personal as well as joined experience and there is a useful distinction to be made between the man's and woman's experience. Pregnancy will certainly intensify the feelings of maleness as well as femaleness—but it will also bridge that separateness. While envy may be aroused in either of them, it will only be those who need to be it all and have it all, a small and troubled group, who will not be able to renounce such wishes and other interferences in the interest of their fuller participation and meaningful sharing in the development of their family.

Comment by:
Henry B. Biller
Helene Arnstein has written a very well-conceived and important discussion. The neglect of the husband during the wife's pregnancy is very much related to the relative lack of attention given to the father's role in our society.

Some males who have developed strong masculine interests and modes of social interaction still have self-doubts as to their basic masculinity. To such men, approaching fatherhood may be particularly threatening. Underlying sex role conflicts are often associated with an inadequate father-son relationship during childhood.[1] Sex role conflicts for expectant fathers are frequent in preliterate societies in which there is much paternal deprivation during early childhood. Expectant fathers in these societies are likely to stay in bed and act as if they are going through childbirth when their wives are in labor. Such behavior seems related to an underlying feminine identification.[2]

Of course, sex role conflicts are only one of the factors which may contribute to a husband's difficulties during his wife's pregnancy. (It should also be added that fatherhood helps many men to achieve a more adequate sex role development.) One rather obvious problem that may arise deserves considerable emphasis. All too often the decision to have a baby is much more the wife's than the husband's. In general, the socialization of males in most subcultures of our society includes little exposure to the gratifications of fatherhood. A particularly serious situation can arise when the wife pressures or tricks her husband into impregnating her. Having a child should be a joint, well-disucssed decision. The couple that is secure in their mutually agreed-upon decision to have a child is better able to provide each other emotional support and to withstand external pressures such as criticism from the wife's or husband's parents.

There is a great need for additional counseling services for couples in terms of family planning. The growing opportunities for family life education during childhood and adolescence may also help to better prepare prospective parents. Males in our society are in particular need of being exposed to more extensive information concerning pregnancy and childbirth and the responsibilities and rewards of childbearing.

When a wife becomes pregnant it seems advisable that the husband accompany her when she visits her doctor and, if possible, discuss some of his concerns directly with the doctor. Some fathers want to observe the childbirth process. The feasibility of such an arrangement depends on many factors and, of course, is the doctor's decision. However, if the doctor has had several meetings with the husband during the wife's pregnancy, both are usually more comfortable with the doctor's decision. If the expectant father's needs and concerns receive adequate attention during the process of pregnancy, he probably will be more motivated and prepared to positively accept fatherhood.

References
1. Biller, H.B.: Father, Child, and Sex Role (Lexington, Mass.: D.C. Heath, 1971).
2. Burton, R.V., and Whiting, J.W.M.: The absent father and cross-sex identity. Merrill-Palmer Quarterly 1:85, 1961.

10. Antipathy To Marriage

JOHN J. SCHWAB

Pessimism about marriage, if not antipathy toward it, has been expressed for centuries by poets, philosophers, and social scientists.

An old German proverb states that "Matrimony is a reverse fever, it starts with heat and ends with cold." And a French proverb tells that "A deaf husband and a blind wife are always a happy couple." In commenting on a widower's early remarriage, Samuel Johnson said that this represented "the triumph of hope over experience." Shelley asserted, "A system could not well have been devised more studiously hostile to human happiness than marriage." Also, it is poignant to note that the greatest love story in the English language, *Romeo and Juliet,* contains the lines, "She is not well-married that lives married long; but she's best married that dies married young."

Western society's literature is studded with such doleful aphorisms which denounce marriage. These statements articulate the individual writer's feeling that traditional monogamous marriage begins as a holy alliance, but rapidly becomes a drab and fettered union and ends as a state of bondage. We should note, however, that such views about marriage are stated by men, many of whom chafe at socially prescribed, if not enforced, monogamy.

Women's demands for equality

In modern America, antipathy toward marriage is expressed openly by certain Women's Liberation groups. Traditional marriage, they assert, is a form of tyranny and enslavement for women. Accord-

105

ing to our conventional system, they think that a wife not only relinquishes her name but also loses her identity as an individual person. In seeking equality for women, the liberation groups proclaim that conventional marriage must be altered drastically, not just reformed.

Obviously, there is a great deal of truth in the point of view which sees women constrained by marriage, confined by the roles of housewife and mother so that they are deprived of the opportunity to develop as individuals, intellectually and culturally. Undoubtedly, housekeeping can be evaluated as drudgery, and the care of the children as tedious and irksome when it is a 24-hour-a-day job. Housekeeping can be a lonely, restricted, unintellectual routine way of life which is also a demanding one when the wife is compelled to be a maidservant as well as a "mother, mistress, and daughter" to her husband, and a sympathetic, nurturing caretaker for her children.

In modern America, many women are torn by role conflict. Educated and competent, these wives know that they could perform as well if not better than their husbands at work and in society at large. In being limited to the roles of wife and mother, they feel cheated. They know that they are deprived of occupational and professional opportunities, and they feel that they are also deprived of the opportunities for self-expression and spontaneity.

There is little doubt that such complaints are valid, but our social turmoil and rapid culture change may be just as responsible for the plight of many women as the conventionally prescribed marital role. Rightfully, they feel cheated; labor-saving devices (which proliferate in the average middle-class home in suburbia) should have provided time for the housewife to follow her intellectual pursuits, engage in creative activities, work part-time, or at least have sufficient leisure. However, the typical suburban housewife now has to use the extra time provided by the plethora of appliances just to chauffeur her children and manage the household, so that the family can live with a modicum of comfort and dignity. As Margaret Mead has pointed out, the average housewife is an administrator and consumer, with little time or opportunity to be a producer, to devote herself to basically satisfying functions, and to fulfill a meaningful personal role.

Married women patients in psychotherapy express an antipathy toward marriage on the grounds that they are trapped by the increasingly complicated tasks required to maintain their households and care for their families. Most of them do not blame their husbands or even conventional marriage for this state of affairs. Generally, they are depressed; they express little anger toward anyone or anything, although they deplore the conditions of modern life and accuse themselves of having failed, as well as being "failures."

In the last few years, for the first time that I have observed, a number of young single women in therapy have stated that they definitely do not plan to get married until the form of marriage is changed, or unless there is a major sociocultural change which insures the rights of women. Furthermore, the threat of overpopulation produces worry and even guilt among mothers of several children, pregnant women, and also young women who look forward to motherhood. They ask whether it is right to have children, not only because of the dangers posed by the rapidly increasing population but also because they are concerned about both our societal decadence and the possibility of a deteriorating quality of life. Many women, including those seen in psychotherapy, are alarmed by the incessant wars, violence, the problems of youth, and the conflicts which characterize our contemporary scene. Motherhood, once deemed indispensable for role fulfillment for a woman, and once thought of as a joy if not an obligation, is now questioned—"Is it right to bring a child into today's world?" And their concern about today's world is only a preface to their fear and horror about the world of 2000 A.D.

In view of the widespread anxiety and guilt concerning woman's essential biosocial role, parenthood, and mothering, it is not surprising that traditional marriage is foundering. It appears that many of our institutions are crumbling in this era, which the poet Robert Hazel has termed "the post-Christian." In a decadent age, lacking an ethic and with little sharing of sentiments so necessary for societal integration, traditional institutions seldom endure, or, if they do, survive in different, generally cleansed, simpler forms. With the threat of overpopulation, concern about social unrest, and fear of the future, antipathy toward marriage and experiments with kibbutz-type child rearing indicate possibly that even the family will not endure as the basic societal unit. A sociosexual basis for antipathy toward marriage, therefore, appears to be a product of our sociocultural turmoil.

Ambivalent religious attitudes

In the past, antipathy toward marriage has been grounded in ambivalent religious attitudes toward the flesh. Although the Old Testament presents Adam and Eve as the first couple, and Noah and his family were enjoined to "Go forth, be fruitful and multiply," many of the Biblical accounts of marriage describe varying forms and usually associate marriage with kinship and property. Examples are Jacob's polygamy and David's concubinage.

Coincident with the decline of the Hellenistic world in the second and first centuries B.C., a number of reform movements sprang up in the Near East. Most of them were ascetic; in fact they valued celibacy as

superior to marriage. Asia Minor was in a decadent, calamitous condition, stricken by want, disease, and war, and unnerved by social
disorder. The premium on asceticism and celibacy can be traced to the
influence of early Manichaean philosophies which, in turn, were probably derived from some aspects of Zoroastrianism. The Manichaean
philosophy proclaimed that there were two powers, good and evil,
spiritual and material, the kingdoms of light and darkness.

Wake, in his book, *The Development of Marriage and Kinship*,
explains that the philosophic speculations of the Manichaeans held
that the individual's soul was a small portion of the universal soul, or
light, and that when it was "seduced by the fatal attractions of matter,
it was said to have fallen into the *paths of generation. . . .*" Birth was
looked upon, if not as an evil, yet as the source of evil. Such a
philosophy, again in Wake's words, '. . . was to provide a means of
escaping from the dreaded cycle of material existence." He tells that
Saturninus, one of the earliest and most celebrated of the Gnostics,
taught that marriage was "instituted by the powers of darkness, for the
purpose of perpetuating the race of their partisans, therefore it was
the duty of men endowed with a ray of the Divine light to prevent both
the diffusion of this germ of celestial life and the propagation of so
imperfect an order of things."

This antipathetic attitude toward not only sexuality, but also legal
marriage, was adopted by a number of reform groups in Asia Minor
before the time of Christ. Furthermore, it appears to have exerted a
profound influence on early Christianity.

The Essenes, a monastic, pre-Christian, Jewish sect in Palestine,
were known for their stringent asceticism and celibacy. They de-
nounced all marriage. But even earlier, the apocryphal book, *The
Wisdom of Solomon* (probably written in the third century B.C.), states,
"Blessed is the barren that is undefiled, which hath not known the
sinful bed: she shall have fruit in the visitation of souls. And blessed is
the eunuch which with his hands hath wrought no iniquity, nor
imagined things against God: for unto him shall be given the special
gift of faith."

By its tolerance and by the doctrine of forgiveness, exemplified by
the story of Mary Magdalene, early Christianity attracted many
women. And in proclaiming the sacramental nature of marriage, early
Christianity firmly established monogamous marriage as the best,
indeed the only acceptable, form. But even monogamous marriage fell
short of the true ideal—the celibate life devoted to good works and
dedicated to Christianity. Paul's doctrine, "Better to marry than burn,"
articulated Christianity's scale of values, a scale which was repeatedly

affirmed by the great theologians such as Augustine and Pope Gregory The Great.

Many early Christians followed the ideal. They lived in communes or together in groups in the deserts and mountains of Asia Minor and Egypt and, when persecuted, even in the catacombs in Rome. Their renunciation of the flesh and their antipathy toward marriage may have been responsible in part for the persecution of Christians by the Romans, even in the first century A.D. In order to lessen sexual attraction as well as to mortify the flesh, Christians did not bathe or tend their bodies. It is reported that some bathed less often than once a year, and that others even rubbed their bodies with dung to increase their sexual repulsiveness. Their reeking bodies must have appeared rank and offensive to Roman society.

The promise of ultimate rewards for chastity and celibacy was announced in the apocalyptic vision of John. The first 144,000 seen by him with the Lamb on Mt. Zion were those who "have not defiled themselves with women, for they are chaste"; they were to be redeemed from mankind as "first fruits for God and the Lamb." This attitude toward sexuality, marriage, and even the birth of children was responsible in part for the decline in population in the Roman Empire. This trend continued even after Constantine was converted and Christianity established as the state religion. Gibbon maintains that the Christian influence contributed to the decline and eventual fall of Rome. Even the previously mentioned doctrine of Paul, "Better to marry than burn," was a compromise; if one could not live a chaste life, it was better to marry than to fornicate. But sexual activity, even in a consecrated marriage, was still viewed as a concession to man's carnality, short of the ideal celibate life of the chaste and the pure.

This ambivalent attitude of the Church toward marriage and procreation continued through the centuries. As late as 1543, the Council of Trent declaimed in ringing terms, "If anyone saith that the marriage state is to be placed above the state of virginity or of celibacy, and that it is no better and more blessed to remain in virginity or in celibacy than to be united in matrimony; let him be anathema."

The Christian ideal—the renunciation of the flesh—has exerted manifold influences on marriage, offering consolation in this life and promises of heavenly bliss to the unmarried who remain pure. Also, the Catholic Church provides a calling and a sanctuary for those who embrace the Holy Orders, and even a marriage for nuns (the Brides of Christ). The Church's ambivalent attitude toward sexual activity is responsible, at least in part, for sexual disharmony in marriage. Exhorted to remain chaste during adolescence and young adulthood, threatened by the fires of Hell and eternal damnation, men as well as women have sexual difficulties which detract from marital happiness. A generation ago, countless women confided to their doctors that sexual activity was an obligation, a wife's duty, which was not only devoid of pleasure but indeed a source of unhappiness and misery. And with the increasing sexual freedom in America today, their plight at times is even greater than it was in the past. They are caught in a bind—tempted by opportunity and license, but constrained by the precepts and the exhortations of the Church. The following case history illustrates the dilemma of a young woman who developed an antipathy toward her marriage.

Case history

A 28-year-old, devout Roman Catholic woman who has been married for 5 years sought psychotherapy because of recurring fears that she was going to harm her two small children. She grew up in a second generation Irish Catholic family in a small town. Her parents were aware that they belonged to a minority group; consequently, they strove toward respectability. Her father became a successful businessman, and her mother was preoccupied with keeping their suburban home as clean as possible. Their social activities were exclusively related to Church functions.

Shortly after learning about masturbation at the age of 16, she became convinced that she had sold her soul to the devil. At first, this belief was directly asssociated with feelings of guilt about masturbation, but after a few months of deepening conflict the belief reached delusional proportions, so that she thought any illness or misfortune which befell her family or close friends in the Church was the result of her alliance with Satan.

She began to engage in a grotesque series of compulsive acts which required two to three hours of her time before going to bed at night. She had to arrange all pointed objects in her bedroom (hangers, toilet articles, shoes, etc.) in one direction. This, and other rituals, had to be repeated a set number of times. If she made an error in the increasingly elaborate sequence, she would not only have to begin from the start but also repeat the entire performance a number of extra times. Finally, her exceedingly prolonged compulsive activities alarmed her family who mentioned them to the priest. Apparently, he had been concerned about her detailed recital of trivialities during confession; he supported the worried parents' belief that she needed psychiatric treatment.

During her last year of high school, she went to a psychiatrist in a nearby metropolitan area for weekly psycho-therapeutic sessions. By the end of her last year in high school she had improved remarkably. She had only a few symptoms during her 4 years at a women's college. During her last year of college, she became engaged to a bright, stable engineering student who was attending a nearby university. Although he was not a Roman Catholic, she decided to marry him anyway because he agreed that physical intimacy between them prior to marriage should be limited to necking, and he consented to have their children brought up as Roman Catholics. She now tells that she saw him as just the right personality type for her—he is quiet, calm, and remarkably stable, while she, in her own words, is "much more emotional."

She sid not enjoy sexual intercourse during the first year of marriage; she would masturbate following intercourse in order to obtain some satisfaction, but increasingly she became concerned about the lurid fantasies accompanying masturbation. She became pregnant toward the end of the first year of marriage, and then was troubled by the fear that she would give birth to a monster or that her baby would die. Her obstetrician and her husband provided substantial reassurance and support during the course of the pregnancy; but after delivery, she had to be referred for psychotherapy because of her recurring thoughts that her baby had died and that she had been supplied with a substitute from an unwanted pregnancy while she was in the hospital.

Six months after the birth of her first child, she became pregnant again, and again she developed symptoms similar to those which had troubled her during her first pregnancy. After the birth of her second child, she believed that it, too, was not her baby; that hers had died during pregnancy and that she had been supplied with a substitute. This belief subsided; her husband convinced her that it was nonsense. During the last two years, however, she has feared that she would harm her children, notwithstanding her husband's support and his repeated calming statements telling her not to worry.

She has re-entered psychotherapy in the hope that she can "learn how to control such thoughts." In the first interview, she said that she wished to obtain psychotherapy also because her present life is unsatisfactory in almost all respects. She spends many hours each day watching soap operas on television, neglecting her children and her housework. She is fascinated by the life of her younger sister, an unmarried graduate student who lives a life of "freedom." The sister has shared a number of apartments with young men, has traveled extensively, and has experimented with the "Hippie life." The younger sister loudly extols the principles of Women's Liberation, insisting that marriage not only deprives women of their freedom but also degrades them. The sister ridicules the patient's already feeble housekeeping efforts, sternly declaring that she will never spend her time "picking up a husband's dirty socks."

In recent sessions, as her recurring obsessional fears of harming her children have significantly diminished, she has been discussing her negative feelings about marriage. She tells that she is trapped in a boring, humdrum existence. Even though her husband is a quiet, considerate, loving man, she views her daily life as being equivalent to that of a servant. She is beginning to see that the hours she spends watching the soap operas, mainly concerned with sexual and medical problems, have provided some vicarious thrills for her, even entering into her fantasies during masturbation (sexual intercourse is still relatively unsatisfying). Highly emotional dramatizations of sexual license, medical problems, mental illness, mistaken paternity, etc., have become fuel for her discontents and appear to have reinforced her obsessions. At the psychiatrist's insistence, she has recently begun taking some advanced courses in her special field, English Literature, and is beginning to think about completing some additional course work so that she can teach in another year or two. She has also begun to recognize that she is flagrantly envious of her younger sister's freedom.

Living in suburbia as a member of the educated technological elite in our society, she is surrounded by married couples whose life styles are characterized by mobility, increasing affluence, and secularization. Their numerous divorces and remarriages indicate that Herbert Otto's "serial monogamy" is the predominant form of marriage for this group in our society today. And the sexual freedom associated with the affairs, divorces, and remarriages in middle-class America is pale compared to the more vivid sexual activities of the young, exemplified by her sister's life.

Rapidity of culture change

She, and many others, particularly in middle-class America, are disoriented by the rapidity of culture change. Not only are the new sexual attitudes (perceived as both tempting and threatening) in conflict with traditional marriage, but indeed, the entire value system associated with the Protestant Ethic is being assailed as irrelevant. The family is no longer a group of producers working toward a common goal; instead, the husband is usually employed away from home and is involved with highly specialized activities which cannot be communicated to the wife and children, who are preoccupied with managing the home and the pressures of school. In view of the concern about overpopulation (which strikes at the very foundation on which monogamous marriage is built), the new sexual freedom, and the rapidly changing if not chaotic life styles associated with fragmentation of the family, we should anticipate increasing antipathy toward conventional monogamous marriage.

It appears that the form of marriage will change. Already we are witnessing polyandry; among some of the poorer, small hippie groups, one woman lives with several men. Various types of polygamy can be observed among the young. And in some of the communes, true group marriage is being practiced. Companionate marriage is openly advocated by many as the only form which has meaning in the light of our modern day nihilism. The advocates of companionate marriage argue that it is the only form of union between man and woman which has any validity. It differs drastically from the premarital experimentation and the secret intimacy practiced a generation ago. Its advocates insist that their companionate marriages entail a commitment to sharing and loving, that it has a cultural reality, and that it possesses more "real" human values than traditional institutionalized marriage.

Comment by:
Janet Zollinger Giele
After reading "Antipathy to Marriage" one can picture a number of vectors that may explain the Women's Liberation movement: the collapse of religious values that renounced the Flesh, the population problem which makes woman's breeding role less valuable, the demands and constraints placed on the educated woman when she is the mother of small children, and perhaps elements of personal pathology that may push particular individuals to find the monogamous sexual arrangement unsatisfactory. Schwab's case study shows the way these factors all meshed in one individual.

An alternative to the case study presented here might be one that chose a woman of Protestant or Jewish background, who has three or four children and loves them, got a Ph.D., publishes, is married to a successful husband, combines both career and family, seems to accept the traditional monogamous marriage, but is presently either active in or supportive of various efforts to improve women's wages and job positions either in the universities or in certain professions. I personally know a number of such women.

The comparison between these cases and the one presented in the article alerts us to the different combinations of variables that may ɔalesce in any one individual and yet produce similar results. These ‚ndividuals, different though they are, all support some form of change in the woman's role. Perhaps one of the most fruitful distinctions that could be introduced here is expressed in two separate questions: (1) what kind of people support change in the form of the family: and (2) what kind of people are disturbed by lack of educational or job opportunities for women. It may not be that women who reject or accept tradition in one area are willing to reject or accept it across the board. In this connection, I find it interesting that the patient described by Dr. Schwab, though starting out by having very destructive feelings toward her children, and resentful feelings toward her marriage and the traditional female role, is being guided toward advanced education and a job outside the home. Presumably she has maintained a family relation with her husband and children. Is then the central issue in her case "antipathy to marriage" or is it rather antipathy to the traditional female role?

After reading this case one might well ask whether the monogamous family will be eroded or actually stabilized by change in the feminine role. While many people have long assumed that letting women out of the home would be the ruination of marriage and the family, it seems to me entirely possible that women with interesting work to do might be less dissatisfied with their family life than those women forced to derive all their satisfaction from it.

Nevertheless, the anger expressed by the young woman patient in the form of antipathy to marriage is suggestive. Although the end result of her therapy may not be an overthrow of her marriage but widened opportunities for pursuing her own interests, it is possible that an ability to express dissatisfaction against traditional marriage was a way station on the road to more basic innovation in her role as a woman.

Perhaps the place of antipathy to marriage in this young woman's therapy is an indicator of the way in which experimental forms of marriage are related to the Women's Liberation movement in the larger society. Those expressing anger toward traditional monogamous marriage may be doing so for very deep psychological reasons. But their example and their experiments may become a liberating force for a younger generation of women who wish to marry but who want a better role bargain than women were ready to settle for in the past. Under such conditions, marriage, even monogamous marriage, could very well continue but with a different allocation of role responsibilities between men and women. Then the predominant change to observe would not be the abandonment of marriage but the retention of marriage with an accompanying change in men's and women's roles that demanded more of others in the care of the family and released women for greater involvement in the world outside it.

Comment by:
Marijean Suelzle
Antipathy toward conventional monogamous marriage must be analyzed in terms of the sources of the antipathy in order to comprehend the range of new alternatives being explored. As Dr. Schwab points out, this antipathy has its roots in ambivalent religious attitudes toward the flesh.

Christianity began as a small sect within Judaism, gradually making converts from other nationalities. It contested the Roman government, the center of political power in Europe, for control of marriage and family matters. Christian beliefs were formed from an ancient philosophy of dualism which held the demands of the spirit and the flesh to be mutually exclusive. They were also formed in reaction to Roman law and custom which punished celibacy and tolerated divorce, infanticide, and prostitution. Virginity was put forward as the ideal, followed in increasingly less desirable order by celibacy after marriage, and fornication. Whereas they had begun by attacking the more blatant evils of Roman life, Christianity fell into the trap of conceptualizing marriage as a purely sexual union.

The formal code of behavior, the single standard of abstinence for both women and men, did not perfectly correspond with actual behavior. The informal standard of behavior was a double standard, with both written punishments and social censure being greater for women than for men. Women occupied a paradoxical status. On the one hand women and men were conceived of as equal in the sight of God, both being possessed of divine souls. On the other hand, the idea of the inferiority of women was pronounced.

Women, personified by Eve, were assumed to represent the evils of sex and to be unwholesome tempters of men. Women, personified by Mary, were placed on a pedestal and were assumed to represent compassion, tenderness, fragility, empathy, love, and motherhood. The two images were not combined in the same woman. Wives, mothers, and potential wives and mothers were idealized after the image of Mary. Prostitutes, servant girls, and women from lower socioeconomic classes were exploited as sexual objects after the image of Eve. Only men were allowed the full range of sexual experience from casual encounter to permanent relationship as husband and father.

The limitation of women's roles extended to other spheres of activity. The double standard in religion and sexual relationships was carried over into education, business, politics, and the family. Despite a 72-year struggle to attain the right to vote, from the Seneca Falls convention in 1848 to the granting of woman suffrage in 1929, a period which saw many other improvements in the status of women, women are still discriminated against in education, employment, and politics. The Women's Liberation movement observed that men had placed women on a pedestal only so that men did not have to look them in the eye!

The Women's Liberation movement has its roots in many contemporary social changes: greater longevity leaving more time freed from childbearing and child rearing, smaller family size, rising divorce rates, effective contraception with the discovery of the pill, admittance to higher education, an influx of women into the labor market, a concern about overpopulation, church, education, recreation, and public accommodation. The movement has attempted to publicize and augment these changes through an all-out attack on the double standard wherever it persists.

One of the problems faced by any reform or revolutionary movement is the necessity of defining an alternative social structure for the one it wishes to replace. The most simplistic solution is a negation of that which is. This kind of solution has been more often attributed to the Women's Liberation movement than it has been advocated by its members themselves. Thus, opponents argue that members of Women's Liberation want women to become "just like men." The image they invoke is that of the man-hating, castrating bitch dressed in army fatigues and hiking boots. They further predict a trend toward unisex, and end of the nuclear family, widespread promiscuity and child neglect. *The image portrayed of men is a very negative one if this indeed is what is meant by being "just like men."*

The Women's Liberation movement itself has not, for the most part, taken the above approach of simply reacting against what is. Rather the movement has taken the active stance of advocating freedom of choice, freedom to actualize one's own human potential, as a central goal. Along with equality of rights is a corresponding emphasis on equality of responsibility. Neither women nor men are to be constrained by the narrow stereotyped roles of the past. Both roles are to be expanded to include elements of what has previously been termed "masculine" or "feminine."

There is an emphasis on person-centered intimate relationships encompassing the many facets of personality, of which sexual expression is only one aspect. There is a movement away from body-centered relationships which focus on the depersonalized physical act itself. In marriage and intimate relationships there is a movement away from the family as a reproductive unit based on role differentiation toward the family as a companionate unit based on role sharing and similarity of interests and behavior.

The traditional monogamous marriage is regarded with antipathy because of the artificial limitations on personal growth imposed by the expectation of husband/father as economic provider and wife/mother as emotional specialist. The creation of two separate spheres, a "men's world" and a "women's world," has resulted in an emphasis on materialism with children being used as pawns in a power struggle between husband and wife. Since paid work in the labor force is a source of status, whereas unpaid labor in the home is not, women retaliate in their frustrated power seeking with the most powerful weapon they have: "But the children love me more than they love you."

Both women and men are torn by role conflict in modern America. Fathers are alienated from their children while educated and competent women are deprived of occupational and professional opportunities. As the roles of provider and parent are shared both sexes benefit. Men find they enjoy food more when they assist in its preparation, and their children more when they assist in their upbringing. Women have a greater opportunity for self-actualization, share more interests with their spouses, nag less, and are more supportive when they too experience the satisfactions and disappointments of a competitive labor market.

Marriage is becoming more universal, not less. The rising divorce rate does not indicate a disenchantment with marriage, for rates of remarriage among the divorced are also increasing. There is an antipathy toward traditional marriage based on a formal division of labor. But at the same time there appears to be an attraction toward monogamous marriage based on the model of a good friend with whom one also sleeps. People are marrying their lovers to expand the areas of life they can share as equals, not to limit them by assuming subordinate and superordinate roles.

Comment by:
Judith Long Laws
Schwab's initial premise is that marriage is at the outset positively valued by spouses, but as a result of their experience with the institution becomes negatively valued. It is this premise which one expects to find substantiated in the article. However, Schwab links the current

outcry against marriage with historical precedents—the Essenes; the Manicheans—which seem to me not to be parallels, since these ideologies value marriage negatively at the outset.

Again, Schwab quotes male antimarriage sentiments, and then fails to follow up the theme. In what ways does marriage disappoint, constrain, and frustrate men? In my review of the marital happiness literature I have found very little data on this question. Certainly it is appropriate to explore what marriage means for men, both in terms of the present institution and in terms of any evolving or potential institution.

Schwab's focus is, instead, women's experience of marriage. As a feminist, I am sensitive to Schwab's use of a vocabulary that is subjective (referring presumably to what is nonfactual) when he discusses women's discontents in marriage. Compare this language (women *"feel* . . . deprived of opportunities") with the simple declarative sentences referring to macrosocial events ("In a decadent age . . . traditional institutions seldom endure"; or ". . . early Christianity firmly established monogamous marriage as the best . . ."). This tendency is underscored by the author's descent into case history, which obscures any analysis of social structure. Rather, the therapeutic context of the data thus introduced lends itself to a view of the complaint as a symptom—again "nonfactual." The author notes that women do not blame their husbands, or the institution of marriage, for their discomfort, but rather blame themselves. Depression, indeed, is often interpreted to mean anger turned against the self, or intrapunitiveness. It has been suggested that women are trained to "act out" in this way—particularly against their own bodies—rather than taking action against social others or "the system."

By focusing on "psychopathology," the author disarms his critique of marriage. The reader is left with a lot of interesting questions. The author reports that young women are refusing the option of marriage unless the institution is (mysteriously and impersonally) changed. Why do they not believe two motivated individuals can change the institution? What is it about marriage (the initial question again) that transforms lovers into antagonists?

Another neglected dimension is the question of options other than marriage in the lives of men and women. Schwab describes a sort of Parkinson's Law which applies to marriage *for women:* the requirements of the housewife role expand to fill the time available; marriage remains a fulltime occupation for women, in spite of "timesavers." (Cross-cultural data on men's and women's time budgets are interesting in this regard. Both husbands and wives spend more time interacting with their children in a number of European countries, but American wives spend more time in the *presence* of theirs—e.g., taking them to appointments—than any other.) Men's and women's experience of marriage cannot be meaningfully compared without taking into account the fact that marriage has never been construed as a full-time occupation for men. Many studies show that overall life satisfaction (or "happiness") is a function of the resources that persons command. Thus even if marriage were equally miserable for both spouses, the husband has at least potential sources of esteem, self-actualization, and achievement outside of marriage, while the wife (at least in middle-class America) is very likely to have none.

This question of options is relevant, too, to the historical situations cited by the author in which marriage was disesteemed for all. Historically, women have been denied the right to hold property and to enter occupations. What, then, in the absence of options, was women's life to consist of without marriage?

The abrupt ending of the paper leaves us unable to explore the question of the future of relations between the sexes. Will the "sexual revolution" produce more egalitarian relations—outside of marriage or within it—between the sexes? Here I feel that the author while cognizant of the antisexual (and antisensual) ideology of our religious heritage, underestimates the degree of secular puritanism that is still with us. The double standard present in those early doctrines (e.g., men are "*defiled*" by their mutual congress with women) is present still. Women's sexuality is tabooed, proscribed, and controlled in a way that is not true for men. Punitive attitudes toward female sexuality can be found not only in our customs regarding marriage and marriageability, but in current controversies regarding abortion, contraception, and fertility. Even "noncontroversial" aspects of female sexuality like childbirth, lactation, and menstruation are the subject of taboos and extraneous control.

A final question regards the future of marriage. Schwab reports that disillusionment with marriage before the fact is becoming more prevalent. He may be correct; certainly the feminist critique of marriage has become widely accessible through the media. He seems to imply that, being awakened to its pitfalls, new generations will avoid marriage. However, I see no evidence for a decline in the popularity of this doomed option. We may be confronting a situation in which young people march into marriage with their eyes open, armed with despair.

11. How does marital quarreling affect sexual relations? –5 views

ISRAEL W. CHARNY, WARREN L. JONES,
CALVERT STEIN, WILLIAM M. KEPHART,
JAN EHRENWALD

ISRAEL W. CHARNY

It seems to me from the facts available that *some* quarreling is not only desirable but necessary for a productive—and that means sexual- —marital relationship; and that either too much quarreling and hatred or too little quarreling do not nourish the intimacy—and that includes the sexuality—of the partners to the marriage.

What has not emerged as clearly is a *theory* for why this is so; as a result there still are a great many marriage counselors and other mental health practitioners who tend to ignore, or minimize, if not actually deny the fact that some quarreling goes along with good sexuality, because they are not comfortable with interpreting this fact.

My own deepest sense of the relationship between quarreling and sexuality is that marital intimacy requires a healthy balance and integration of love and hate. I see the basic energy system of us human beings calling for a constant putting together of complementary or dialectical qualities such as *good* and *bad*, *strength* and *tenderness*, or *love* and *hate*—that there is something real to each side of life, and in every case when we carry even the seemingly nicer side of life to an excess the result is something monstrous. Each side of a dimension of experience seems to add a meaning to its very counterpart that is sadly lost when one, for example, is either *all* loving or *all* hating. The very tension of the process of putting these complementary qualities together seems to act as a tonic to people feeling and being alive and attractive—and sexual.

121

There are numerous other ways of explaining why quarreling and sexuality go together—many also have the advantage of being far more simple.

Another favorite of mine is that a *genuine* relationship between a man and a woman necessarily involves quarreling around this, that and the other thing—ultimately about the inevitable human short-comings of each partner. A genuine relationship offers each of us the opportunity to look at our short-comings and to be moved to efforts to grow in those regards. And good sexuality quite naturally accompanies a genuine relationship. In contrast, the phoniness of people who are all-nice to each other, with never a pebble to cast at the other or to dodge from the other (pebble here is intended as a miniature of the stone that one casts for much bigger sins!) makes for dull sex.

It is striking to observe that too little quarreling often enough makes for plain little sexual activity at all—so that there isn't even an opportunity for it to be dull.

In clinical practice, I have seen any number of couples who describe their relationship as one of genuine friendship and sympathy for one another—qualities one would ostensibly value in marriage—who add in effect, "But there is only one thing wrong: we have very infrequent sexual relations with each other." Often enough, this is a fact that comes to light indirectly in connection with the fact that the couple has come in for help around *someone else* in the family, such as a child who is suffering a psychological disturbance—often a fairly severe one. Other times, the couple themselves may have come for help for their marriage precisely out of a sense that something is missing. In any case, initially it would appear terribly puzzling why a couple who seem to be doing a better job of getting along with each other than most of us do have so much less of the fun accompanying real sexuality —until one comes to understand how all those *natural* processes of difference, and disagreements, and tensions of intimacy are being suppressed by these too-good souls in the interests of too much peace and quiet and security. The price for such peace and quiet is barely any sex.

The other side of the coin, that too much quarreling turns off intimacy and sexuality, hardly seems to require explanation. What does seem to warrant thinking is how too much quarreling, as well as too little quarreling, both represent failure to create a healthy fusion of love and hate. Each encounter between a man and a woman is a new one. There will always be better moments, and worse moments, and an infinity of moments that are better and worse at the same time. Men and women who know how to quarrel with each other *in the interests of* a greater loving of each other understandably may well achieve a greater breadth in their sexuality too. We might say those who plunge into their marital relationship in more natural risk-taking ways also are likely to enjoy a more healthy sexuality and fun.

WARREN L. JONES

Marital quarreling can, with skill, experience and good intentions produce deeper understanding and an increasingly vital relationship for a married couple. Such assertive communication can enrich a couple's relationship; as a consequence, sexual relations are benefited. Arguments may provide a dynamic, unique experience that may well be enjoyed—yes, enjoyed!—by the married couple.

Differences of understanding, discrepancies in mood and a host of other complications impinge perpetually upon even the most harmonious relationship. The struggle to persevere and be understood in a relationship requires forceful and explicit interaction. Discussions may become debates and debates phase into arguments and quarrels. The challenge in this marital communication crisis is to conquer mutual confusion in favor of clarity, further understanding, trust and affection. Successful solution of these encounters draws upon an inner core of appreciation and admiration. The couple who give to one another in a challenging as well as a tender, loving relationship gain a unique perspective; their physical relationship is a link in a delightful chain. This chain of strength and dynamic growth enriches each and builds self-esteem. The consequence is becoming a more adequate and gratified lover.

The crux of this discussion is to distinguish quarreling that is childish bickering and disruptive to intimacy on the one hand, and quarreling that is productive. Hostile quarreling which demands that the partner provide needs that can be supplied only by oneself becomes a vicious circle. As the individual develops inappropriate expectations of the partner, further dependency and anger mount. Hostile expectations that are impossible to meet lead to frustration, hurt, and confusion. The person eventually withdraws or attacks in an immature and deleterious way.

Basically, a good marriage relationship uses quarrels to clear the air and to gain a meeting of the minds which results not only in intellectual and emotional gains but erotic consummation as well.

CALVERT STEIN

Marital quarreling affects not only the quality, duration, and frequency of sexual response—but vice versa. When quarreling seems to result from unsatisfactory sexual relations, one should also seek other probable causes such as inadequate privacy, procrastination or haste, anxieties regarding health and birth control, relatiation for personal habits, previous rejections, or in-laws and associates who are no longer tolerable. Like other marital encounters, the most satisfying sexual relationships emphasize *giving* as well as receiving.

Habitual non-givers and passive partners have dependent and self-centered personality traits which usually have not changed much since childhood. For these people, sex can be less satisfying than quarreling. The impatient or aggressive partner also has an established pattern. He uses sex to bolster a sagging or deflated ego, to prove his virility, to assert dominance, or to release tensions—including hostility.

For such people, sex is frequently resorted to *after* a quarrel—each partner needing reassurance and proof of devotion. Sex may be used as a temporary truce in the perennial war between the sexes. It may also represent a lifelong struggle for identity and recognition.

Other factors which quarreling and sex have in common include their use and abuse as a defense against boredom; as coverup for emotional depression, gambling, philandering, frigidity, impotence or homosexuality; and as an excuse for physical complaints, excess of food, sweets or drink, overwork or taking off for days at a time.

Many partners can recognize the probable causes of their quarreling, yet avoid analysis of their sexual difficulties. One reason for not seeking help is the belated and reluctant recognition of their strong dependency needs. Financial support by a parental substitute, plus love without the challenges, dangers and degradations of sex, have been the primary objectives all along. A similar pattern may exist when there is a minimum of sex and rarely any quarreling in what appears to outsiders as the perfect marriage.

Nevertheless, quarreling has some advantages for the participants: (1) It can clear the air and relieve tension. (2) Fortunately it is self-limited, if there is no audience to act as witness, advocate, judge or jury. (3) If nothing else, quarrels afford a needed interlude and change of pace. (4) Quarreling may even have erotic aspects which can heighten the libido of the participants. (5) A variety of aches, pains and even menstrual tensions are often relieved by quarrels as well as by sex. This is accomplished by the resolution of emotional unfinished business with parents, siblings, and other VIP's as the sex partners take out on each other their pent-up hostilities and other compensations for earlier

resentments and frustrations. (6) There is yet another dividend—
—making up can be most rewarding.

As individuals become more mature emotionally, their needs for
frequent or excessive quarreling diminish. They learn to resolve their
disputes more quickly and peaceably. They avoid previous pitfalls and
learn from mutual experience. What then emerges is a gratifying
discovery of tenderness and love for each other. Such togetherness
replaces earlier emphasis upon rapid or genitally focused erotic pleasures, representing a major achievement toward a fulfilling male-
female partnership.

To accomplish such objectives one needs to follow the example of
the successful host and hostess: make the partner feel like a special and
honored guest; vary the setting, menu, entertainment and surprises;
and consult qualified counselors and specialists as the occasion arises.

Arguments can be prevented as well as shortened by agreement.
The host can at least agree that his guest certainly has a right to his own
opinion. An apology also soothes and calms ruffled feelings. One can
always be sorry for something: "I'm sorry you feel that way . . ." The
"but" can be *thought*, yet does not have to be spoken. Lastly, there is
the time-tested remedy of changing the subject of discussion and
offering other diversions.

WILLIAM M. KEPHART

The easiest-sounding sexual questions—those which seem to call
for a "common-sense" approach—are often the most difficult to answer, and this one is no exception. While I am not at all sure I can
provide a satisfactory explanation, I think I can point out some of the
complexities involved.

To begin with, even if we accept the common-sense answer—that
marital quarreling and sexual discord tend to go hand-in-hand—it is
vexing to try to sort out cause and effect. That is, it may well be that
quarreling has an adverse effect on sex adjustment, but it is just as true
that sexual difficulties may lead to excessive quarreling. Which is cause
and which is effect? It is not always easy to tell. One divorce lawyer,
after listening to embittered spouses "bare their souls" over the years,
remarked that "causes are jumbled, like a drop of bluing in a pail of
water. You cannot tell where the bluing stops and the water begins."

This cause-and-effect or "which came first?" dilemma is one of the
reasons behavioral scientists have found it difficult to come up with an
answer based on empirical research. It also explains, at least in part,

why there is so much difference of opinion on the part of the "experts." Divorce lawyers, for example, often see sexual problems as the root of most marital unhappiness. Psychiatrists and marriage counselors, on the other hand, are more likely to see sexual maladjustment as the result of basic behavioral conflicts.

My own view is that, in many if not most cases, quarreling does have an adverse effect on sex adjustment, but that the *seriousness* of the effect depends not only on the nature of the quarreling but on a number of other factors. Not all of these factors have been identified, but let us look at a few of the more obvious ones.

There are some individuals—unfortunately for the rest of us—who appear to thrive on turmoil. They insist on being where the action is, and if there is no action they can be counted on to foment some. Such people tend to be outgoing types, whose feelings are not easily hurt; indeed, they seem to have the epithelium of a rhinoceros. Is it reasonable to expect these individuals to encounter sexual problems simply because of marital quarreling? Or is it more likely that conjugal quarreling would simply serve as a vigorous prelude to an even more vigorous "make-up" session in the marriage bed?

At the other extreme, there are persons for whom quarreling—of any kind—is anathema. Such persons are easily wounded by verbal strikes, and as a result they come to spend a goodly portion of their waking hours trying to avoid conflict. What happens to these good people when they find themselves in a marital situation where altercation is unavoidable? Is it not likely, under these circumstances, that quarreling would have a grievous effect on sex adjustment?

It is probable, speaking very generally, that the wife is more affected by quarreling than the husband. Her feelings tend to be more sensitive, and her sex drive is not so imperious as her husband's. And since she is more concerned with the affectional rather than the strictly genital aspects of coitus, it would be relatively more difficult for her to immunize herself against the consequences of bickering and quarreling.

Other factors are also involved, however. For example, the importance of sex declines with the passing of years. The effect of quarreling may be one thing for a couple in their 20's or 30's, who are having—or would like to be having—intercourse two or three times a week. But what of the couple in their 60's or 70's, who indulge only once a month?

I could go on. What about such intervening factors as health, children, community interests, finances? A wife whose husband makes $50,000 a year, for instance, might well put up with quite a bit of bickering—and still maintain a satisfactory sexual relationship. But would this same woman be able to maintain the relationship if her husband were earning, say, $5,000 a year?

To sum up: it seems logical to suppose that for a large percentage of couples quarreling would have some adverse effect on sexual adjustment. *The magnitude of the effect, however, probably depends on factors of the kind mentioned above.* The type of research necessary to identify the major factors—and to put them in a rank order of importance—has not yet been undertaken.

JAN EHRENWALD

Quarrels between lovers or marriage partners may be skin-deep, touched off by trivial factors. Or they may express longstanding conflict. If so, the quarreling usually conforms to a readily recognizable pattern and may have a profound effect upon the spouses' mutual sexual adjustment. Paraphrasing a line from a famous love poem, they may ask: "How do I hate thee? Let me count the ways . . ." There are countless variations on the theme, especially if love and hate coexist. The ambivalence may lead to an endless succession of seemingly irrational clashes and reconciliations. They may culminate in a fullfledged sadomasochistic pattern in which hurting and being hurt become the preferred source of sexual gratification.

In its most harmless form, a lovers' quarrel may simply be conducive to one partner's sulking, punitive withdrawal from the other, while the ensuing reconciliation adds zest to their subsequent sexual reunion. The quarrel, in such cases, may serve as a veritable aphrodisiac. Yet, more often than not, habitual quarreling may indicate his or her need to combine the two classical Freudian ingredients of love-making—tenderness and violence—in one climactic sexual experience. (Ethologists like Lorenz or Tinbergen have recently come out with animal observations tending to support the Freudian thesis.)

Certain neurotic individuals habitually channel their hostility into the sexual act. So much so that the fear of losing control, of hurting and subsequently being hurt by the partner, may make him or her temporarily impotent or frigid. For others, coitus may be a barely disguised act of punishment, with the partner serving as a mere scapegoat or a mechanical outlet for pent-up rage and hostility. Some women can permit themselves to enjoy intercourse only if they feel it has been forced on them. Their scenario calls for rape, for being used, degraded, violated, tied-up against their will. Staging a fight, in such cases, serves as an alibi for a nagging conscience, and may become a necessary ingredient to make ultimate sexual fulfillment possible.

But quarreling between lovers and marriage partners may also affect their sexual relationship the other way around. Lack of fulfill-ment often leads to smoldering resentment or open hostility against the partner. The male's premature ejaculation is a frustrating experi-ence to the spouse. It may be aggravated by her mistaken feeling of being personally rejected by a partner who "does not even try," or "does not care" what happens to her. In a similar vein, the wife's inadequate sexual response or inability to reach an orgasm may pro-voke feelings of inferiority and resentment in her partner. Longstand-ing patterns of this lead to a vicious cycle. Chronic irritability, argu-ments and mutual recriminations may become the order of the day—or the night.

The existing sexual maladjustment in such couples often reflects incompatibility in broader areas of living. It may be due to false expec-tations held by one partner in regard to the other, with both having developed an unrealistic image of the respective spouse. Fear of the "bitchy," "castrating" woman, or resentment of the callous, predatory male is a frequent feature of such distortions. On closer inquiry one may find that one or the other spouse is in effect a replica of a signific-ant family member to which he or she had been exposed as a child. The early experience of a bad marital relationship—of recurrent fights between father and mother—is then carried over into their own mar-riage.

What is the remedy for such a state of affairs? The garden variety of lovers' quarrels may merely enliven the marital scene and open a safety valve for occasional interpersonal tensions. In so doing it may bring variety into the established marital routine, sexual or otherwise. A recurrent pattern of open discord and hostile acting out calls for an attempt to open up better lines of communication between the part-ners. The clarification of underlying misrepresentations and faulty perceptions of one another may help. Specific questions to be asked are: How deep is the confusion between love and aggression in his or her mind? Does the need for spicing the sexual experience with an element of violence reach pathological proportions? If so, is there the danger of an existing sadomasochistic pattern getting out of control and destroying the marriage? Can improved communication between the spouses resolve their difficulties, or is it a symptom of neurotic illness which calls for professional help?

PART III

Extramarital Sex

12. *Extramarital Relationships*

JETSE SPREY

Extramarital relationships are not just another form of deviant or "abnormal" behavior, despite the fact that they are considered by many people, even those who engage in them, a form of deviance. Extramaritality deserves to be studied in its own right, in its complexity, and in all its possible forms of interdependency with marriage, not merely as a violation of the latter. It follows then that when we try to explain extramaritality, we must begin and end with its interconnection with marriage itself. In other words, it is not the "extra" that concerns us, but the "extra" in the "marital."

All the data presented in this paper are there to illustrate, or at best to question, generally held assumptions, and are not intended to prove hypotheses about extramarital conduct. Their main purpose is to create a realistic perspective and illuminate the complexity and many-faceted nature of our subject matter.

The sources of my data are questionnaires (completed anonymously) that were distributed over the past years to small audiences such as P.T.A. groups, wives of graduate students, career women, and parents. The response rate varied between 60 and 80 percent. My case material is unsystematic and often impressionistic. I am a family sociologist, not a marriage counselor, therapist, or divorce lawyer. I have found that many individuals who are, in one way or another, involved in an extramarital relationship like to discuss their stiuation with someone who has the professional neutrality of the social scientist, but is not associated with counseling or therpay. Family sociologists make good sounding boards because they can be expected

131

to have a legitimate interest in extramarital behavior, but do not require their informants to define themselves as "patients" or needing "professional help." Many of the people I talked to who were or had been involved in an extramarital relationship referred me to others they knew in similar circumstances. Therefore, the case material reported here differs from that often used by clinicians in that it reflects the attitudes and conduct of people who did not seek professional help, and who on the whole have not expressed any intention of doing so.

In addition, there is the wide range of data reported by others such as journalists, clinicians, and lawyers, as well as the personal documents and testimonies that keep appearing in the newspapers, magazines, and other material that reaches a broad part of the population. Most of this, unfortunately, is unreliable and unsystematic. But because our dearth of information on extramaritality is such, we are in no position to ignore any source of insight which comes our way.

Public and professional views of extramaritality
Each contact between a married person and anyone other than his or her spouse is by definition an extramarital one. However, this is not the way in which most people, either professional or laymen, perceive it. On the whole, the term "extramarital" is associated with a sexual relationship of some kind. To provide some insight into the public definition, small groups of housewives (altogether 43 middle and lower-middle class women) were asked which of the following descriptions they associated with the notion of extramarital relationship.
  (a) A sexual affair between two people of the opposite sex of whom at least one is married.
  (b) A friendship between two people of the opposite sex of whom at least one is married.
  (c) A combination of (a) and (b).
  (d) A friendship between two people of the same sex, of whom at least one is married.
  (e) All of the above.

Seventy-four percent selected the first statement (a) as the proper definition. 23% took the choice of (c), while 2.3% chose (e). When asked which of these alternatives they considered potentially the most damaging to their marriage, 39 of our 42 respondents marked (a), two selected (b), while (c) and (e) each received one choice. It is interesting to note that among those who associated "extramarital" with both sex and friendship and therefore picked definition (c) for the word, most singled out the *sexual* affair as potentially most damaging to their marriage. As one put it: "I select (a), (b) could sometimes be forgotten where (a) most likely would never be forgiven; (a) is really the most damaging but to some people with real jealous minds (b) could be just as damaging." This type of comment reinforces my impression that most wives recognize the fact that there remain unshared and "unconquered" domains in their spouses' lives and in their own as well. Such unshared realms, in the case of husbands primarily occupational, should leave room for friendships and colleague relationships even with members of the opposite sex. The ambiguity and uncertainty enter only at the question of how far such relationships, especially the heterosexual ones, should go.

For example, in response to the question of whether or not a working wife has the right to establish friendships with male colleagues, 18 of the wives in this group said "yes," 21 gave a conditional "yes" answer, while 4 answered "no." All conditional answers reflected the problems associated with the limits of such contacts. For instance:

> Yes, providing their friendship stays within the boundaries of their working hours and within their place of work. *No* personal contacts after working hours. Dangerous!!!!

or: Yes, as it relates to the job. And socially only on a basis of married couples together.

Typical of the few "no" answers is the following comment:

> No, I do not. She has made her choice and should not need other men in her life.

Many spouses, husbands as well as wives, seem to have few illusions about their abilities to share in everything that concerns the lives of their respective spouses. They do not seem too upset about this. When, for example, a larger group of wives was asked the question: "Do you feel that a wife can provide the interest in her husband's occupation that a colleague (male and female) can?", 30 out of a total of 65 answered with a flat "no"; 21 responded with "not sure", while 14 said "yes." Apparently, and not too surprisingly, the type of work of the husband made a difference here. Twenty-two of the women in this sample were wives of graduate students — from this category 18 answered "no," (81% as opposed to the 46% negative response from the group as a whole) and only 3 said "yes." Many women in this group indicated that they didn't have very much of an idea what their husbands' work was all about.

What does the foregoing add up to? Statistically speaking, very little. But on the impressionistic level, a number of things suggest themselves. The reality of marriage is such that, for many couples, large parts of their lives are not shared. In an increasing number of societal spheres such "open" domains are shared with others, men and women, married and unmarried. This trend can only be expected to increase. The response to the potential challenge of such extramarital involvements—sexual or nonsexual—seems to be that as long as there is no actual sex there is no danger. A questionable assumption indeed, especially in an evolutionary period for marriage when increasing stress is being laid on the interpersonal rather than the contractual aspects of the marital bond. No wonder that so many spouses, male and female, appear baffled and defenseless when confronted with extramarital entanglements in their lives.

Types of extramarital involvement

One of the first impressions one gets in talking to various people about extramarital behavior is that the great diversity of involvement defies any categorical use of the concept "extramarital." We can only begin to understand it if we define our terms carefully.

First of all, we must distinguish between sexual and nonsexual extramarital involvements, keeping in mind of course that some relationships may progress from the one into the other. A primary distinction between these two types of extramaritality is, of course, the different relationship of each to the marital bond. Which of the two poses the gravest threat—or greatest aid—to marriage? As mentioned earlier, many people see the relatively new phenomenon of friendship between married individuals in a different light from sexual affairs. Terms like "infidelity" and "adultery" are reserved for the latter category only. Still, with the increasing accent on the interpersonal nature of marriage in our culture, the extramarital sex per se may not really be as great a threat as emotional extramarital intimacy. Illustrative of this is the fact that those couples who are making joint extramarital games of their married lives, the so-called "swingers," go to great lengths to keep their mate-swapping procedures on a strictly impersonal level.

A second basic distinction is that between short and long term involvements. It is tempting to equate this with the difference between casual and serious affairs, but in view of the fact that some casual affairs may last a long time, this seems invalid. I know of at least one casual sexual relationship between two people, both married, that has lasted more than ten years. How, to take another example, do we categorize a life-long friendship between two people that had its beginnings in a fairly brief intense extramarital sexual relationship? I know of some in which occasionally, depending on the circumstances, sex still occurs but has been delegated to a very minor part in the context of the total relationship. Many marriages show a similar course of development.

Another factor to be taken into account is the location in which the extramarital encounter occurs. Many brief sexual affairs happen during conventions, vacation trips, and other out-of-town stays. Traditionally, such away-from-home type affairs have been mainly male activities, often involving prostitutes or other semi-professionals, but I believe this is gradually changing. Women, including married ones, are increasingly participating in previously all male occupations. I know at least a few professional women who consider a sexual fling a desirable part of professional meetings or business conventions.

A fourth factor to be considered is the marital status of those participating in extramarital relations. Logically speaking, there are three possible combinations: (1) both parties are married, (2) the male is married, the female is single (3) the female is married, the male is single. It seems likely that when both participants are married their relationship may be different from the other two possible combinations. The fact that not one but two divorces stand between their affair and marriage may well create a psychological climate quite different from the others. I consider this distinction particularly relevant in understanding those affairs, or friendships, that manage to exist over considerable time in some kind of symbiosis with the marriages of those involved. I also believe, without any formal evidence, that many of such extramarital relationships, if given the option of marriage, would lead to bad marriages. In other words, in addition to the assumption that some marriages need extramarital involvements of the spouses to survive, I feel that the reverse is equally true; some and perhaps many extramarital affairs depend on the marital status of both its participants to survive. For one thing, the fact that marriage is out of the question facilitates a complete concentration on the rewards of the relationship per se. These may be manyfold—emotional, sexual, and economic. It is my experience, supported by the writings of others, that congenial, nontraumatic extramarital relationships are most likely to occur in conjunction with the stable marriages of those involved.

Finally, when we use the marital statuses of those who engage in extramarital relations as a criterion of analysis, the classification "single" must be further categorized as to the previous marital histories of those involved. Morton Hunt's description of the "world of the formerly married" provides enough ground to suggest this.

One last aspect of the situation that must be considered is the presence or absence of children, especially minors. Parents with small children who engage in extramarital behavior are in a very special situation, and most of them, in my opinion, are quite aware of this. Again, the accent lies not so much on the behaviors and attitudes of the children per se, but rather on the specific interdependence between the "extra" and the "marital" which results from such a condition.

So far we have listed separately a number of presumably relevant attributes of extramarital relationships. This is, of course, unrealistic. They will occur in a wide variety of combinations. In some cases the effects of certain factors may reinforce each other, in others the reverse may be true.

In either case the pattern of the extramarital relationship raises questions about the marital relationship: What is the connection, if any, between the quality of a given marital bond, the types of careers of the spouses, and the kinds of extramarital life of either spouse? May we assume that the types of extramarital behavior sets of spouses engage in are a function of the kinds of marriages they have? Or perhaps the opposite situation—the kinds of marriages people have are a function of extramarital conditions—may provide greater insight into behavior patterns? I believe this to be the case, but until I can assemble relevant data I have little more than impressions to substantiate the idea.

Practical aspects of extramarital activity

So far we have considered the sociological and emotional factors of extramarital relationships. There are also some purely pragmatic considerations. First of all, to start an extramarital relationship, and especially to maintain one, people need the opportunity to be together. This means they need a few scarce commodities; time, a place to meet intimately, and last but not least, the financial resources to cover the necessary expenses. In other words, each extramarital relationship, some types more than others, depends on a specific opportunity structure. The latter functions as a necessary, but not a sufficient condition, to the existence of any form of extramarital behavior, except that existing in a person's fantasies. A few illustrations may clarify this point.

A more-or-less permanent place to meet is a necessary condition for the survival of any extramarital sexual affair because motel rooms lose their charm after a while even for those to whom money is not an issue. The fact that single individuals are likely to have a place of their own makes getting together with a married partner a great deal easier and less traumatic. There are other pertinent factors connected with the meeting place. Some types of community provide considerable more room for privacy than others; through friends or connections, a meeting place may be made available; one or both of the partners may be able to afford to rent a permanent place; yet even when all the above are lacking, some couples are extremely enterprising.

In the light of such requisite opportunity structure it seems likely that much of the hitherto observed and reported—by Kinsey for example—socioeconomic and regional differentials among those who do and do not have affairs are a function of the unequal distribution of the opportunity factor. The opportunities for extramarital affairs present at professional meetings, for example, are not available to spouses who cannot afford or are in no position to travel.

Contemporary society and extramarital patterns

A number of societal factors underlie our rising rates of extramaritality. One is the increased life expectancy of contemporary Western marriage. In the historical period during which our cultural prescription denoting marriage as a life-long bond became firmly entrenched in our mores, the average life expectancy was about thirty-five years, so spouses were obliged to endure each other for no more than ten to fifteen years. At this writing, the expected duration of the average American marriage is approximately forty years.

The increasing stress on the emotional, interpersonal qualities of contemporary marriage is a second factor. Marital and familial bonds in our past, before the 18th century, "did not penetrate very far into human sensibility," as Philippe Aries put it. Now couples work at getting to know every inch of each other's minds—and bodies. This merits attention in view of the proclamation of those who see our current rise in extramaritality as an indication of the deterioration and demise of marriage. I would argue that exactly the opposite is the case; our rise in extramarital relationships reflects—as is the case for our high divorce rate, although in a quite different context—the strength of contemporary marriage. A deterioration of the institution of marriage would be accompanied by a decrease in marriage and remarriage rates, which the statistics show is simply not the case. In fact, many people are trying to enlarge its scope. We already have examples of group marriage and can look forward to the homosexual marriage also. Contemporary extramaritality is no assault on marriage—it represents a frantic effort to come to terms with marriage in its current thoroughly inhumane form.

The much heralded transition from the traditional extended family to its modern nuclear unit consisting of parents and their offspring, in addition to a steady decline in family size, is interconnected with one other major social development: the changing nature of women's participation in society. Women, married and single, are moving steadily into previously all-male occupational spheres. Married women, including those with young children, have been entering the world of work in increasing numbers and there are no indications that this trend will reverse itself.

These appear to be the major societal factors responsible for a sociocultural setting that is conducive to a steady increase in extramaritality. Families are smaller than in the past, while marriages are expected to last many years longer. Women are combining careers and marriage, and consequently engaging in new relationships with men whether as colleagues, fellow workers, and/or as fellow consumers. At the same time, marriage remains the most desirable life goal for both sexes, with an emphasis on the idea that the marital bond consists of total sharing, common identity, and all-embracing togetherness. The increased social and cultural acceptance of nonprocreative sexuality has added another burden to contemporary marriage because of the tendency to see a mutually satisfying sexual relationship as part and parcel of a close emotional bond. This also poses problems of management in the extramarital sphere, especially where heterosexual friendships are present. The union of sex and friendship outside the context of marriage is new in our culture, and is problematic on both the premarital and extramarital level.

Inividual considerations

Few people marry with the intention of establishing extramarital relationships, yet many end up doing it. Why, and under what conditions, do some spouses engage in extramarital relationships? And, equally important, why do others *not* get involved? If we accept Robert Bell's estimate that by age 40 about one third of all married women and possibly 60 percent of all married men have had an extramarital sexual experience, we are left with a sizable proportion of our married population *without* such an involvement. Is it because of no opportunity, no courage, or no inclination? About one year ago I gave a detailed questionnaire about extramaritality to a group of career women; about 20 percent of the respondents admitted to at least one extramarital affair. Lack of inclination despite the availability of opportunity was mentioned by several respondents who did not get involved. In some instances, freindships with male colleagues developed into sexual affairs, but in other instances, they did not. Again, why?

My impression is that a large proportion of people who have extramarital relationships drift into such encounters, and are not motivated by a preconceived, systematically executed plan of action. When a given spouse is psychologically "ripe" for extramarital involvement, the factors of chance and opportunity doubtless play a large role. It is probably true that there are some critical stages in this type of process, particularly when it is a first affair.

What happens is that, over the years, for some the possibility of extramarital involvement becomes increasingly realistic. As one married woman said, "Instead of asking why should I, I began to ask why shouldn't I?" In other cases relationships, especially friendships, seem to creep up on those involved and at a certain point the question of "where do we go from here?" demands an answer. Most people, however, who are having an extramarital relationship cannot explain what really happened to them—in the same way that most people do not truly understand the nature or development of their own *marital* relationship.

Clearly the question of why, and how, some spouses refrain from extramarital relations requires some thought. In some instances, absence of extramarital conduct results from a clear-cut conscious decision, often based on strong ideological or religious commitments. In other instances, there is just no opportunity. There are still, however, those who would not rule out extramarital conduct as a matter of principle, and who also have the opportunity, but who continue to refrain. The following illustrations are examples of precisely this point.

One of my informants, a professional male in his early forties, is and has the reputation of being sexually liberal. He is also very attractive. His marriage is stable but in many aspects is far from a total relationship. Despite sufficient opportunity, both in his daily working environment and at professional meetings and trips, he is quite monogamous. Most of his numerous female friends are professional women, and the friendships are nonsexual. In his own words: My attitude toward easy sex is the same as that toward cheap booze. Who needs it? At conventions and other occasions, I have better things to do than look for new women, and I certainly do not wish to have to go through the old seduction routine with them. I prefer a book, or conversations with friends. This doesn't exclude the possibility of meeting new people, men or women, of course.

To this man, extramarital involvement would mean first and foremost a close friendship of which sex could be a part, depending on the circumstances. Another typical comment is: As soon as you get over the conquest hang-up, casual lays, even with nice women, get to be rather monotonous. I can see just plain curiosity of "How would she do it?" may be a factor to some men, but to me, it isn't worth my time or the risk involved. I just as soon get mine at home.

If we look realistically at the investment in time, energy, and money that an extramarital affair frequently requires, it becomes un-understandable that many sophisticated spouses, both male and female, often abstain from the pursuit of promising leads. One wife says: Sometimes, at a party, during a pleasant conversation, a man asks if he may call sometime. My reaction is, "What's the use?" I am not in the market for a quick lay, and to start something permanent is just too much of a thing.

Comments like these do not necessarily imply a happy home life or a blind acceptance of the monogamous ideals of conventional marriage. They do reflect, in my opinion, experience, maturity, and a sense of self-esteem. Some people in this category may have had an occasional extramarital experience, but they do not make a habit of it. It further indicates that the home situation—with its limitations—tends to serve as a reference category in the establishment of external involvements. Spouses like these are unlikely to engage in relationships with someone inferior to their own spouse. Why should they? I doubt that this is a matter of religiosity. It is more likely due to the fact that there simply is nothing to be gained.

It would be easy at this point to interpret the foregoing as meaning that only the immature, the insecure, and the neurotic among our population of spouses are likely to engage in extramarital affairs. Perhaps they are statistically more inclined to do so. Clinical evidence seems to support this, but it remains an educated guess. I would predict, however, that in such cases the quality of their extramarital involvements will be not better than that of their marriages. But there are also mature, responsible people involved in extramarital relationships. They accept the dishonesty and secrecy associated with their relationships as the price for something they experience as meaningful and helpful to all involved, including those from whom the relationship is kept secret.

On the "extra" in the "marital"

We find it hard to explain why someone who is part of a stable, satisfactory marriage would engage in extramarital relationships, whether sexual or not. This has to do with the fact that in our culture the marital bond has evolved to be the most intimate of all human involvements; a dyadic love relationship which excludes all others except the lovers themselves. To realize the pervasiveness of this assumption one has only to look at the idealistic young couples who have established joint relationships outside of marriage. Problems of jealousy, possessiveness, and exploitation exist that are remarkably like those that plague all married couples. The limited experience I have had with communes both in this country and abroad has taught me that one of the major causes of disintegration and conflict is the formation of pair-relationships that become, despite all rhetoric to the contrary, exclusive of all others.

Basically there are two categories of extramaritality. One is symptomatic of disorganized, deteriorating marriages. We may also find here a relative overrepresentation of spouses who have personality traits that tend to make them, without professional help, poor risks in close interpersonal relationships of any sort, marital or extramarital. Many of the case studies published on extramarital conduct appear to fall into this category, I believe, because they are for a variety of reasons more easily accessible. This category of marriages has its own complex problems, and the extramarital conduct of its participants is part and parcel of it.

I am most interested in the other category of extramarital behavior, that associated with stable marriages. If we realistically think about "cure" or "change" with regard to this kind of extramaritality, we have no choice but to ask "Cure what? Change what?" It is here that we are confronted with the more basic question of whether the kind of bond we expect in modern marriage is humanly possible. I would suggest it is not, but for reasons that have little to do with human nature. If we, for the moment, contemplate a world consisting of only two people—a dream apparently associated with the utopias of many romantic lovers—there would be no one to *exclude,* which would make the relationship in question totally empty and meaningless. In other words, the more exclusive and intimate a human bond becomes the more it will depend on qualified others to be excluded. Marriage is not a static structure, but an ongoing event that depends for its survival on a continuous process of reaffirmation and mutual rediscovery. This, I would suggest, requires a continuous involvement with others——extramarital involvements. What kind—sexual, fantasized, friendship? I simply do not know because no one, to my knowledge, has studied extramaritality from this perspective.

One of the important implications of this view of extramaritality is that it raises some very basic questions about marriage and our participation in it. As one married career woman put it:

I never realized that I would be able to have so much of what is really meaningful to me outside of my marriage. My work is a major part of my life, but I can only share it with some of my friends.

This woman has a close friendship with a male colleague that completely excludes her husband, but in no way makes her feel guilty.

Sometimes such friendships turn into sexual relationships. This may be the beginning of the end for the relationship, but also may be the end of the beginning. I know of affairs like this that have been going for years. This demands considerable interpersonal skills, and a clear conception by both of what the relationship in question means and what the marriages involved mean. Somehow, each must be brought into line with the other.

Finally, we are left with one more important question. Given the fact that some extramarital relationships may actually be supportive of marriage, what can be done to make them less distasteful and more acceptable on their own worth and therefore less difficult for those involved? My answer is that, short of changing our expectations about marriage, nothing can or should be done. I completely agree with Spurgeon English's contention that extramarital relationships need to be managed discreetly and kept "free of the anger of others."

The urge to "come clean," often rationalized as a belated return to "honesty," reflects, in my judgment, little more than a selfish desire to lessen one's guilt at the expense of someone else's feelings. Those who feel the need for honesty should announce and discuss their extramarital inclinations beforehand, and when feasible incorporate them into the negotiation of their marriage arrangement. This is, of course, actually done by some spouses and advocated by those who favor a so-called "open-ended" type of marriage. How many spouses will, in fact, be able to do this successfully remains a question to be answered in the future.

I suggest that the reason for secrecy in so many contemporary extramarital involvements lies in the fact that the marriages in question are *not* open-ended and cannot tolerate the "honesty" that goes with the kind of soul-baring propagated by representatives of our growing guild of encounter-groupers and sensitivity experts. The motto of these people seems to be "one cannot make an omelet without breaking eggs." I would go along with that, but my image of an intimate human bond, such as the marital or parental, is not that of an omelet, totally blended, but rather of a relationship which despite its closeness leaves the personal integrity of its members intact.

Intimate human relationships are quite vulnerable and fragile. This fragility is, paradoxically, their main source of strength because it brings with it the need for continued protection, reaffirmation, and involvement. Most important, however, it requires respect for the uniqueness of the intimate other. Such protection and respect involve secrecy and dishonesty from time to time. As one man said to me:

My wife and I now each go to our separate ways. We can sleep around when we like, because neither of us really cares anymore.

It is in that type of situation that honesty no longer can do any harm.

Bibliography

1. Aries, P.: Centuries of Childhood (New York: Vintage Books, 1965).
2. Boylan, B.R.: Infidelity (Englewood Cliffs, New Jersey: Prentice Hall, 1971).
3. Cuber, J.F.: The mistress in American society. Medical Aspects of Human Sexuality 3:81, Sept. 1969.
4. Cuber, J.F., and Harroff, P.B.: Sex and the Significant Americans (Baltimore: Penguin Books, 1966).
5. Bell, R.R.: Social Deviance (Homewood, Ill.: Dorsey 1971).
6. English, O.S.: Values in Psychotherapy: The Affair: Voices, Vol. 3 (Winter, 1967).
7. Hunt, M.M.: The World of the Formerly Married (New York: McGraw-Hill, 1966).
8. Hunt, M.M.: The Affair (New York: World, 1969).
9. Neubeck, G. (ed.): Extra-Marital Relations (Englewood Cliffs, N.J.: Prentice-Hall, 1969).

13. DEBATE:
Is Marital Infidelity Justified?

Yes: O. Spurgeon English
No: Melvin S. Heller

Dr. Heller: I would like to point out that a couple of years ago my good friend and esteemed colleague, and my adversary for this occasion, startled a number of people by publishing an article in which he recommended affairs for married people as a preferable alternative to divorce, high blood pressure, murder, coronary heart attacks, and all of the internal sufferings which afflict people who endure unendurable marriages. It landed like a bombshell in our psychiatric community.

Dr. English: In my 38 years of psychiatric practice I have seen many people who benefited from, and whose marriage had been helped by, an affair. I came out in favor of affairs after seeing this a good many years and observing the positive results, while seeing only an occasional case that came to grief. And when it came to grief, it was usually a case of bad judgment or because someone felt it couldn't continue without a complete confession. It wasn't his sense of morality that caused him to tell somebody, because consciously and rationally he didn't consider it immoral. It was because he couldn't stand it emotionally. He couldn't cope with the anxiety of being caught or the anxiety generated by his conscience. And by conscience I mean his incorporated values of others—not truly his own.

    That constitutes a very important distinction to be made right away. So many people said, "Morally this is bothering me so I'm going to tell." It didn't bother them morally at all—they saw no harm done to anyone by their infidelity—and they would have continued if they didn't need some help with their attempt to balance their very own convictions against those they heard from parents and church—often parents who were carrying on an affair themselves while preaching chastity to their children. They hoped the spouse would not give them the same double-talk as their parents did. So they finally told somebody, and then trouble began. In their extreme tension they thought that if they told their husband or wife "they will understand and then I'll be comfortable." The husband or wife rarely understood. They have not understood in the past and there aren't many husbands or wives who understand now.

I want to add that in addition to Dr. Heller and I battling this issue, our discussion is partially intended to get the opinions of people here of various ages and from different walks of life whom we invited to comment and ask questions in order to find out what they think of this highly charged matter called the sexual affair.

Dr. Heller: Let me ask if we want to differentiate between the affair and the casual sexual encounter outside of marriage? I would think the affair involves a meaningful, ongoing relationship rather than a casual roll-in-the-hay, so to speak.

Dr. English: I wouldn't attempt to make such a distinction because I think there are some continuous ongoing affairs which go on very well for a while and then become burdensome. Both people try to be authentic but can't break it up when it has reached its end. It's like a poor marriage when a divorce is delayed too long. On the other hand, there have been single encounters that that have had great meaning for people. One couple I know had been very interested in each other as youngsters, but beyond their twenties couldn't culminate their feelings with the intimacy which they both desired. Yet, after a great many years and a great change in circumstances, the wheel of fortune brought them together again and sexual relations occurred once and it was of such meaning that neither of them has been able to forget its high value, in spite of the fact that they remain married to their originally chosen mates.

Audience: As an advocate of affairs, would you not hope that this last couple that you were describing might try it again? Or is this to be their one and only gratifying experience for the next ten years?

Dr. English: I think that depends upon the capacity of a mind to enjoy and remember. After all, how many times do we get to Venice? How many times do we get to Tokyo? How many times do we experience other beautiful things in life?

Dr. Heller: I would hope that we get to bed a lot more often than we get to Tokyo!

Dr. English: Repeated going to bed can get to be very boring, and a beautiful feeling of a one time intimacy can thus be ruined by realities which a brief encounter can avoid, leaving the romantic experience uncontaminated by some of the realities of marriage or a long time affair. Consequently, I just can't say that a single exposure of selves to a meaningful experience is inferior and two hundred are superior.

Dr. Heller: I'm wondering if you can dignify an encounter such as happens to a large number of men (we've all heard about traveling salesmen) who will on occasion, when the opportunity presents itself, indulge in an impersonal sexual encounter. And it is meaningless in terms of not having any knowledge of, or particular consideration for, the person with whom they are having little more than genital friction.

Dr. English: I object to your denigrating a single encounter. No sexual encounter is meaningless.

Dr. Heller: I'm not saying it's meaningless. I'm saying that having it with an individual about whom they know little or nothing, they probably project onto the partner characteristics that person doesn't have at all. They are having sex with a stranger to whom they attribute certain characteristics.

Dr. English: Aren't you forgetting that no man really knows a woman until he goes to bed with her?

Dr. Heller: It's an interesting dictum, but I know people who have gone to bed with other people and still don't know them, or even themselves.

My chief point is that as an affair becomes protracted and meaningful, significant damage can be done to the sexual partner, to oneself, and to children of both if they are sufficiently young to need both married partners involved with each other. I think that's damage of a much higher order than the damage that can be done if a salesman goes to a meeting in another city and in the haze of a few drinks finds himself sexually involved, only to wake up the next morning, go home, and forget about it.

I think if you're going to carry on with an extramarital partner on a regular basis, there are certain predictable consequences. One of them is that if the relationship is meaningful it is going to dilute the sexual interest in the spouse—which the spouse may be delighted to experience, by the way. Probably there are all too many spouses who would be only too glad to have this occur. I think this is an inevitable accompaniment of affairs, as I have seen them in my patients. That's one kind of danger in an ongoing affair not present in a chance encounter.

Dr. English: I don't think that a meaningful sexual experience is ever harmful. It's the confused attitudes and self-defeating behavior of the people having the affair that make their positive experience turn negative or indifferent in the end.

Audience: I would like to speak up for the ladies. If a person's marriage is a good, meaningful relationship, why should that person have affairs? By the time you have met your partner you should have experimented enough and finally have found the person that you're congenial with, compatible with, and get the greatest enjoyment with. Doesn't that rule out the need for other partners?

Dr. English: Even in the presence of a happy marriage, an extramarital sexual experience can be enjoyable and pleasurable and imaginatively creative while it happens, and can be retained in the mind as a good, happy, or positive experience with some contribution of imagination or inspiration in it. The person's marriage doesn't have to be filled with grief or contention for an outside sexual experience to add something worthwhile to his or her life.

I would like to say this in another way: I am sure there are people who could devise a limited diet for me that would keep me alive and healthy as long as I live. But I could get awfully tired of this monotonous diet. It might keep me alive; it might keep me healthy. But I'd get tired of it. I would want some variety. Marriage as an institution will keep one alive but it doesn't give many of the extras that people desiring an affair are looking for.

Dr. Heller: You make too light of the possible harm. First distinguish between the "discovered" affair and the "discreet" affair. I think you must grant that the affair discovered is frequently used as a kind of bomb, a piece of blackmail, or relatively violent resolution of a preexisting problem. And so, I hope you are not advocating that people involved in affairs make announcements of that fact, especially to their spouse who is always the last person to know.

The discreet affair is consistent with a great deal of feeling in this country that the major crime is getting caught, not what you do. That equates fudging on the profound commitment of marriage with such things as fudging on your income tax; and that vows and oaths mean little. Some people feel pretty smug about their derelictions, until caught, that is. Would you differentiate, as I do, between the "hidden" or "discreet" affair and the bungler who gets caught, most likely at his or her own doing?

Dr. English: Getting caught's not a crime—it's a misfortune.

Dr. Heller: Oh, but it's unconsciously determined, and frequently as a kind of desperate maneuver in an already destructive relationship that should be improved, rather than further undermined by the addition of new weapons such as unfaithful sex behavior.

Dr. English: I would prefer for the time to speak of the affairs as such without yet getting into the question of those who trap themselves. I think those instances are people who don't enter an affair with love and consideration of all parties and hence must trap themselves.

Dr. Heller: Okay, let's do that. But I also would like to ask you what you think of a relationship based on a lie—and I do favor the deceit over the cruel truth, in such instances.

Dr. English: I don't object to the role of a liar. It may sound shocking for me to say that, but I say it with this in mind: I think most great men and women have died with many secrets in their hearts that they couldn't share with anybody. I think that if people are going to live and live importantly, occupy important positions and be of social value they just can't share everything with everybody. There are some things that people in positions of responsibility have to hold within their minds. And if being a parent and marital partner isn't a position of responsibility, I don't know one more so. I'm going to hurriedly throw this in: of course the whole business of secrecy could be dissolved if people would just become generous enough to allow their mate to enjoy something with another person they can't provide; not because they are inferior people but because they possess only one body and one mind.

Dr. Heller: Now, let me introduce another concept with reference to affairs. I have seen a variety of women who have had affairs and came to my office with problems. I think I have yet to see a woman who is happy in her affair, who is not desperate to convert that affair into a marriage. At the beginning they think they can establish ground rules about what their relationship will be, when they can meet, what they will mean to each other. But eventually these limitations start to erode, and usually the woman wants more. I wonder if an affair as it is experienced by most women is something she wants to convert into her definitive and final marriage?

Dr. English: That may be true but I think it's neurotic. It's all part of the guilt associated with "cheating." To that word and to that comment I would like to say that I don't regard the affair in anyone's life as "cheating" anybody of anything. Most times it is contributing. Women should learn to regard it as merely an imposed evasion put upon good people who don't want to make trouble. It's an evasion imposed upon them because somebody can't stand to face the nitty-gritty truth about sex and its meanings. They can't stand to face the truths of sexuality. Marriage should not have to be a contrived or schemed matter. It should stand on mutual attraction and goals.

Audience: It may mean the end of a beautiful affair.

Dr. English: Right. If you want to end a beautiful affair, get a divorce and remarry.

Dr. Heller: But if the affair is good she wants to live with the guy, wants to cook for him, wants to go to bed with him every night. She'd like to be with him in the open.

Dr. English: My dear friends, there's a Southern European proverb that says that marriage is a yoke it takes two to carry and sometimes three. And today maybe four.

Audience: But it's a Southern European proverb—I don't know if it's an American proverb.

Dr. English: America can still learn from Europe.

Dr. Heller: Let's talk about the children. I remember as a child it was hard for me to envision father having intercourse with my mother, let alone my father having intercourse with another woman. Now I think it's worth asking what young persons would feel if they discovered that their father was having an ongoing affair with a woman while married to their mother. And how would they feel if their mother were having an ongoing relationship with another man?

Is the affair really an unsharable secret that the man or woman has to carry to the grave? Or is it something you can sit down and say, "Dear son and daughter, your mother and I have been married for many years and we love you children, but we can't really gratify each other sexually, and rather than die of high blood pressure I have discovered this lovely lady who can really gratify me and I her, and so this is the way I've made my adjustment, and I wanted you to know this. Among the various legacies I've left to you is this little piece of confessional wisdom." Is this what you would advocate, and what would a child feel about such news?

Audience: Dr. Heller, are you saying there are never any circumstances where an affair should take place?

Dr. Heller: I would say there are circumstances in which I, despite my very dim view of this type of thing, would urge and help certain patients to indulge in affairs. The first one would be circumstances in which the spouse is by reason of physical incapacity unable to participate sexually. Unfortunately, married persons sometimes develop multiple sclerosis, incapacitating infectious diseases, or other chronic conditions which render them incapable of participating in a sexual act. The spouses of such individuals may sit remorseful, guilt-ridden, abstinent, or rely on masturbation; I would certainly urge them to discreetly and lovingly avail themselves of sexual gratification. But I wonder if, even for that individual, meaningful sexual gratification is not inevitably accompanied by a rapidly developing emotional involvement which soon robs the crippled spouse of whatever meaning existed in the relationship? I don't think you can open a hole in a pot without something leaking out.

Audience: Going beyond that, suppose there is a mentally crippled spouse who's not responsive, then would you advocate an affair?

Dr. Heller: A mentally crippled spouse, I suppose, is to be regarded as potentially curable. I think we have gone beyond the days, in psychiatry, where we feel we are dealing with incurables in back wards of mental hospitals. If you are dealing with an extreme mental disturbance where the mate has been institutionalized, resulting in a physical kind of divorce which has not been sanctioned by law, that person has a right, in my opinion, and probably a responsibility, to attempt fulfillment in life.

But if the mate is simply troubled or sexually unresponsive, I think the solution is an amelioration of her condition rather than a self-righteous seeking of another bed-mate.

Dr. English: It seems to me that I heard you in a mental health inconsistency; to wit, that if a person married to a mate who is physically ill or emotionally ill enters into an affair, the pitfall is that they're going to become emotionally involved. Well, since we believe emotional involvement is a healthy state of affairs and a necessary state of affairs for personality balance and personality efficiency, it seems to me that it should not be regarded as an evil. When the person they are married to is incapable of involvement, I don't see how an affair must cause harm. You can't do harm to a person who can't feel. And if "A" can't feel and "C" can, and "B" gets involved with "C" this is the best kind of balance we can make in an imperfect world. I think we oldsters have talked enough for the moment. These young people here ought to make a comment because I daresay they probably see this from a totally different angle than we do.

Audience: I was wondering how many summit meetings there will be on this topic in the next decade or so? Or will it get to the point where people will simply shrug and say what's all the fuss about? There seems to be so much less guilt now. Instead of the affair, we're having parties where it's a mutual thing—the "swinging" mate-swapping parties, the orgy scene, and so forth. I've read about them, and they say it's much more acceptable because it's by mutual consent and there's no guilt afterwards, there are no hang-ups afterwards. I wonder if in a few years this will be a very commonplace thing? Sex is not that important.

Audience: I want to agree with Dr. English that just because you're having an affair doesn't mean you want to terminate your marriage. But if you tell your spouse you're having an affair and continue in an affair, how can the spouse say, "That's very good, you go right ahead"?

Dr. English: She's horribly afraid the marriage will be terminated because that traditionally has often happened in the past, or she may be bound by false pride to end the marriage. Therefore one shouldn't tell because we don't want to move the Viet Nam war over to this country, with fighting in every home.

Audience: I really don't think there has to be a war about it. I think, first of all, if the marriage is going there's a lot of trust in it. You're not going to break this trust if you're not going to tell. If you're having an affair and you still want to keep your marriage, if you believe in your marriage, it's not having the affair that's going to break up the marriage. It will probably bring more things into your marriage that are good, and if you have a decent understanding with your spouse to begin with, this trust is just reinforced if you tell. You discuss it.

Audience: When you tell your spouse, are you then going to continue the affair or are you telling your spouse when it's over?

Audience: No. I'd tell him when it started.

Dr. English: You would then assume that you could continue the affair?

Audience: Yes.

Dr. Heller: Would you tell your children, too?

Audience: Yes. I think the more people you can be very close to and communicate with the better your life is. So why should you say, "All right, I'm getting married. This is the only person I can get really close to?" You're limiting yourself. You're limiting your mind; you're limiting your experience; you're limiting your life.

Dr. English: You are very eloquent.

Dr. Heller: How many children do you have? And would you tell the children?

Audience: I don't have children.

Dr. Heller: Therefore, I say that you haven't reached that stage which some of us older fools have reached when we feel we are not as important as our offspring during a certain stage of their existence. One of the things you owe your children, it seems to me, is some support of their mother or of their father, a support which is undermined by extramarital sexual involvement.

There is no greater way that I could harm immature children of mine than to rattle their mother by indicating she is inadequate female companionship for me. They can't take it out on me. I am big, strong, and resourceful. But the young children are the ones who are going to sit and take from her the behavioral by-products of her depression, of her anger, and her despair. And if you haven't been raised by a woman who is filled with despair and depression, you can't know what I'm talking about. There are few more devastating experiences in the life of a very young child.

Dr. English: Are you saying that her point of view couldn't be imparted to children without harm?

Audience: From the way this young lady spoke, I think she has a beautiful, healthy outlook on all types of relationships. And I don't think she would shortchange or harm her kids if she had a dozen affairs going.

Dr. Heller: How about if her husband had a dozen affairs going? She'd be sitting there holding down the fort. If she loved her husband and felt emotionally deserted by him, or felt that she was not needed by him, or that she was not the single significant sexual person in his life, and if this went on for a long period of time, and there she was with one or two or three or four children, I wonder if she would then have such a starry-eyed view?

Audience: I don't think your point is well based. An agreement between husband and wife would eliminate the pain of suspicion, the anguish of humiliation, the destructive deceit, and so on. These are the things that really affect the children.

Dr. English: What I think we've heard from these two young people is a totally new set of values which we of our age can barely grasp. Whether I can grasp it well or not, I certainly wouldn't think of asking any questions about the welfare of their children. I think their children will fare very well with their united point of view.

Audience: They might fare better. You see a lot of kids from homes where nobody's strayed and they're all miserable.

Dr. Heller: I, too, have seen a lot of adults who came from seemingly stable homes who are very upset. But I have seen many more adults as psychiatric patients who have come from broken homes, at times when they were pre-schoolers of three, four, five years of age.

Audience: But you're talking about a broken home where there is animosity between the husband and wife.

Dr. Heller: Right. And adultery without animosity—despite the proclamations of "swingers"—boggles the mind as far as I am concerned. There aren't many spouses I have encountered who would have such a beautiful, altruistic, trusting, and loving attitude toward a recurrently wayward mate.

Audience: I don't think I could feel too accepting of infidelity if I were married. If my husband came home and told me he was having an affair I'd be crushed. Intellectually I don't think my reaction is right, but emotionally I know that's how I'd feel.

Dr. English: You think that you'd be crushed because you're afraid of something?

I'll remind you of a definition of love which says that when you love someone you want the best for them. Couples who love each other and are on the same wave-length should be willing for the other person to have the best that that person felt he needed for himself.

Dr. Heller: Why can't you be the best for them? Isn't that what marriage is intended for?

Audience: Dr. English, do you think monogamy is against human nature?

Dr. English: In society there is a wide range of people. Some people are more impulsive, some have more integrity, and so on. There are some limited personalities and there are some very broad spectrum personalities. But there are some people, male and female, who have a very broad spectrum personality and one person isn't necessarily going to meet all their needs. If you've got a broad spectrum individual married to an archconservative then there's going to be tension, there's going to be pressure. You can't confine a broad spectrum personality—people with many antennas out, people with many interests, people with many needs—with a convinced conservative. Some people see no need for an affair but they shouldn't legislate for all, and they are the kind who like to do just that. They would be like one of those who couldn't use a million-dollar yacht if he were given one. If you don't need it, you don't want it; if you need it, you need it badly.

I think if a person with real integrity, a thoughtful person, feels that the growth of his personality and his happiness and welfare require an affair he should have it because if he doesn't he's going to cheat his mate. In the long run he or she will sense an undercurrent of resentment, a feeling of being duty-bound rather than bound by love, that will be more destructive to her life than if there were a sexual experience with another, which left the more sensual one content within their relationship. If deprived of an affair, his spouse becomes his enemy.

Dr. Heller: You're saying that there are many who require a polygamous relationship?

Dr. English: I'm saying that there are some people for whom it's entirely necessary. That's all there is to it and histories of these people prove it. It's necessary if they are going to live. They can do without it but they're going to die within gradually. And they may die prematurely and they may also become misanthropic and difficult to live with as time goes on.

Dr. Heller: Well, that's as good a rationalization as I've heard today, and I've heard a number of them.

Dr. English: Well, you've uttered several. Please allow me one.

Dr. Heller: You know, we must remember that we're talking about affairs involving partners to a marriage. Those people have a responsibility in a contractual relationship and have made each other certain kinds of commitments: to love each other and to care for each other, and be available to each other. I wonder if you're available to each other if you're off being available to someone else?

Dr. English: Certainly.

Dr. Heller: Well, you can do it with a large enough bed, I suppose.

Dr. English: Do you desert your wife when you go fishing or play golf?

Dr. Heller: Not unless you have strange relationships with fish. But I think we are talking about a special kind of sexual intimacy. And certainly that is not threatened by a reasonable amount of fishing or a limited amount of golf or something else.

Dr. English: I get the impression from you and other people there's an aura of mysticism and magic surrounding sexuality. And yet if we are accurate in memory we realize that whenever people have a sexual relation, when it's over they simply put on their clothes and go home. Both get up and dress and go home, and start thinking about something else fairly promptly. These things don't have such long reverberations as you're implying. And I don't think they need to.

Dr. Heller: Some of the best sexual experiences a man or woman are capable of are terminated by falling asleep with each other. The sad thing is that you have to put on your pants and go home. That's the sad thing about an affair.

Audience: Suppose after the first decade of marriage one person felt the need to acquire many more sexual relationships, with other people, and the spouse did not. What then would happen to your marriage?

Are there many people who can indulge in affairs satisfactorily, or are there very few people who can carry it out discreetly and healthfully and not get into trouble emotionally?

Dr. English: Well, the number of people I know is relatively small. I can only say there are more carrying it out discreetly and with meaning and value than those who are not. The ones who run into trouble are the ones who have a neurotic tendency which forces them to be found out. They do some of the most blatantly silly, obvious things to get caught—things a child of 7 or 8 wouldn't do. But those who are able to control their behavior, those with any maturity, are having affairs successfully and valuably far more than those who are not.

An important element is knowing how to limit an extramarital involvement. A very capable young psychiatrist at Harvard made the excellent point that one of the things adolescents of this country should be helped with is the ability to tolerate separation or termination of relationships. We talk about getting involved, but nobody has said much yet about getting uninvolved. There is a way to get uninvolved and we don't know much about it as human beings.

Dr. Heller: It is your premise that an affair can be therapeutic to a member of a marriage, is it not?

Dr. English: Would you call growth synonymous with therapy?

Dr. Heller: All right, fine. Growth-promoting. Is there such a thing as a growth-promoting affair? Let me further ask you, Dr. English, if one is developing one's multiple facets and if one affair is good, could not one say that maybe two ongoing affairs might be better? And, if you're strong enough, why not three? As long as the strength holds out, why not develop a number of facets simultaneously?

Dr. English: You've got to get your work done. You have to carry out the trash, and you want to play a golf game once in a while, so you've got to limit this somewhere.

Dr. Heller: Would you say, therefore, that the limit ought to be two? One's spouse and one's girlfriend or one's boyfriend and one's husband?

Dr. English: Unless someone's a superman, I'd say that ought to do it.

Dr. Heller: Well at least we've established some limits. Of course, I think the ancients and some of the contemporary Arabs probably outdo us.

Dr. English: That's right.

Audience: Dr. Heller, you made some comments on the effect on children if there is an affair. Now, I haven't heard you say anything about the effect on children if the relationship between the spouses is bad. I think the effect could sometimes be much more harmful than if someone was out having an affair, having a relationship that is gratifying.

Dr. Heller: I think this is the rationale of one aspect of Dr. English's thesis. But I am not arguing against divorce as a solution—I am generally against adultery. Dr. English states, and with a considerable amount of experience, that some poor marriages are maintained only so that the children can be sheltered and nurtured by two responsible parents, one of whom is involved in an ongoing affair.

I think that most often the straying wife or husband becomes emotionally involved with the person with whom he or she is having an affair. Then the marital stability begins to totter, and either the affair is given up, often with a great deal of recrimination, or there is separation or divorce. So, practically speaking, in the experience of patients with whom I have consulted the affair causes more harm than good.

Dr. English: I don't think that we should say that everybody must be limited to one woman or one man. If they've got a larger personality, I don't know why they couldn't have ongoing relationships with two or more other personalities. It seems to me you're talking about limiting the human personality as if it were a weak, feeble thing.

Dr. Heller: Well, I would respond to that by pointing out the capacity that people have to help each other grow in a one-to-one relationship is enormous. Maybe even infinite. And I think that one can get much from another human being—maybe not everything but probably more than one could experience in a lifetime if they really worked at it. Generally, an affair is a kind of cheating, and often to oneself, of an opportunity to create a really intensive relationship with another human being. There is a great reward in sticking it out through thick and thin.

Dr. English: I didn't know that you and I were at such opposite poles. Let's drop sex out of this, and change the sexual matter to an energy expenditure. I'm sure that my wife's energy expenditures in many pursuits have influenced me favorably, and mine have influenced her. And, not mentioning sex at all, I think the energy expenditure on different personality-bolstering endeavors makes one a better person and subsequently a better companion. And, if sex happens to be one of the rewarding endeavors, why condemn sex so much? Why is sex the thing that causes everybody to get in such a tizzy?

Dr. Heller: I think you recognize as a fellow analyst and a fellow psychiatrist that sex is an enormously unique and powerful factor in human existence. One's sexual expression with a partner can be an enormously intense experience, and I believe if one takes away from one's chosen partner the exquisite intimacy and gratification sex has to offer, there is no way to make up for this to the partner.

How many times, for example, can a man or a woman have sex in a week or in a day? And if you're having sex with a girlfriend or a boyfriend, the marriage partner is going to come up shortchanged, unless of course they don't want sex relations. This, as you know, is very often the case. But even that situation can be improved if a solution other than infidelity is sought, since infidelity only hardens the estrangement.

Would it not be better to try to have a more intense, more frequent, and qualitatively better sexual relationship with each other rather than seek sex elsewhere?

Dr. English: Dr. Heller, I know that you play the violin, and I know that you bought a bass fiddle, and I know you play the piano. Now suppose that your wife said, "Don't you dare buy a bass fiddle, don't you monkey with the piano keyboard, you stick to that violin or you're going to go to perdition"?

Dr. Heller: That's what my violin teacher told me. And that's why I'm not a better violinist.

Audience: Dr. English, I think you're being a little unrealistic. I think people who get involved in affairs do not have exquisite intimacy with their mates. Something is lacking at home. If it's all so beautiful at home there is no need, and I think people who have an affair have a need.

Dr. English: Yes. You mean a man can be better husband than his wife will permit him to be.

Dr. Heller: I think we're always discussing the guy whose wife is a poor bed partner.

Audience: How about vice versa?

Dr. Heller: I think that when women are involved with a man who is to some degree impotent, it is sometimes because she has rendered him so. And I think that wherever there is an affair the unfaithful partners are married to people who are to them sexually inadequate. I have yet to see an adulterous woman or man who felt that their spouse, over a long period of time, was sexually competent or gratifying.

As human beings we make comparative values. A child finds a stone that looks beautiful, and saves it until he finds a nicer one. When we're involved sexually, the first time is great, or the first girlfriend is great, or the first boyfriend is great. But the repeated experience pales, the sense of wonder diminishes, and a new person seems greater.

Similarly, the affair is a more moving experience, and the person devalues the sexual experience with the spouse.

Dr. English: First you say sex is the most glorious, wonderful thing, and then it's the one terrible, rotten, destructive thing. I don't think it's as grand as some people have implied; I don't think it's as terrible or awful as some people have implied. When we get talking about it, we seem to think it's either going to kill us or take us to glory. I don't believe either one.

Dr. Heller: It's a shame that it doesn't take you to some kind of glory. You know, I think that's one of the great things sex can be—a momentary glimpse of glory. Feeling something like a king, speaking from a man's point of view.

Dr. English: Someone has said that the sexual relation does occupy the position of giving people the highest sense of self awareness. Now, I believe that. But, I still don't think it should be rated as a hundred and everything else dropped below fifty. I think there are some things that come up around ninety, eighty, seventy-five, and so on. Learning. Music. Travel. Dancing. Driving a sports car. Playing tennis. I could name ever so many things I think come close to sex, and probably beat sex with some women. Some of these frigid American wives—these things could beat sex with them any day!

Audience: I feel sort of the way Dr. English feels. Sex is just one of a lot of things that can be rewarding, meaningful, and I think in order to be a full person you have to be able to do a lot of things.

Audience: While I was listening to everybody talking the thought came into mind about how our society imposes rules and laws which deny our human feelings. Marriage is kind of a restriction. In one respect it's good and it's beautiful, but I don't think you should be restricted and say "Well, I'm just going to stay with you the rest of my life, and I'm not going to look at another woman or a man." That's denying that you're human. If you're human you have feelings. You have desires. You want to talk to other people.

Dr. Heller: Maybe we ought to talk a minute about marriage. Let me state that I feel that the real purpose of marriage is to have children. I cannot see any other reason why two rational people would enter into a lifetime contract with each other at a time when they hardly know anything about themselves, let alone the person to whom they are devoting themselves for all eternity. But I think that if you have children, then you enter into about a twenty-year stint, more or less, in which you have mutual responsibilities involving dependent human beings with whom you have a kind of sacred protoplasmic trust. This is what civilization is all about.

During that period of time you owe each other and the children something, namely, an inviolable, trusting family unit. If there are no children involved, I would make an entirely different set of rules. But after you have spent twenty years rearing children, you've shared a family life that is unique and you have built something in the bank of human experience together that you ought not to dismiss too lightly.

Dr. English: That's true. Are you implying, however, that the children are going to be devastated if they know that their father had an affair?

Dr. Heller: No, but I think they'll have a better start in life if the parents stay together and behave like reasonable people. When parents have a sexual wanderlust they really are not drawing the heavy cart of all their children's needs.

Dr. English: Stay together and not have affairs although miserable or incompatible?

Dr. Heller: I believe that the greenery on this earth is for children. Just picture a world without children who have experienced love and devotion and affection and parental teamwork. Then I think we would have a hideous demise of any hope for improving life, improving human values, improving a sense of real love and responsibility. If love is, as Dr. English said, wanting someone to be happy, married couples should devote themselves to this enterprise.

Dr. English: That's wonderfully poetic and sentimental, but you know most parents think children are a pain in the neck.

Audience: Perhaps, Dr. English, your advice on infidelity for a member of your family would be different than for a patient who consults you.

Dr. English: I have no different rules for patients and my family. My suspicion is that it's possible an affair might enhance the marriage because there might be a higher general level of satisfaction. I have no qualms about supporting an affair under certain circumstances.

However, I would do everything possible to have the kind of relationship that Dr. Heller was talking about; I agree that if you can make the marriage beautiful, if you can be on the same wavelength, and have the trust, the interest, the love and respect that's desirable, an affair would be unnecessary. I would support an affair only in a situation where you were not getting all the satisfaction you would normally get or seek in a marriage.

Audience: I love the idea that one could, and perhaps owes it to oneself, to have multiple personal relationships in one's life. I can see where that would be very beautiful and extremely satisfying. But I don't see it working personally for me because I think that too many layers of guilt and emotionality would come to bear. I don't see that it could truly work. In a sense, I feel kind of brainwashed by my husband's concepts. But I tend to go along with him because I think, in the long run, they're pretty valid for us. I truly can embrace your idea. I think it's a beautiful idea, but I don't see it working for my generation.

Audience: I find it very hard to speak of the affair, or to generalize, because the affair can have one million faces. I think for some people it can be great. I think for others it's just like eating watermelon—it ain't worth all the mess.

Audience: I think it all depends on the person, and I think if it enriches that person you should do it.

Audience: I feel there is no such thing as infidelity, and I feel that if we can share our food we must share our love and emotions as well.

Audience: I disagree with extramarital affairs. I'm conservative and I don't think there's any room for it. I'm married to one man and that's all I want.

Audience: I found the man of my life and I don't want any extramarital experiences. He's the greatest.

Audience: Either because of a sexual relationship which has not worked out, or because of a lack of communication, those who can find relief, happiness, solace in another relationship should have such a relationship. I don't agree that it should ever be talked about or told to the spouse.

Audience: I make no moral or value judgments. For those people who feel the need, and who are strong, healthy, and discreet enough, I say go ahead. And just hope that most people wouldn't.

Audience: Well I'm still old fashioned, I guess, although I'm the youngest one here. I hope that I just never have the need for an extramarital affair.

Audience: I think that you can't tell people what their morals should be. It's dangerous to tell people to have an affair or not have an affair.

Dr. English: I'd say I take a positive stand toward extra-marital affairs because they represent an extension of the need of human beings for a wider human involvement with their fellow man. I would not say that an extramarital affair is always necessary. But, in the same manner, many human activities are not necessary but still might be beneficial. Human growth and love should not be legislated. When they are, in my opinion, society suffers.

Dr. Heller: I think the last thing I would say, in summing up, is that one's spouse ought to have the right of first refusal, and one ought to bring one's sexual business and love to them first. I view infidelity as a threat to marriage, and until proven otherwise marriage is the best arrangement thus far for child rearing that we have. To advocate affairs is one more gesture toward destroying the fabric of our social structure. Religion has already lost much of its impact, and we've shot all kinds of other institutions to hell. One of the few institutions we have left is marriage. I think you're endangering it at a time when I'm a bit frightened about the future of civilization. We have certain responsibilities along with our copulating, and the protection of our marital, child-rearing units constitutes an awesome trusteeship which our generation shares with countless generations of parents who did right by their children in the past—and hopefully with future generations of parents who will continue to do so.

14. A Positive View of Adultery

LONNY MYERS and REV. HUNTER LEGGITT

The myth that our society is virginal before marriage and monogamous afterwards was exploded over two decades ago by the famous Kinsey studies. Our experience goes a step further and challenges the widely promoted view that the Ideal Marriage for Everyone is sexual monogamy with complete honesty between partners. In sharp contrast to the popular view that extramarital sex is always destructive, we believe that the story of extramarital sex as a *positive* experience needs to be told.

We are all familiar with instances in which extramarital sex is handled carelessly, the results are messy, fraught with jealousies, fights, and broken homes. We all know that it can be part of personal and interpersonal disturbances. However, our study forces us to recognize that these widely publicized unfavorable histories, while descriptive of certain real and serious problems, are only part of the story. The other part of the story is that extramarital sex can be positive. It can be related to maturity, personal growth, better marriages, and joy.

We knew that both responsible and irresponsible, happy and unhappy people are sexually monogamous. The surprise was that some marriages improve when one or both partners engage in extramarital sex.

We knew that extramarital sex in our society has many risks and dangers. We also knew that sexual monogamy has risks—including stagnation, boredom, and loss of outside interests. The surprise is that to take the risks of extramarital sex may avoid some risks of monogamy, sexual and otherwise.

165

We thought that people were driven to extramarital sex because either the marriage or the marriage partner was inadequate, but we discovered that it occurs whether the marriage is "good" or "bad." Often it fulfills needs which could not be fulfilled by any single relationship, within marriage or otherwise, no matter how "perfect."

We believed that a feeling of guilt is usually associated with extramarital sex. But we discovered that the persons we interviewed felt little or no guilt. And yet they were fully capable of experiencing guilt—for example, about striking a child, acting out of racial prejudice, and so on. Several stated, however, that they "would feel guilty" if, as a result of their extramarital sex lives, they neglected their families, became hostile to the sexual advances of their mates, or destroyed someone else's marriage. But they took unusual precautions to avoid these outcomes. In fact, most felt themselves to be "on the same team" with their lovers, with a real sense of respect for their obligations and marriages.

The cases we report are all of middle and upper class people over thirty years old. All are affluent and mobile. All but one live in large cities, suburbs, or near college campuses; the other is from a small town. We have changed a few unessential details and have used pseudonyms throughout. We make no attempt at in-depth psychological study. We simply described a life style, and draw some conclusions.

Occasional, casual affairs

We found this to be the most common form of extramarital sex among those whom we interviewed. We present two typical histories—one a high school teacher, the other a business executive —each of whom described his marriage as "good," to illustrate that an occasional affair need not be a threat to a good marriage.

Jack is a 39-year-old high school physics teacher married seventeen years; he sees himself as overweight and short on sex appeal. But he has a warm pleasant face and his eyes sparkle as he talks about his several affairs: "Usually it starts out as a casual sex experience with someone I like. But it develops into a friendship with sex just part of the relationship. These affairs have helped me feel much more tender and affectionate at home. I do have a good feeling of stability with my wife and children, without the frustrations of sexual monogamy.

"Yes, I've experienced times when a woman became too emotionally dependent on me. I've had to end the affair." Of course, the woman suffered. So did Jack. But who is to say they would have suffered less without the affair?

Jack now feels that this kind of suffering can be avoided by getting involved only with women who have "roots." They have a firm commitment to their marriage, or if single are deeply involved in a career and not looking for a husband. "It's like trees," Jack said. "If two trees are firmly rooted, they can safely mingle their branches. That's a responsible affair. But if a deep-rooted tree intertwines his branches with a sapling and a wind comes along, the sapling gets pulled up. I have deep roots at home. So I've learned to pick women with equally deep roots. That way, nobody gets toppled. In fact, it's very pleasant."

Jack has also enjoyed intimate "affairs" without genital sex. He does not believe in the double standard, and would allow his wife the same freedom.

Don describes his marriage of twenty-two years as "absolutely great: a warm, close relationship to my wife and two sons." During the early years of marriage, life was filled with gratifications at home, despite the presence of his chronically ill mother. At that time, he felt a great deal of pressure to "make it" professionally. But once he achieved business success and the children left home, he experienced a "surplus" of energy and warmth and simply not enough outlet. At the same time, he had more time and money. Typical of people in his wealthy suburb, sexual opportunity was everywhere, the risk minimal, the need for intimacy and variety growing, and Don began having affairs. There were a few awkward moments when his wife discovered he wasn't somewhere he said he'd be. But the years went on, and the marriage relationship continued "great."

When his mother's illness took a turn for the worse so that she required round-the-clock care, the burden was crushing. "My wife needs a change," he told us. "I wish some handsome cat would just swoop her up and take her off for a passionate, romantic weekend. The nurse can take care of mother." He honestly wants his wife to have an opportunity to "get away" and enjoy an interval of freedom from worry, and believes a romantic escape would probably be most effective. But there is no way that Don, being also involved with the burden, can provide this escape. He knows how much his affairs have helped him, and wishes she could enjoy the same benefits.

But his wife (a 45-year-old woman steeped in the habits and righteousness of sexual monogamy) probably could not handle a lover, even were he to appear. "It's too bad," the husband said. "I really wish she could. She needs something, and I can't think of anything else that could provide such real escape."

Controlled response to passionate extramarital love

We found this sort of affair less common, but definitely dispelling the myth that "true love" cannot be successfully handled as an extramarital affair. It is quite possible to love more than one person at a time. Here, each affair was a deep emotional involvement that did not destroy (or demonstrably weaken) anyone's marriage; in fact in some cases it enhanced the marriage.

For fourteen years, Delores enjoyed a secret, sizzling-hot affair with Lyle, a brilliant surgeon with an attractive wife, a good marriage and two healthy sons. Delores had married too young, and speedily outgrew her accountant husband, whom she described as "cold . . . disagreeable most of the time."

Delores and Lyle never demonstrably robbed their spouses of family-sharing time. Over and over again they denied themselves the opportunity to picnic together on the beach, to go off together for the night or weekend. For fourteen years, until Lyle was killed in an auto crash, they met almost exclusively for short periods in the afternoon, often using only their lunch hour.

Who knows what Lyle's relationship with his wife would have been without this affair? Delores describes him as the kind of man who would have had another lover if not her, a man no one woman could satisfy. He wanted both the comfort of a wife and the excitement of an affair. With her, he had a cooperative, responsible, and discreet lover. With someone else, who knows? As for Delores, without this affair she might have divorced and remarried. Like other women we interviewed who are responsible and who enjoy extramarital sex, Delores learned to "make extra time" for Lyle in order to avoid neglecting her family. For example, she organized her marketing efficiently so that instead of having an hour for coffee with a girl friend she would meet Lyle.

We are convinced that Delores and Lyle were desperately in love, yet able to limit their relationship in order to function within the social structure.

So were Anne and Michael. The idea of extramarital sex seemed absurd to Anne. Then, twelve years ago, when she was 37 years old with only one of her three children still at home, Anne fell deeply in love with Michael.

As the months went by, she continued to resist sexual involvement with him. Meanwhile, he continued to offer gentle, open, and persistent invitations. He was most understanding of her reluctance and never forcefully urged her to commit herself to a sexual relationship. To this day, Anne is not sure what did it, but after a year and a half she began to meet him for sexual intimacy, and continued to do so two or three times a month for five years until Michael's business transferred him out of town.

Anne described her affair as a "deep, passionate love." She has enjoyed several "casual" affairs since then, without the deep emotional involvement. "My sexual friendships are a great remedy for loneliness," she told us. "I truly have no regrets." She often thinks of the months of mental anguish spent for making up her mind those twelve long years ago. She believes she made a good decision which indirectly strengthened her mediocre marriage.

Fred is a 36-year-old auto repair shop manager. He has been married for ten years and loves his wife very much. For over a year, he felt "turned on" by Ginger—a strikingly beautiful and vivacious woman with a cold marriage. Finally, they arranged to meet alone.

Ginger is extremely passionate when they are together, but she continuously wrestles with the "morality" of her affair with Fred. She recognizes that it helps her feel "alive and human" and at the same time she is troubled by the contrast between her own experience and her moral indoctrination. She repeatedly threatens to end the relationship, but as of our interview it was still flourishing. Fred described it as a deeply emotional relationship that goes way beyond sex.

Fred told us, "The last eighteen months with Ginger have changed my whole life. I feel a lot happier and more fulfilled. The whole world seems brighter! My wife doesn't know why I'm feeling so good, but she likes me the way I am now, and my sex life at home is really better."

This torrid relationship between Fred and Ginger has added vitality to Ginger's life, perhaps making a bad marriage tolerable, and has demonstrably improved Fred's marriage. He is against the double standard, and would not deny his wife the same electrifying experience.

Extramarital sex and ideal marriage

In the above histories, several participants said that "Yes, I love my husband" or "We have a great marriage." Here, however, we are describing persons whose marriages are even *more* ideal: passionate, exciting, and close. They speak of their marriages with such tenderness, warmth, and devotion that one is quickly aware that no one else could ever "hold a candle" to their spouse. Among these, we found both enthusiastic and committed sexual monogamy, *and* extramarital sex.

Steven's marriage is right out of the storybooks. He describes it as "ideal" and "loaded with enjoyment." During twenty-four years of marriage, he has "never been bored" with his wife. She is a "typical home-loving soul." They live in a suburb. He commutes each day while she gardens, refinishes antiques, and prepares gourmet meals. Now in their late forties, they have sexual relations almost every night. But that is only part of the story.

Steven has been an outstanding athlete since junior high school—not only on the court and field, but a "sexual athlete" as well. He is not a "Don Juan" proceeding from one seduction to the next. He is keenly aware of the danger of women-without-roots becoming too dependent on the affair. So virtually all of Steven's lovers have been married women who needed that special bit of extra attention, of romance, of mutual temporary ecstasy he could provide, or the rare single girl who is firmly "rooted" in a career or other commitments.

"I always explain how much I love my wife," he said. "It is important for me to make that clear. I become involved in affairs only as a supplement, an addition, not a substitute for any lack whatever at home. I simply have more need for intimacy and more sexual energy than my wife can possibly absorb."

To have denied himself the affairs and to have described the frustration that resulted to his wife would have been honest—and cruel. Had he even described the level of his *needs*, his wife would have been miserable for she prides herself on meeting his needs.

In meeting his own needs, Steven likes to enrich the lives of women who are, to some degree, unfulfilled at home, yet who are strongly committed to their families. "And they feel safe having an affair with me," he said. "They know I will never leave my wife for anyone else, and I will do nothing to disrupt their own marriage commitments."

Whenever he has sex with another woman in the afternoon, he always makes love to his wife that night (if she wishes to), making doubly sure he is not taking anything away from her.

His wife is equally open in her intellectual attitude toward sex, we learned when we interviewed her, but emotionally she is very possessive. "She would be deeply hurt if she knew about me," he said. "She couldn't imagine my sharing the kind of sexual closeness we have with someone else."

Steven's wife is very proud of her husband. She claims she is "sexually satisfied and then some" and feels her marriage is tops. And we would agree with her. They both speak in glowing terms of each other—and seem to be two of the luckiest people in the world.

The moral of their story seems to be that consideration for the feelings of others may require withholding the truth.

Frequent, casual affairs

Here we are describing married persons who are committed to their marriages as a first priority and have had a hundred or more sex partners. Some developed the freedom of casual sex only after marriage. Others started before marriage and continued to enjoy casual sex—which then becomes extramarital sex—since marriage.

Because having so many different sex partners is stereotyped as irresponsible behavior, we feel a need to stress that all of these persons were conscientious and socially responsible. Their uniqueness appears to be simply an apparent freedom to participate in sex whenever and wherever a reasonably safe, attractive opportunity is presented which does not conflict with family, work, or other obligations. Their questions seem to be: Is it feasible? Will it be enjoyable? Is it reasonably safe, so that my enduring relationships will not be threatened?

By the time a person has accumulated this much sexual experience, the variety of possible aftereffects is well known. Few men, but more women, admitted to having made some wrong decisions, but quickly added that there are no areas of life where one expects to always make the right decisions!

With rare exceptions, spousal attitudes ranged from a reluctant tolerance (in an instance where the affair was discovered) to a presumed "utter devastation if he found out." These critical attitudes were attributed to upbringing—reinforced by the mass media, sex educators, and textbooks that present frequent casual sex as the behavior of the irresponsible, the inconsiderate, the compulsive, or the neurotic.

None of the people interviewed expressed guilt about their casual sexual activities *per se*. If given a chance to live life over, none would choose a sexually monogamous life.

Corrine is an extremely independent woman—yet very domestic and proud of her home and family. She has been married for seventeen years and has three sons. Her husband is dedicated not only to his work, but to a number of social causes. Despite his admirable dedication and humane conscience, he is *not* a fun-loving person. In many ways, the marriage is "cold." They have sex rather routinely. Corrine enjoys it and rarely turns him down, even though it falls far short of the ecstasy and abandon she is capable of enjoying. Yet she respects her husband profoundly, is deeply committed to the marriage, and needs the stability he provides.

Although Corrine goes out often, she is very conscientious about arriving home at the anticipated hour, dinner is always ready on time, and so on. She told us how well her children do both socially and in their school work and—more important—that her children are happy. Officially "unfit" as a mother, this woman appears to be the model of vital and responsible motherhood.

When asked how she was able to break away from tradition, Corrine admitted that her father was "very radical" in his ideas, believed in total equality for women, took life quite seriously (as does her husband) and worked hard to live up to his ideals. She also mentioned her best friend, an unmarried woman, is a "swinger"and introduced her to many other swingers. This friend has occasionally made her apartment available to Corrine. In addition, Corrine (a gifted amateur photographer) attends meetings and shows when family obligations permit, and these offer an opportunity for discreet, casual sexual relationships.

She has had two "serious" love affairs—both men becoming her good friends, good friends of each other, and also good friends of her swinging girl friend. All four are dedicated to two principles: love without possession or exclusion, and love and let go.

Corrine is a rarity. We have not interviewed anyone else remotely like her. Although not typical, she demonstrates what is possible side by side with a deep commitment to marriage, and her story confirms that partners in a cold marriage need not grow cold to fit the marriage.

Stanley is a 48-year-old traveling salesman who estimates that he has had over two hundred sexual partners, all brief encounters with no serious affairs.

He lives in a small town and always returns home with eager anticipation for the warmth and coziness of his home and family. He loves his wife, has a "good marriage," and truly enjoys his relationship with his growing boys.

He sees no harm whatsoever in his sexual excursions; they have almost no effect on his marriage—and would not hold it against his wife if she did likewise.

Forbidden fruit

These two cases involve persons who feel they have been deprived of warmth, love, and sexual response because of the prohibitions expressed in traditional sexual mores.

Lester, a 68-year-old man married forty years, feels "gypped." His only reward for a lifetime of sexual monogamy is incredible frustration, a keen sense of lacking warm, loving memories, and an abundance of "what a fool I was" despair. He feels that he was led to believe "all sorts of lies." But now, it's "too late."

When Lester remembers moments when he could have entered into meaningful love affairs but refused on the grounds of "virtue," he feels deep sadness and regret—even guilt—for having "held back from life."

He and his wife have had no sex since he retired early over ten years ago because of illness. The illness did not decrease his ability to have sexual intercourse. It simply created a convenient time to end what had become dull anyway. We found him typical of many men (and women) in his age group who are living proof of the observation that doing without extramarital sex does not guarantee future rewards.

Irene is keenly aware that she has lived for years in a home without love; although to the outside world hers appears to be a "successful" marriage. She and her husband enjoy the same music, the same friends, and fishing. Her husband has sex with her in a very routine manner, leaving her without satisfaction most of the time. Aside from the "sex act" (which is the proper term in this case), there is no cuddling or spontaneous touching between them other than, of course, *pro forma* kisses when he leaves for work.

During her thirty years of marriage, Irene has broken out of the strict monogamy pattern twice. One of these was brief but radiantly intense: "It made me so happy, I was afraid someone would ask what had happened to me." But both times her sense of guilt forced her to break off the affair. Meanwhile, her investment in her marriage is so tremendous she feels caught. "I need love," she said, "but I can't live the lie of an affair."

Psychotherapy did not make her husband more warm and understanding, nor did it loosen her own inhibitions against extramarital sex. The therapist's value judgment that "extramarital sex can only be destructive and you should work harder on your marriage" was accepted by Irene because "Dr. Smith is an authority"—even though her own experience contradicted his view.

If a cold partner cannot change, and one is not willing to divorce, and extramarital sex is desired but denied, is "virtue" its own reward? Irene says her virtue is not rewarding. Her plight echoes that of those whose personal growth and emotional reward are blocked by "moral rules" which they have internalized without critical examination.

Extramarital sex with the spouse's approval

These are couples who approve (not just tolerate) each other's affairs with different degrees of communication about specific activities:

"It hasn't always been this way," said Charles, "but after eleven years of sexual monogamy our marriage was on the rocks and something had to give." Married for seventeen years with four children, Charles and Sylvia openly discuss their extramarital sex, group sex, and homosexual experiences. Each has had sex with many partners in the past years, with the spouse's knowledge and encouragement. Charles has had group sex, including experiences with homosexuals, and has no hesitancy or shame in discussing these adventures with his wife. They feel that their marriage is secure and unthreatened by this attitude. They both have responsible jobs and are highly respected in their community.

"The first time Sylvia broke out of her cage into an affair, and then told me about it, I was so angry I smashed every dish in the house," Charles admitted. "But it turned out to be the beginning of a real relationship. I was suddenly face to face with my own possessiveness and fear of life. I had my foot on Sylvia's back. On my own back too, afraid to be honest about my own curiosity and desires."

"It isn't our sex life *per se* that really has made the difference," Sylvia concluded. "It's that we've learned to let each other be, not to cling, and at the same time to be honest, to really relate to each other. If this leads to extramarital sex and talking about it with each other, well that's part of being human. Having experienced it both ways, I wouldn't want it otherwise."

Joe and Emily have worked out a different pattern. For the last twenty-five years of their fifty years of married life, they have included another woman as part of their "family." In addition to this special person, there are others who share concern and intimacies with them—sometimes with, and sometimes without sex. The members of this "larger family" consult each other before making important decisions; they have changed jobs and relocated in order to live in the same city with other members of their "family"; they have asssisted each other in the rearing of their children. This is not a "group marriage," and has not been without its problems over the years. But there is a deep understanding and loyalty, and a sharing of love and intimacy. Looking back over a half century together, this couple is deeply in love, and feel self-respect for having lived according to their conviction that loyalty, responsibility, and caring can extend beyond conventional limits.

For Glenn and Marcia, knowledge of "with whom" is tolerable, but an enthusiastic reporting of details is less so. Married eight years, each agrees that affairs "do happen" and also agrees (at Marcia's insistence) to spare each other the specifics of where, what, and how good.

It didn't always work out according to this agreement. Marcia's first affair was destructive. She wasn't home when the children returned from school, meals were poorly prepared, and she became hostile to her husband's sexual advances. The couple have relocated in another city, and Marcia has entered into a new affair which she is handling discreetly and responsibly. Glenn learned of it only after a year, and is not disturbed by it. He too has had affairs during the eight years.

Glenn and Marcia agree that the destructiveness of her first affair was due not to her so-called "infidelity" but to her obvious lack of concern at home and to gossip in the community.

Homosexual affairs

We interviewed several persons who are committed to their mates and families, and who have experienced varying amounts of extramarital homosexual sex:

Ted, 43 years old, has a comfortable but unexciting marriage, a "good sexual relationship" with his wife, and an arrangement by which he has one night a week "out"—which he spends invariably with homosexual friends. He is grateful that he has been able to assimilate bi-sexuality into his life without a complex system of excuses and absences.

Lynn's homosexual activity started with a heterosexual friend, more or less out of curiosity. She got pleasure from stroking the female body, which she found attractive. "But," she said, "I don't feel turned on when I see attractive girls in public." She also had several heterosexual affairs. She doesn't have any idea if she'll ever have another homosexual experience, and won't push it.

A growth experience

These people strongly feel that their extramarital sex has helped them grow as human beings—more sensitive to human needs and more aware of human potential.

Alicia had a cool, though not hostile, marriage and after a period of indecision divorced her husband. During that time, she had an affair with a married man. It was "stars and fireworks and the whole bit." But unlike other persons whom we interviewed, she was unable to transfer any of its afterglow to the marital relationship. Her lover's marriage was also "fair," but he had no intention of divorce: children, stability, and other reasons. The point here is that her affair helped Alicia to make her own decision regarding the divorce. She did not get the divorce in order to marry her lover, but the strength and self-affirmation of the affair gave her the confidence to decide. "I have more confidence in myself now," she said.

Will's growth experience happened when he took his children on a vacation trip and met a middle-aged woman without her husband, whose children were the same age as his own. He described her as "warm and open—easy to talk to." They soon found they had many interests in common. She had experienced affairs before, and realizing he was very shy she proceeded slowly. It wasn't until the fifth day that he recognized she had been gently pulling him into bed.

Will could hardly believe what was happening! Born and reared strictly, he was a virgin when he married. His wife had a chronic illness with acute exacerbations, and he would go as long as five years with no sexual outlet. He never masturbated. Understandably, Will was frightened that he couldn't "perform." He hadn't even held a woman close to him for over four years. But his new friend reassured him that closeness was a rewarding experience in itself, and that the act of intercourse was not essential to a good feeling of warmth and intimacy.

He told us that he had never met anyone like her. He never had dreamed that anyone "nice" could have affairs without guilt. He has rethought many values as a result of this experience and has gained a good feeling about himself. The growth experience has gone beyond sex. "I have gained a sense of power, of self-determination. I don't feel so victimized by my home situation; I don't resent my wife's illness nearly so much." The affair seems to have uncovered new depths of Will's potential. "I feel I can better handle nonsexual relations now," he said. "And who knows" (with a shy smile) "maybe I'll have another sexual one some day."

Conclusion

We limited this report to a small series of cases where the positive aspects of extramarital sex far outweigh any anxiety or negative experiences. The purpose is to offset the equally stereotype destructive effect of extramarital sex so widely publicized. We are fully aware that the entire gamut exists, that there are vast numbers, probably a majority, that fit neither category, that are neither as rosy as the cases we present, nor as miserable as the cases routinely described. We suspect most affairs are of such complex nature that whether the net result is helpful or harmful remains an enigma even to the participants.

How is it that extramarital sex helps preserve some marriages and enhances others? We would not pretend to know all the answers. Based on our interviews:

Some people are discreet and considerate of their marriage partners, and are careful to keep their affairs from impinging on their marriages.

Some affairs provide temporary respites from problems at home. They provide new perspectives (like a good night's sleep) so the problems can now be solved or else lived with.

Some affairs help people to expand their sexual and relational repertoires when the alternative would be to feel stifled by the marriage and resentful of the spouse.

Looked at in perspective, some affairs are acts of kindness towards partners who are seriously ill, preoccupied, or exhausted by chronic problems—for whom the "should" of sexual or emotional response would be just one more burden.

Some affairs fulfill the felt need for a variety of sexual partners. A clear example is the bisexual man or woman for whom no single relationship can fulfill both desires.

Many affairs fulfill the needs of both partners in the affair, so that neither is being "exploited" by the other. An example is the temporary arrangement of two people who are each separated from their spouse for too long. How long is too long depends on the people.

A few affairs are just "madness" in the sense praised by Zorba the Greek—madness that some people need and that is clearly an exception to their usual routine—the exception, as it were, that proves the rule.

We would emphasize that on the basis of our case histories, extramarital sex is far less likely to preserve or enhance marriage when the spouse knows about it. This point is also confirmed by Kinsey in Sexual Behavior in the Human Female, especially on page 433. Show and tell often turns out destructively. But when a marriage allows some privacy and freedom for each partner with no questions asked, affairs stand more chance of working and benefitting the marriage. The privacy and freedom may be circumstantial—like out of town business trips. Or it may be an agreed on part of marriage, a possibility we expand on in our forthcoming book about freedom and privacy as Marriage's Fourth Compartment (Nelson-Hall, 1975).

We found extramarital sex coexisting with both "good" and "bad" marriages. It may simply satisfy needs that could not be met by any one relationship, no matter how "perfect." Hence there is no reason for anyone who discovers that his or her spouse has extramarital sex to conclude, on that basis alone, that "My spouse no longer loves me," or "I have failed as a marriage partner."

If we can accept these facts, we may be able to work towards reducing the harmful consequences of such assumptions as that the uninvolved ("innocent") spouse is supposed to feel angry and jealous and the involved ("guilty") spouse is supposed to feel ashamed and humiliated; or that the best thing is for the "betrayed" spouse to become "very brave and understanding" and the "prodigal" spouse to humbly beg forgiveness and promise never to err again. The most prevalent misguided assumption is that extramarital sex per se is a primary cause of marriage failure, or for that matter, of marriage success.

Some recent changes in our society increase the incidence of affairs. We can now recognize that some of these changes also make it more possible for affairs to be beneficial rather than ultimately destructive. The changes include:

Effective contraception, and legalized abortion. Of the two, contraception is clearly preferable. But to know that abortion is there as a "fail safe" clearly makes a psychological difference. Perhaps it also makes an ethical difference in deciding whether or not to have extramarital sex, if consequences are a consideration. There are times when recourse to abortion probably makes the difference between an affair turning out destructive of the marital relationship, or not.

There are precautions to decrease risk of VD and even if you catch it doctors can cure it.

A contemporary life style that for many people includes frequent trips away from home plus the anonymity of large cities. This maximizes opportunity and the chance that discretion will succeed. It gives circumstantial privacy and freedom to each spouse—both the one who goes and the one who stays home. Increasingly, they both go—to different places.

Today's "nuclear family" of just one man, one woman, and usually some children, puts more strain on the family than ever. Who is there to divert and chauffeur the children, help with the dishes, listen to one's complaints, rub one's back, unclog the drain, and then make love? Just one other adult. If that can make you important to each other, it can also make you tired. If it makes marriage more important, it also makes marriage more likely to fail, for who or what can live up to all those expectations? Either we think of ourselves as Superpeople, or modestly admit that as the French proverb suggests, "Marriage is a yoke that sometimes takes three to carry." The psychiatrist O. Spurgeon English adds, "And conceivably, even four." (See chapter 13)

Transience—each year one out of five Americans moves. This makes spouses "portable roots" for each other, on the one hand; but it also accustoms people to establishing and breaking off relationships. For an increasing number of people, affairs seem to help them cope with this transiency. An affair is a way to enjoy some intimacy when there is too little: she goes ahead to her new job in San Francisco, he stays in Boston with the house and children until the school term ends. Either or both may have an affair in the interim. An affair can also be a way to enjoy some intimacy when there is too much. Not that there is too much intimacy at home (though that too might be so), but that there is too much going on at home in terms of financial worries, moving plans, selling the house, and reassuring the children, to enjoy the intimacy that might be there. People tend to get snappy at moving time. There are times, for some people, when it's hard to enjoy sex in a context that is a constant reminder of problems. But at such times, the release of sex may be even more needed.

Finally, rising expectations. We expect everything to get better and better—not merely income, employment, housing and cars, but also personal relationships and sex. After reading some articles published lately, one would believe that at the least marriage should combine the intensity of a T-group with the excitement of an X movie. However, some people seem to understand the limits of one person and one relationship and, rather than condemning their marriages as "failures" when these expectations aren't met, they seek some of this closeness and excitement outside the marriage.

Given these features of today's world, we believe that the professional involved in marriage counseling is wise to recognize that extramarital sex can be helpful both to the individual and to marital relationships, even as he recognizes that it harms other individuals and relationships. There is no scientific evidence that sexually monogamous couples have more (or less) fun in bed, or have better (or worse) overall relationships than couples in which one or both spouses have extramarital sex. The appearance of extramarital sex may at times signal a shy and hesitant but positive step toward discovery, trust, the risks of growth and love. Like a fawn venturing into the meadow, the least scent of disapproval sends her scurrying. Rather than frighten her away from life, we would throw our weight on the side of realistic and supportive evaluation, a feat made almost impossible by the preponderance of hostility toward extramarital intimacy. We seek to promote evaluation on the merits of each individual case; we deplore the blanket negativism so often expressed by professionals.

In a society where all public values are stacked against it, a warm human event takes place and its meanings and effects are often contrary to the predictions of experts in human behavior. So it is with extramarital sex. For in the last analysis we live as individuals, not statistics. Each moves in a unique context of personal morality and responsibility. And if we do not know what is dispiriting or energizing, meaningful, or insignificant for us as persons, then who will tell us?

Comment by:
David R. Mace
During the depression I lived in a slum in London, England. I knew a young man, John, who was very devoted to his ailing mother, very kind and generous to their neighbors and friends, and loved and respected by all. He had no job, yet he always had money to spend. This was a mystery to others, but not to me, because he had confided to me that he was a burglar. He broke into wealthy West End homes, sold what he stole, and used the proceeds to make others happy. So far as I know, the police never caught up with him. He did good to many, and did little harm to those whom he robbed.

This article provides us with similar examples of people who seemingly turned into good what has been traditionally viewed as evil. Such human stories illustrate the principles of the relativity of ethics. We sometimes speak of people who could "get away with murder"; and I have no doubt at all that there are human situations where murder would be an act of kindness to all but the victim.

Every marriage counselor could provide his own repertoire of cases in which extramarital sex seemed justified by unusual circumstances, or even turned out to be good for the marriage. He could also, of course, give plenty of instances where the reverse was true. We certainly need a sense of proportion about such matters.

I have no doubt that many robberies can be justified. And as long as they remain infrequent, society can absorb them. Provided most citizens respect private property, a good many burglars can operate without destroying public confidence. But let burglary become frequent, and people react by double-locking their doors and sleeping with loaded guns at hand. Let burglary become commonplace, and society would be forced to give up the concept of private property altogether—a change which some consider highly desirable.

Likewise, let extramarital sex become commonplace, and radical cultural change would become inevitable. There is much truth in the rabbinic saying that the commandment against adultery is not so much an injunction not to meddle with your neighbor's wife, as a warning not to unsettle the foundations of human society. A society in which all married people considered themselves free to engage in extramarital sex, and did so on a large scale, would be radically different from our present culture. Some people sincerely believe it would be a better society — but we have absolutely no proof of this, and the experiment could conceivably be disastrous.

We are all aware that the institution of marriage is having its troubles today. The mood of many is to offer a solution in terms of loosening the tie between husband and wife. I personally do not find this convincing. I prefer the opposite course—that of marriage enrichment. My long experience as a marriage counselor suggests that dull, boring, unhappy marriages represent either mismated couples who would be better to go their separate ways; or more often, couples whose relationship is tenuous and superficial because they have never made the real venture to which marriage invites them—the venture of commitment to the shared life, which in my opinion offers the most richly rewarding of all human experiences.

G.K. Chesterton once said that Christianity had not been tried and found wanting, but had been found difficult and not tried. This may also be true of modern marriage—it has disappointed us not because it does not work, but because we have not committed ourselves to the necessary effort to make it work successfully. I doubt whether increasing our freedom to engage in extramarital affairs would take many of us far in that direction.

Comment by:
Gordon Clanton
In a time when institutions as basic to human happiness as marriage and the family are being seriously questioned, *it is important that people know what their options are.* We are social creatures who give shape to our world on the basis of what we learn from one another's experiences.

My own research, like that of Myers and Leggitt, has discovered a great deal of nondestructive extramarital sex—or "constructive adultery" as some call it. Other researchers report similar findings. This new material is a valuable complement to studies which have chronicled those affairs and flings which have caused great trauma in the lives of the persons affected. We are learning that there are many kinds of marriage and many kinds of adultery, that all monogamy is not blissful and healthy and that all adultery is not painful and sick. We are learning that marriage is not monolithic but rather that it is a resilient ever-changing human invention which will continue to be reshaped in response to human needs and in light of the new things we human beings learn about ourselves. We are discovering that even adultery and homosexuality, once seen as the antiheses of happy marriage, can sometimes be accommodated in a relatively stable marriage which serves the best interests of the two persons involved and of those among whom they live.

Sex research will serve us best if it will report the successes and failures of others in enough depth so that we can really learn from them. In so doing such inquiry suggests to us some of the limits of our freedom as we seek to construct our own versions of workable emotional relationships. If it is to serve us in this way, sex research must continue to be willing to ask the difficult questions, the questions which many people would still rather silence. Those who tell the stories which reflect our changing sexual consciousness must resist the temptation of minimizing the conflict and pain which often mar sexual experimentation. It will not do to replace uncritical condemnation of adultery with uncritical approval.

Let me mention two important interrelated questions which bother me, questions on which I would like to see more research and reflection. (1) As research and reportage and life experiences make us more and more conscious of our options, of the wide range of possibilities within an expanded understanding of marriage and fidelity, is it not desirable that married persons (and others similarly committed to one another) talk about their feelings about extramarital sex and the possibilities of their becoming sexually involved with another *before* either of them actually acts on an extramarital urge? Perhaps marriage counseling and premarital counseling could urge the confrontation of these questions before the need arises in order better to equip persons for life in a world in which nontraditional options abound. I suspect that extramarital sex can be discussed with less deception of oneself and one's partner *before* an actual adulterous involvement begins.

(2) Is it ever better to hide an affair or the desire for an affair from one's spouse? I know that compelling arguments can be made on both sides; it is no easy matter. But the argument *My spouse would be happier not knowing about my affair* can be an exercise in self-deception and an evasion of responsibility. Sometimes the emotional cost of years of deception is more than psyches can afford.

I hope that papers like this one can catalyze candid conversations about the pros and cons of extramarital sex among concerned professionals and between sensitive spouses.

Comment by:
James A. Peterson
This paper by Myers and Leggitt is a courageous beginning of an investigation into an area of human behavior that has been neglected in almost all previous studies. Extramarital sex is ubiquitous and pervasive and, consequently, needs the attention of carefully designed inquiries to test its impact on interpersonal and intrapsychic health. One of the virtues of this presentation may be the fact that the conclusions the authors reach may become the questions in further investigation. As a social scientist I have great difficulty in regarding those conclusions as anything more than rather loosely worded hypotheses drawn from a preliminary look at the data.

The authors indicate that they have made no attempt at "in-depth" psychological analysis and, I would submit, neither have they attempted in-depth interactional analysis. They "simply describe a life style" and then draw conclusions. But what we have is a rather naive repetition of stories told to the authors with all the defensiveness, problems of recall, and projection that characterize first interviews in a therapeutic setting. Without a far more elegant method of investigation I would think that the authors would exercise a great deal of caution before they proposed what affairs may or may not do. We are dealing with one of the most profound experiences human beings may experience and judgments ought to be cautious and restrained until a number of in-depth studies begin to indicate some possibility of consistent findings. If the scientist does not have that humility he may himself contribute to a mythology as destructive as those he abhors inherited from the past. Or he may fall prey to accepting persons' rationalizations of behavior as a real measure of the results of that behavior and these two are widely separated.

Nevertheless I am pleased that this piece was written and that the two authors have set themselves in this line of investigation. I would hope that they will (a) continue to write about the subject and (b) develop their methodology of inquiry. They have a monmoralistic stance which is essential if they are going to explore this field. In their conclusions they have made statements (which I wish they had raised as questions stemming from their case histories) which are important for future study. But before they can come to guidelines which are useful to the family analyst or the family therapist they need to be sure their interviewees are representative of all the possible subjects in each given class; that they have measures so they do not mistake rationalizations and projections for real effects; and that they have some way of contrasting one class of interviewees who have had affairs with similar groups who have not, so that having had extramarital affairs is the primary significant difference. Their conclusions may be absolutely right but we do not know that yet.

Comment by:
Silas L. Warner
The positive aspects of extramarital sexual experience are mainly in the minds of the participants. In the vocabulary of the younger generation, it is usually an "ego trip." These conclusions are based on in-depth clinical studies and not only subjective reports of life styles. While the experience undoubtedly is "pleasurable," "mind-expanding," and "uninhibiting," it usually has negative long-term effects, especially on other family members.

The typical individual motivation for extramarital sex turns out to be a strong sense of personal inadequacy coupled with hostility and excessive narcissism. When each spouse has such problems and they agree to allow each other to experiment sexually it seems like a perfect solution. However, they are usually starting a vicious cycle which requires repeated novelty in the form of a steady stream of new partners. If any lasting sexual attachment does occur it introduces a triangle which cannot be resolved without great pain and sacrifice.

I would estimate from clinical experience that about 90% of extramarital sexual experiences result in decidedly more negative than positive results. In the other 10%, there seem to be some situations in which extramarital sexual experience does lead to positive short- and long-term effects.

There may be benefits in a marriage in which one member has a relatively strong, mature personality and the spouse is neurotic and immature. The stronger partner becomes increasingly frustrated with the spouse's limitations and becomes sexually involved with another more mature individual. This can lead to a divorce and remarriage or a prolonged affair. If the children can be intelligently coped with during and after the divorce all parties may benefit by the new arrangement. A prolonged affair may be brought on by the weaker partner's steadfastly refusing a divorce and the stronger partner's being unable to leave. Neither spouse is very happy with this situation but both fear that it could be worse. The sexual partner outside the marriage is also frustrated and only partially happy. This situation can continue until the children are grown up. By that time the married couple are so entrenched in the marriage that they usually elect to sustain it and the affair fades out.

There are rare instances of reasonably mature spouses who want to stay married but seem incapable of having satisfying sexual experiences together. They both elect to have an "arrangement" in which each is free to have extramarital sexual experience as long as it is done discreetly. This seems to work, especially if they are motivated to preserve the marriage because of other (nonsexual) mutual satisfactions. Their character defenses are usually so fixated that neither psychotherapy nor extramarital sexual experience can enable them to enjoy each other sexually.

There is one other rare situation in which a married couple is young and, like siblings, are too competitive toward each other. Both feel frustrated and angry and one or both find substitute sexual partners. If the marriage can survive this, there may be a maturing effect which makes them more appreciative of each other. This stems from an internal psychological shift which is enough to unplug the logjam which originally stymied the marriage. However, psychotherapists should not prescribe extramarital sexual experience because there is a strong probability that it will create more problems than it will solve.

Comment by:
John F. Cuber
In these days of groping for knowledge concerning aspects of sexual behavior which run counter to the conventional wisdom, I find it exceedingly rare when two studies done independently by persons who did not know each other reach virtually identical conclusions. This is, nonetheless, the case with Dr. Myers and Rev. Leggitt's article and our own chapter on "Other involvements" in *The Significant Americans*. Partly, of course, this unusual convergence may result from the fact that both studies involved the same kind of people—above average in education, occupational status, urban residence, and so on. Nevertheless, Myers and Leggitt's cases sound almost as if they came from our own files. A further replication which should be mentioned is that in the six years since our book appeared, many cases have come to our attention, both volunteered and sought-out, which underline the same protrait.

More specifically, both studies have found that extramarital sex relations do not necessarily hurt existing marriages and may even help not only to maintain them but to enhance their richness. Moreover, these persons involved in extramarital affairs typically do so with little immediate or subsequent guilt. Where the spouse is apprised of the fact or finds it out, acquiescence if not approval is not unlikely—even if sometimes reluctant. Finally, extramarital relations occur both in good and bad marriages, although, as we have pointed out, the causes are somewhat different in the two circumstances.

Practically all of the above generalizations clearly run against the traditional grain. It seems almost inconceivable that some people still fail to comprehend that a break with traditional etiquette and morality does not necessarily result in the heinous outcomes which are so confidently predicted. It is a little surprising that, as Myers and Leggitt pointed out, although "the myth" that our society is monogamous "was exploded over three decades ago by the famous Kinsey studies," there is still a pervasive supposition to the contrary. One wonders how long it takes for a culturally entrenched belief to yield to empirical reality.

The Meyers and Leggitt report has reawakened my consideration of a very basic theoretical question about sexual behavior among persons already mated to someone else: Is it an example of what psychologists call "coping behavior"? That is, do extramarital relations arise chiefly out of frustrations or disappointments in the prior mating? Or is there a general tendency in the human species for polygamous experience? Most of our contemporaries have been raised on a repressive sex ethos, which I suppose prejudices the case for the coping behavior theory. I am inclined to think that the repressive ethos has simply resulted in the atrophy of a more generalized sexual aggrandizement which is basic in human nature. But whether right or wrong, it is certainly worth consideration along with the more conventional view.

15. How Does an Affair Affect a Marriage? – 7 Views

JAMES L. FRAMO, YEHUDI A. COHEN, HERBERT A. OTTO, CAROLYN SYMONDS, ALBERT ELLIS, LYNN G. SMITH, JAMES R. SMITH, LEON SALZMAN

James L. Framo

My observations are based on material obtained in marital therapy sessions—the setting most likely to reveal a depth view of this deeply personal issue. I treat husbands and wives together, largely because when a marriage is in serious trouble the likelihood of divorce is much greater if the partners go to two therapists separately, or if only one goes for treatment. When I see a couple I consider that I have three patients; the husband, the wife, and the relationship; sometimes the relationship cannot or should not be saved, in which event "divorce therapy" is indicated.

Exploration in marital therapy can reveal, considering individual motivations, that an affair was destructive in intent, designed to get rid of the mate; that it was a chance by-product of other marital problems; that it had little to do with the mate at all; that it was designed to arouse the partner's interest; that it was based on revenge for real or fancied hurts; that the lover or girlfriend was a way-station on a route back to the mate, etc. Interactionally, extramarital affairs may be built into a marriage as a necessary ingredient to maintain the balance of the relationship cannot or should not be saved, in which event "divorce therapy" is indicated.

When an affair is revealed in marital therapy, the reactions of mates cover a wide range—all the way from encouragement, through seeming indifference, to being shattered. In some cases the mates ignore the more obvious hints and don't want to hear about the affair because then they'd have to do something about it. People who have liberal attitudes about their mates having an affair may suddenly shift when the abstraction becomes a reality, when they know for sure. Those partners who react initially with mild upset and curiosity often have a delayed reaction; I've gotten to the point where I can predict when I will get a request for an extra therapy session. Some partners are truly devastated and rocked to the very foundations of their personality. Psychotic reactions, suicide, and murder in response to affairs appear in the newspaper every day, but when it's handled in conjoint therapy by a competent marital therapist, and the meaning of "infidelity" is explored, the dangers are minimized. Some mates react with blandness to the news of an affair; their partners usually perceive this reaction as the most hostile of all. One husband smiled through the whole thing until his wife hit him. Some partners are overforgiving and blame themselves, and still others have taken a "scientific attitude" about the matter, handling it like a research problem.

What are the long-range consequences of affairs on marriages? It is rare for the affair itself to break up the marriage. In some cases the affair turns out to have a therapeutic effect by revitalizing a depleted relationship. In others, the basic trust never gets reestablished and the heightened suspicion gets incorporated into other problems that the couple have. In most cases the couples move beyond the crisis of the affair and begin doing the real work of therapy—involving the original families of these adults, learning to deal with issues between them, the work toward developing a separate self, couples group therapy sessions, etc.—but therapy is another story.

Yehudi A. Cohen

The phrasing of the question is unfortunate because it presupposes only one type of marriage: "a marriage." There are many types of marriage, and the variability is almost as great in a complex society like ours as it is among the world's cultures. One of the things that anthropologists have learned about marriage is that the relationship between spouses depends in large part on the nature of their relationships with other people outside the household. I can best illustrate this by describing two types of marriage; they are extremes, and there are several shadings between the two. For example, as in many "ideal" middle-class marriages in a modern society when a married couple are not intimately involved with networks—like relatives—outside their immediate household, they tend to "put all their emotional eggs in one basket." In such marriages, spouses tend to become emotionally inbred, as it were, sharing the same interests, having the same friends, going out and entertaining together, and sharing mutually in household tasks, like dishwashing, care of children, cooking, and cleaning. Emotional life is very intense in such marriages, and people have no other social—or even physical—places to which to go when the going gets rough. There is no other network to which they can turn for solace or support during emotional crises and none that can serve as a buffer against the "isolated nuclear family."

Hence an affair carried on by one member of such a marriage may have more drastic consequences than in other types of marriage. When, in a marriage like this, sexual exclusivity (or fidelity) is interpreted as symbolic of a more general loyalty and commitment, an affair by one is often seen by the other as rejection or abandonment. With nowhere to go, the sense of emotional pain may become too much to bear; likewise, the sense of guilt in such an emotionally inbred situation may also be too much to bear for the perpetrator. It is at this point that all hell breaks loose.

At the other extreme is the marriage in which one or both members are regularly and intimately involved with relatives or other networks outside the household. In such marriages, the spouses diffuse their emotional attachments. They tend to maintain financial privacy vis-a-vis each other, have separate interests and friends, go out and entertain independently of each other, and each has clearly defined and separate household tasks which they do not share.

In this kind of situation, extramarital sex, at least on the man's part, may not have the same emotional impact as it does in the first type of marriage, or the impact will be different. A wife, for example, has other groupings to which to turn for comfort and a sense of belonging; not having anchored herself to her husband so exclusively, she can use a variety of rationalizations—such as, "that's men for you"—to blunt the sense of rejection and abandonment that she may feel. This is not to say that a hellish storm will not result, but—it seems—for quite different reasons and with different quality than in the emotionally inbred family.

I suspect that, as in most societies, extramarital sex tends to elicit more extreme reactions when carried on by women. Although there is not much good information about this, I also suspect that this too varies with the type of marriage in which people live. In the emotionally inbred marriage, for example, the general equality that tends to prevail between spouses probably extends to the ways in which people respond to each other's affairs; that is, men in these marital situations probably feel the same way about their wives' affairs as the latter do about their husbands'.

Herbert A. Otto

In a recently published volume edited by the writer entitled *The New Sexuality* (Palo Alto, Science and Behavior Books, 1971), Dr. O. Spurgeon English, Professor of Psychiatry at Temple University, had some very stimulating comments to make in his article "The Positive Values of the Affair." I too would like to begin by commenting on some of the positive effects of an affair on a marriage.

The partner who is having the affair often notes a greater openness in communication either in himself or in the partner—although mention of the liaison is usually excluded from this. At the time of the affair one or the other member may make a greater effort to please the other partner thereby affecting a temporary improvement in the relationship (the affairing partner from a sense of guilt or to divert suspicion, the other partner because he senses something is wrong). New variety is sometimes introduced into the sex life by the affairing partner who may have acquired a different outlook on sexual experiencing or perhaps some new approaches or techniques. Paradoxically a few instances have come to my attention where the affairing partner claimed a greater appreciation and love for the spouse was developing as the affair progressed.

On the other side the usual effect of an affair on a marriage is first of all to introduce a sense of disturbance. In most instances on some level of awareness the non-affairing partner picks up that a new element has entered *their* relationship. This often induces an added level of strain in both partners as the suspicious (or unsuspecting) partner begins to probe to find out what is amiss. A number of women have reported that they would have "little accidents," i.e., burn a meal, fenderbend his car, etc., while they were having an affair apparently in an attempt to invite hostility and some form of punishment. One affairing partner made this illuminating comment—"I spent a great deal of energy planning and plotting on keeping from spilling it—as a consequence I had less to give at home." Another often reported effect is a subtle (or not so subtle) denigration of the other partner by the affairing partner—"I couldn't give him (her) credit for anything he (she) did." Also in a great many instances there is a diminishing of the sex life as the affairing partner invests his sexual and psychic energies elsewhere.

In the final analysis the affair becomes a catalytic force in a marriage, disturbing a static or seemingly frozen situation which had not been meeting the needs of one or perhaps both partners. Thus the affair can be both a cry for help, a reaching for health, or the acting out of an inner disturbance.

Carolyn Symonds

There is no specific answer that can be made to this question, many variables are involved. There is a question of the short range effect, or the long range effect. The effect on the individuals involved can be different from the effect on the marriage relationship.

Men have traditionally had more access to occasions for secretive affairs than have women. A great deal of this is due to their occupations which take them out of the home, permit them to travel, to go to meetings and conferences, and to meet new people in far-away places. This has been somewhat acceptable for men. Women who had affairs had to be much more discreet. But now, with a Women's Lib Movement going on, women are beginning to ask for some of the same opportunities that men have had. In the long run this may democratize our society and the marriage relationship—but in the meantime there will be some unhappy people and some broken relationships.

A woman came to me for counseling who came from a very traditional background and had never questioned her marriage relationship. When she took a professional job and began to travel, she also began to have extramarital experiences. Only then did she discover how sexually incompetent her husband was. After this variety of new experiences she was not willing to continue a marriage with the very dull sex life she found herself confronted with. The problem as she saw it was how to reeducate him without letting him know of her new experiences, or without doing great damage to his ego.

It is probably safe to say that in a traditional marriage without close communication between the parties, if the man has an affair very little harm will come from it—even if he is discovered; if the woman has one and is found out it may dissolve the marriage.

In a more modern marriage where the participants try to have close communication, and try to keep each other informed about what they are thinking and feeling, the subject has probably already been discussed at great length between them. When and if it happens with either or both of them, they are ready to explore with each other the negative and positive aspects of what has occurred. This can and often does happen in mate swapping (swinging) situations. Each is geared to identify with the other so that one gets enjoyment when the other has enjoyment. This can be beneficial to the individuals as well as to the relationship.

Some of the people dropping out of the mainstream of the society, especially the younger ones, are rejecting the current societal values. The strict separation of male and female roles is a tradition that is being questioned. As the separation of sexual roles diminishes, the concept of monogamy as we know it receives serious question. Perhaps in a few generations the question under discussion will be meaningless. The concept of "affair" may have changed considerably, and perhaps "marriage" as we know it will be nonexistent.

Albert Ellis

How does an affair usually affect a marriage? No one accurately knows. Almost all studies that have been done on this question—and, all told, they have been damned few—query fairly liberal, relatively unguilty individuals who are willing to admit that they have had affairs and to openly discuss them. Such individuals commonly report that their extramarital relations had no particular effect on their marriages or that they helped improve their relationships with their mates. And they are probably reporting correctly. But many other adulterers who are more conservative and infinitely more guilty about having affairs—and who consequently hesitate to report or discuss them —might well have more unfortunate consequences to relate. And where are such respondents easily to be found?

That adultery *must* affect a marriage adversely is, of course, non-sense. I have personally spoken to literally hundreds of individuals during the last thirty years who swore otherwise and who seemingly had substantial evidence to back their claims. Both wives and husband have told me that the only or main thing that kept their marriages together was a hot and heavy love affair on the side. One such wife has stated, "If I hadn't carried on a relationship with Bill for the last six years, I would have gone absolutely crazy with my husband's dullness and lack of sexuality. Little does he know how grateful to Bill he should be!" And a husband: "I really care for my wife and we have a great deal in common. But without the great warmth which I receive from my secretary when we get together once or twice a week, not even my love for my two children would have kept me living at home. Between the two of them, I have almost everything. With my wife alone, I just couldn't take it."

Other spouses to whom I have talked—many of whom have not been clients of mine but "normal" human beings whom I have encountered at various points in my life—have expressed less extreme but nonetheless anti-monogamous sentiments. Said a 33-year-old mother of two children: "I certainly don't *need* an affair to keep my marriage alive, since I really get along quite well with my husband in most ways. But meeting my lover regularly is far more exciting than reading a new novel, and many of the things I have learned from him have helped enrich my relationship with George." And a 56-year-old grandfather:

"I can't think of any woman I'd rather be married to than my wife. I am almost panicked whenever I think that she might die before I do. But I don't think my sex life with her would have been worth a damn had not I kept up a series of affairs with several much more sophisticated and sexy women. If she ever discovered how I really learned to satisfy her, she'd probably die!" In my book, *The Civilized Couple's Guide to Extramarital Adventure* (New York, Pinnacle Books, 1973), I present many more instances where adultery helped make a marriage more tolerable or more enjoyable.

The other side of the story is much grimmer. For I have heard countless regrets, usually by women but also by men, about extramarital affairs; and not a few of these affairs have led the mates involved to become disillusioned with, less attracted to, and ultimately alienated from their spouses. In many of these cases, these marriages would have been poor anyway; but in others, the outside affairs significantly contributed to their dissolution. Not that this necessarily was all to the bad. Scores of mates to whom I have talked—and, again, wives tend to stand out in this respect—remained supinely tied to an individual whom they did not love, honor, or cherish, for fear that they could not possibly make a good sex-love relationship with anyone else. Just as soon as they engaged in a satisfactory (or even an unsatisfactory) affair, and thereby discovered that their love and marital horizons could be much wider than they had previously imagined, they stopped putting themselves down and wisely brought to a legal conclusion marriages that had for years existed in name only.

Is there any moral that can be drawn from these seemingly contradictory data about the good and bad effects an affair may have on a marriage? One mainly: that all general conclusions in this regard are likely to be misleading. When adultery ensues, some marriages gain and some lose; some mates are happy and some are miserable; some offspring of marriages benefit and some suffer; some friends and relatives of the spouses mourn and some are deliriously happy. By and large, it is not the having or not having of the affair that greatly counts but the reasons for doing so and the attitudes of the adulterer toward having it. The hardheaded realistic, nonguilty individual more often than not has considerable success with his or her extramarital relationships and suffers few major consequences. The thin-skinned, unrealistic, guilty individual tends to rarely engage in such affairs, and bleeds considerably when he or she does so. Today's women, who still tend to be more conventional and anxiety-ridden about sex and love relationships, flagellate themselves for their adulteries more than men do, and consequently enjoy them less. But a new breed of husbands and wives is slowly arising, who consciously face their nonmonogamous urges at the time they marry (or soon after) and who allow each other and themselves openly acknowledged and guiltless extramarital adventures. The indications already are that the effects of this brand, of honest, civilized adultery on marriage are generally good and that out of such experimentation a new, sexually and amatively non-exclusive kind of one-to-one mating may gradually develop.

Lynn G. Smith and James R. Smith

Since we are at a point in time when extramarital sex is occurring in increasingly differentiated forms and contexts, it is only to be expected that the responses to extramarital sex and thus its effects on marriages are also becoming increasingly differentiated. The spousal discovery of an affair is becoming increasingly unlikely as our curiously liberal society moves in the direction of acknowledgement, discussion, and acceptance of extramarital sexuality, a direction preceded by our relative acceptance of premarital and postmarital sexuality.

One general effect of an affair is that it tends to make life more exciting; whether or not it satisfies, produces conflict, destroys, or uncovers a new dimension of life, it certainly intensifies. On the positive side, it may renew dialogue, reawaken sexual interest, constitute a source of sexual knowledge, deepen a variety of extramarital ties, and overcome the isolation concomitant with monogamy and sexual exclusivity. On the negative side, it may create a communication barrier, destroy trust, stimulate destructive jealousy behavior, signal a rejection of the primary partner, and engage feelings of insecurity and inadequacy. But what determines whether a positive or negative effect will prevail?

After having studied cases of consensual adultery for the past five years we are in a position to hypothesize that the major factors determining the effect an affair has on marriage are (1) whether or not the spouse knows about it, (2) whether or not it violates the marital ground rules and agreements, ultimately whether or not what we call primary allegiance is violated, (3) whether it arises from positive or negative motivation, i.e., whether the marriage is basically satisfying or not, and whether the motivation is primarily "want" or "need" or oriented, (4) the meaning assigned to the affair by the spouse, and (5) the levels of trust, communication, and intimacy present in the marital relationship. Other factors which seem to be of lesser importance are the level of self-esteem of the spouse, whether it is the husband or the wife who has the affair or both, and whether the affair is based upon primarily emotional or sexual factors.

If the spouse doesn't know about the affair, then the effect on the marriage may be relatively small until it is discovered and only then may marital difficulties arise—in which case it is the knowledge of the affair rather than the affair per se which has the primary effect. And yet twenty years ago Kinsey reported that of the women who had engaged in extramarital sex half of their husbands either knew about the affairs or suspected, yet in half of those cases such knowledge had not resulted in any serious marital difficulty.

The secrecy and deception which characterize the conventional clandestine affair do, however, constitute a breach of trust, a violation of traditional marital ground rules. Such trust, once lost, is difficult to regain, as many a child learns after being caught engaging in the forbidden, particularly in the realm of sexuality. Suspicions linger and give rise to dissension. With the knowledge and consent, and perhaps participation, of the spouse as present in consensual adultery or comarital sexuality, the divisive effects of secrecy and deception may be circumvented. Many couples, no one knows how many, have openly and honestly faced their desires for sexual sharing with others, and have reached an understanding that allows, even approves, of extramarital sex under various conditions and in various situations. These new ground rules, however, are just as important as the usual monogamic rules, for if they are violated, jealousy and other negative reactions have been shown to recur, though with perhaps less intensity. Primary loyalty to the marriage, signified by adherence to the ground rules, remains important for a feeling of security.

The meaning assigned to the affair in the total context of the marriage is another significant variable. If the marriage is basically sound, then an affair is likely a supplementary source of gratification rather than a substitute for marital gratification. If the marriage is basically sound, then even a discovered deception will tend to have a less negative effect. But the ultimate effect on the marriage depends not only on the individual's motivation, whether positive or negative, for having an affair, but also on the spouse's interpretation of what the affair means. Obviously a husband or wife who believes that an affair means their spouse no longer loves them will feel and act differently from the husband or wife who believes that it is just a sexual attraction which will most likely burn itself out in due course. Self-esteem, including a sense of personal adequacy or inadequacy in sexual matters, is undoubtedly an important influence in the type of interpretation or meaning which will be assigned to the partner's affair. And it makes no small difference whether there is a relevant peer group or subculture which is supportive or critical of the behavior in question.

In sum, an affair in the context of deception and dissatisfaction certainly has a different effect on marriage than an affair in the context of consent and approval based on mutual esteem and love. And the time is long past when expectations which actually aggravate the situation are appropriate. To approach an "affair" as primarily a "problem" or as an indication of problems elsewhere may be the surest pathological, neurotic, or otherwise destructive type of behavior.

Leon Salzman

Adultery is a widespread phenomenon which can be largely attributed to the failure of marriages to fulfill the needs of the partners, rather than to the more popular rationalizations regarding man's innate polygamous tendencies which cannot be satisfied with a monogamous social arrangement. Whether, in fact, monogamy, polygamy, polyandry, or any other arrangement for fulfilling the sexual needs of man are biologically determined, in the long history of monogamous relationships in the Judeo-Christian culture, adultery can be best understood as a consequence of unfulfilled needs, sexual and otherwise, within the marriage.

Adultery is less widespread when marriages are freely chosen rather than arranged and when the partners are mature, considerate, and truly like each other. The widespread phenomenon of adultery in both highly moralistic religious cultures and sexually liberated cultures says more about marital customs, economic and social instability, and the paucity of tender, loving marital partnerships than about man's propensity toward sexual infidelity. This issue is not fundamentally altered even during prolonged absences or illness of one of the marital partners. Under such circumstances masturbation rather than infidelity is the form of sexual outlet that is more common. While some psychiatrists always consider adultery in either partner to be evidence of disturbed interpersonal living, and therefore a psychiatric problem, I do not find that this is necessarily true. Disturbed marriages and disrupted interpersonal intimacies do not necessarily involve neurotic or psychotic manifestations in the partners requiring psychiatric intervention. Divorce is neither irrational nor evidence of psychic malfunctioning. It is more often the inevitable consequence of a marital situation badly conceived and without any reasonable basis for sustaining it.

How an adulterous affair will affect a marriage relationship depends upon the capacity of the partners to tolerate less than the ideal sexual and nonsexual exchanges between them and their readiness to communicate to each other the existence of such affairs. Ordinarily it may be an unnecessary and explosive intrusion for the partners to inform each other of the existence of their infidelity. However, in the guise of honesty some individuals insist that the partner be informed in the expectation that the ability to communicate this fact may lessen their guilt and avoid the partner's indignation. At times they expect to be rewarded for their honesty, but such admission often serves as a means of tormenting and punishing their partner. On the other hand, communicating such information to the partner may be an appeal for help in terminating the affair so as not to disrupt the marriage.

This was precisely the situation with a man of 40 who had two children with a woman he insisted he loved even though she was an unsatisfactory sex partner. When his girlfriend separated from her own husband and initiated divorce proceedings, he panicked and told his wife about his affair. She immediately called his lover and terminated the relationship with an emphatic and permanent rebuke to the woman while toward her wayward husband she was supportive and rewarded him with additional affection and concern.

Under other circumstances the presence of an adulterous affair permits a wavering and unsatisfactory marital situation to continue. In these cases the adulterous affair is usually kept secret from the partner and it allows the marital relationship to proceed because the discontents which produce the adulterous affair can be tolerated. One dissatisfied wife maintained several affairs with the explanation that these affairs made it possible for her to remain married to her husband. She had no intention of abandoning him and the children, but she was also losing interest in her husband and in order to continue in the marriage she had to be involved sexually elsewhere. Under these circumstances there is very little anxiety and very little guilt and therefore these adulterous affairs rarely come to the attention of either the partner or the psychiatrist. When they do for other ostensible reasons there is little impetus to abandon the adulterous affairs.

On the other hand, adulterous relationships can be the final straw that breaks the back of any weak marriage. The discovery of the adulterous affair forces the final break in the marriage which ultimately results in separation and divorce. These are the situations where divorce would have probably followed even if there were no affairs.

The growing interest in marital swinging is an aspect of adultery in which there is mutual agreement to accept the partner's activities. Here it is in the open, known to all, and frequently does not disturb the existing relationships. However, one should recognize that under other circumstances this behavior can be enormously disruptive in spite of the agreement of the partners in advance. In spite of all the proclaimed virtues of swinging, coupling, triad, or communal relationships, there is considerable jealousy, rivalry, and open hostility which make such arrangements unstable. This is true in spite of the realization that it takes a particular psychic structure to contemplate and enter into such arrangements in the first place. These sexual experiments as the alternatives to nuclear family arrangements require not only free and revolutionary individuals but also uncommitted and unrelated individuals as well.

While monogamy may not be a natural or preordained innate state of adjustment, it is clearly one in which the difficulties of relating to another human being are minimized. In the presence of tender consideration for one's partner, it is the basis for the most stable relationship particularly where each partner manages a reasonable amount of both sexual and nonsexual satisfaction. Under these circumstances adultery should be unneccessary and, if it appears, it can be enormously destructive. Such damage is not due to the jealous or selfish demands for loyalty or fidelity but rather to the tendency to feel deprived of the attention and affection which is given to the adulterous relationship. Consequently the partner feels cheated, humiliated, and rejected which can only lead to a disruption of benevolent attitudes in the relationship.

16. The Office Wife

JAMES A. PETERSON

I was sitting on the sands of Waikiki some time ago with a discussion group of young men and their wives talking about the problems associated with secretaries, when a middle-aged woman came by and stopped to listen. She was not part of the group but she soon became a part. Just as I paused after making a point about the unfairness of competition between the wife and the secretary, she proclaimed with great assurance her conviction that "the secretary always wins." Having given a climax to the discussion, she left. The late Edmund Bergler, famous psychiatric consultant on sex and divorce, would have objected very strenuously to her conclusion.[1] He felt that she rarely won. Furthermore, he felt that if she had won she would not have followed up her victory because her participation was really on the basis of a masochistic need to fail, and not primarily to achieve a permanent and lasting intimacy.

What are the motivations of "office wives"? There are many and we will attempt to assess some of their psychological and social characteristics, as well as look at the social and economic structure that almost inevitably produces intimacy between a businessman and his secretary. Undeniably, most men are devoted to their wives and families. In fact, the prime impetus for business success rests in the wish of the man to prove to his wife that he is worthy of the dreams which he instilled in her in their courtship, and to confirm to his children and to himself that he is an exemplary provider and father. However, observation has led to the conclusion that, given our present social organization, a person whose marriage is deficient in various regards may be overly susceptible to the potential emotional outlet of an "office wife." And here I am using the term wife in the sense of a companion toward whom one feels loyalty, and with whom one shares emotions.

We begin by describing the roles of modern executive secretaries to justify that conclusion, bearing in mind that the discussion pertains primarily to the minority of men who are unable to maintain the balance in their lives necessary to derive deep rewards from their home lives. It is also pertinent to consider that even among such men, those who are too absorbed in their occupations to reap satisfactions from their marriages may very well be disinclined to seek similar interpersonal satisfactions extramaritally. The following analysis is an effort to put into perspective the occasional man-office wife relationships which do occur.

"Polygamy" in American life

A young executive, a manager, or an independent entrepreneur often lives in a frightening world of competition where his possible successor lurks at the next desk or across the street. Further, his sense of self-esteem comes primarily from his economic success, and not because he is a "good man," "an honest man," or "a good father and husband." He authenticates his self-image partially in the approving eyes of his boss, and partially in the symbols his money buys which are on exhibit at the curb in front of his home and in his home.

The person who shares the important business moments which contribute to success and to failure is usually the secretary who typed up the proposal and who shared in the planning for the effort. She knows more about the problems involved in the transaction than the man's assistant. Furthermore, she knows more about the man. She sees him intimately for eight hours a day and, providing she has the kind of sensitivity such secretaries must have, knows how to buoy his spirits or share his enthusiasm. As time goes on she becomes indispensable not only in arranging for his airplane transportation and his hotel reservations, but in reinforcing his flagging zest or tempering his optimism.

In such a situation emotional dependence of one on the other is bound to occur. There is no point in saying to a businessman and his secretary. "Do not allow intimacy to grow between you." It is inevitable that they will share meaningful moments of their common activity. If some concern, if some tenderness, if some gratitude develops, it is difficult to draw a line at the precise point where that tenderness should not be expressed. In fact, the growth of feeling between a man and his secretary is often so gradual and so insidious that when they become aware of it they are shocked and chagrined.

There is a well-known sociological proposition (and perhaps sociologists make too formal what every layman can simply observe) that the more frequent the interaction, the greater the possibility of persons liking each other. I would add that when that interaction concerns those things that are crucial for one's success, liking may turn to loving.

But there is more to be said about this than a simple recitation of the social organization of the modern office. Another matter is the distance between a man and his wife. He gets on the train or into his automobile in the morning and spends a rather long time away from home. His mind is gradually disoriented from the breakfast scene until he begins to anticipate the office. If his secretary is there to greet him warmly and to outline his tasks with efficiency, he also looks forward to seeing her. Then he is with her and he is not with his wife.

During the creative and tumultuous part of his day he is with the secretary. After eight exhausting hours, and this does not count commutation time, he returns home. By now the workday is over and he is not about to enjoy presenting a warmed-over version of the day's problems and achievements to his wife and children. The office is a psychologically different world and he leaves it when he travels home. In one sense he must leave it behind for his wife is simply not familiar with his work. At the beginning of their marriage she may· have worked gallantly to understand what he did and what it meant to him, but as he progresses and his involvement becomes more complex she simply does not know enough about his work to discuss it meaningfully.

Increased estrangement at home

Many times, the wife's focus of attention grows away from him and toward the duties of home, motherhood, and community. One of the most insightful discoveries of Blood and Wolfe's study of husbands and wives[2] was their analysis of the increasing differentiation of role tasks with the passage of years. With each passing year there is more and more role differentiation, so that the involvements of the husband and the wife become fewer and fewer as time goes on. This includes the difficulties and complexities of the husband's work.

Perhaps a husband and wife "ought to" share their most meaningful experiences when apart, but our studies indicate that they do not. The ground for that kind of sharing is lost early in contemporary marriage. Often a very responsible mother becomes so engrossed in the trials and triumphs of raising her children that she gives scant attention to her own mental or esthetic growth. If her husband is in a business or profession which demands increasing mental acuity and social awareness, he may come to feel that there is such a great differential in their growth that his wife is boring. My office rings with the reiteration of the phrase: "She bores me." Of course in some instances this can be a rationalization or justification of his affair with the office wife. But there is no doubt, given the role differentiation of our society, that lag in growth rates often occurs.

A further complication comes out of family structure. A century ago when the family was extended there were dozens of significant other relatives available for emotional interaction. In our society, in which almost every family has a nuclear structure consisting of only husband, wife, and children, the emotional demands are overwhelming. The modern family turns in on itself. For many persons modern marriage demands too much. When a woman has small children, who are particularly exhausting in their persistence, she may not have a great deal of sympathy and tenderness left for her husband. And, if early in the relationship he gets an impoverished response from her, he may early learn to turn to his secretary or someone else for his emotional nourishment. Fifty years ago he would have been able to turn to his mother, his aunt, his sister, or any number of others who had primary relationships with him. Today he has only his wife and she may not be able to meet his needs.

There is also the situational contrast which I have often labeled as unjust. The husband leaves his wife while he is scrambling to get to work on time and his wife is scrambling to get the children to school on time. He comes home often to a harassed and tired wife who has had the children all day. Her appearance and her spirits both may be drooping and dejected. On the other hand, he never sees his secretary unless she has both physical and psychological makeup. He sees her generally at her best and if she is ill or tired she avoids coming into the office. His wife has no such escape. In a somewhat more profound way he associates his wife with all of the history of their relationship. Undoubtedly there have been unpleasant and boring periods in the marriage. There would also have been these times had he been married to his secretary, but he does not know this. Their possible interaction has not been tested by being thrown into the crucible of continuous, week-long intimacy during which it is impossible to maintain masks or poses.

Sexual involvement with the "office wife"
Still, not all of the intense office relationships have sexual connotations. Gordon Cummings, one of my graduate students, studied married men and women who appeared to be having affairs and found that in one-fourth of the men and in about half of the women their relationships did not involve sexual intercourse.[3] Cuber and Harroff in their study, *Significant Americans*,[4] adopt the term "office wife" to describe these relationships but point out that: "We use the phrase *office wife* for this widespread relationship with some hesitancy, since it conveys sexual meanings which the facts do not always justify." There can be warmth without physical demonstration and tenderness without touching. How then do we account for the relationships that go on to include full intimacy? Cummings' study[3] gives some answers. He found that there were two aspects to almost every affair that could be described as etiologically significant: there were the deprivations at home and the attractions away from home. He found the following factors highly associated with the production of deep involvement:

1. Poor sexual adjustment in the marriage
2. Finding the other man or other woman a challenge
3. Being "in love"
4. Having an unaffectionate mate
5. Involvement in a marriage that never was good
6. Enjoying the company of the other man or woman
7. Feeling sympathy for the other man or woman
8. Getting revenge
9. No specific reason

It is interesting that only one-third of the males thought that their motivation for such an affair was rooted in their dissatisfaction with their home sexual partner. We make the inference that companionship and emotional interaction are more significant variables. But, inevitably, when a person other than the wife supplies the basic answers to a man's deepest needs, he is prone to symbolize that response physically as well as emotionally.

There is a further comment to be made regarding the sexual aspects of these involvements. Man is a creature of habit and this is also true of his sexual behavior. After ten years his sexual contact with his wife is often not a very zestful or creative experience. Wives are particularly bitter about this fact. Furthermore, the habits which are developed by a young man and a young woman in early marriage, which are often inept and far from satisfying, persist into later years.

Consequently, the man often feels that he is missing a great deal in the routinized sexual interaction with his mate. He fantasies all sorts of new experiments with someone else, but somehow not with his wife. Because an affair is a new conquest and it involves new approaches, he may find his new bed partner much more gratifying than his wife. If he does, this reinforces all of his other feelings for her. Whether he would maintain the same thrill if he were married to her for some years is another matter.

Despite the fact that the sexual aspect of the union with the office wife may be more stimulating than with his wife, my impression is that the woman who interrupted our oceanside conversation was wrong and that the office wife does not always win. The office wife may achieve a good deal of emotional response, a sense of important and creative sharing in significant work, and a degree of sexual fulfillment, but I do not think that she often replaces the other wife. There are many reasons for this. One of them is the very large sense of responsibility that many men have to a wife of many years and a growing brood of children. Another is the family image that looms large in the selection of candidates for advancement in any industry. Another is the deep suspicion that a girl who will be an office wife may also turn out to be a faithless "home wife." There is still enough hangover of the double standard to make this factor weigh heavily in the minds of some men. Sometimes, too, the office wife prefers that arrangement because she states very frankly that she is not about to become the home wife, for she "knows" the man will become involved with his next secretary or someone else. Experience, after all, is a great teacher. There is often an age difference, and if the office wife wants to have a home and children she prefers to do that with someone her own age who will not die and leave her with sole responsibility to raise the children and manage the home.

Why secretaries accept such relationships

What are the psychological characteristics that motivate secretaries to accept such relationships if they are often dead-end marital streets? Their motivations are as varied as their life histories. One young woman confessed to me that she had gone through a series of such affairs as "revenge" because another woman had taken her husband. Others are desperately lonely and pay any price for a period of tenderness even though they suspect it has a termination point. Still others are physically motivated. They have strong sexual drives and need fulfillment but they do not necessarily want yet to be tied down in a marriage. Still others go about establishing relationships in which they are destined to be deprived and hurt.

I know others who are calculating and determined predators who choose their love objects as skillfully as they choose their clothes. Life is defined as tough and the victory goes to the most persistent and clever. They are manipulators who set a goal and often reach it. In contrast there are the naive ones who step by step became involved until they were deeply emotionally and sexually entangled without really knowing how they ever reached that point. Each person who presents such cases to the counselor brings his own unique life history and his own peculiar profile of personality variables. Sometimes these involve high sexual drives, but not always.

The after-office wife

There is another phenomenon in our social and sexual relationships which involves married men and secretaries, but in a slightly different way, which must be mentioned to complete the picture. This relationship is between a single girl and a married man and takes place after office hours. It may involve a secretary but generally she is the secretary to someone else. This relationship has been called the *Cocktail-Lounge Model* by the two sociologists, Roebuck and Spray, who studied them for two years.[5] Secretaries make up 33 percent of the women involved in these semistable and semicommitted affairs.

The reason for labelling the relationship by the name given is because first contacts are made in a high-class cocktail lounge, although as the evening progresses the couple generally retires to the secretary's apartment. The authors found that the secretaries tended to remain in such relationships for approximately one or two years. They then "dropped out" to be married (or re-married) and others took their places. The men do not drop out but only change partners. During the two years of the study not a single marriage was reported disrupted by these affairs and they were characterized as "happy and successful." The authors concluded that there is a functional value to these relationships in that they enable women to postpone marriage until a proper mate is found, and they contend that it helps the men maintain marriages that might otherwise have been broken. The same reasoning might be applied to the functional utility of office wives.

Conclusion

The explanation of the phenomenon of the "office wife" is seen to involve both social and intrapsychic factors. One cannot account for the high incidence of such affairs without having reference to the urban economic organization which makes such relationships inevitable. They are the products of structured office interaction. On the other hand, one also has to include in the explanation the structure of the contemporary family, because its size and complexity raise significant questions about its facility in meeting profound emotional needs of the husband and wife. Where it does not meet those needs, individuals turn to other sources of gratification. But each marriage has a history, and we have seen that the tendency is toward alienation of roles and interests which truncates companionship and motivates again toward other relationships.

It is not possible to classify the intrapsychic motivations of the females who become involved in these intimacies because their needs are enormously varied and individualistic. This is likewise true for men, and some proof of this is seen in the fact that while we use the term "office wife" in a meaningful percentage of cases there is no sexual aspect to the relationship. Men, as well as women, have other needs beside sexual contact. It may well be that these other needs often are the basic ones which only later are expressed sexually. In any case, these relationships seem to be institutionalized in our society. How functional they are for marriage and the "home wife" we do not know and will not know until far more definitive research has taken place. At least some of our observers feel that they do contribute to the stability of the marriages of the participants.

References

1. Bergler, E.: The Revolt of the Middle-Aged Man (New York: Hill and Wang, 1957).
2. Blood, R. O., and Wolfe, D. M.: Husbands and Wives: The Dynamics of Married Living (New York: Free Press, 1960).
3. Cummings, G.: A Study of Marital Conflicts Involving an Affair by One of the Partners. Unpublished Master's Thesis. University of Southern California, Los Angeles, 1960.
4. Cuber, J. F., and Harroff, P. B.: The Significant Americans (New York: Appleton Meredith, 1965).
5. Roebuck, J., and Spray, S. L.: The cocktail lounge: A study of heterosexual relations in public organization. Amer. J. Sociol. 72:388, Jan. 1967.

Comment by:
Sylvia Clavan

It is possible that the role of "office wife" described by Dr. Peterson may soon become an anachronism. Two current social phenomena could change the occupational structure so that the relationship depicted would become less probable.

The first trend, and possibly the more important, is that of feminism in the U.S. today. As women strive for more equitable status in the work world, it is likely that their career pattern will change from partial to total commitment. With a higher level of education and gains in occupational opportunities, it may be expected that the role of secondary or peripheral worker will not be acceptable to young women entering the labor force in the decades ahead. Female liberationists have also been reevaluating the male-female relationship in all its social aspects, and have become increasingly aware of the subordinate position traditionally expected of them. This new consciousness plus higher aspirations for full participation in their career choice combine to inhibit overlap of the sex and work roles necessary to "office wife" status.

The second trend is purely statistical. The U.S. Department of Labor predicts that eight out of every ten women will eventually enter the labor market. A work force of about 100 million is anticipated for 1980 to produce needed goods and services. The number of women workers is expected to continue to increase faster than that of men workers in the years ahead.[1] An increase of women workers, including a significant number committed to realization of their potential through careers, suggests possible changes in occupational assignments. Put in another way, there may be a move away from characterizing certain jobs in sexual terms as being appropriate only for males or only for females. Sexually undesignated employment want-ads already reflect this move. Thus, distribution of secretarial jobs could conceivably be more evenly divided among men and women according to ability and interest, rather than ascribed by sex.

More crucial, perhaps, than the subservient occupational role suggested by "office wife" is the male-female relationship involved. It is not possible to predict what correlative changes may occur among men as women begin to compete with them in areas traditionally considered to be male. Jessie Bernard states, "For women, the revelant problems have to do with the implications of sexuality for equality; for men, with the implications of equality for sexuality." [2] Dr. Peterson suggests that in an "office wife" situation emotional dependence of one on the other is bound to occur. It is possible that as more women move toward self-realization, men, too, will become more aware of their own human attributes and have less need for an "office wife" relationship.

References
1. U.S. Department of Labor: Handbook on Women Workers. U.S. Government Printing Office, Washington, D.C., 1969.

2. Bernard, J.: The status of women in modern patterns of culture. The Annals 375:3, 1968.

Comment by:
Robert N. Whitehurst

Dr. Peterson has developed some perceptive insights into the relationship between modern marriage and the person who serves in another intimate capacity in the life of many men—the secretary. It may or may not be that men who develop sexual relationships with secretaries are unable "to maintain the balance in their lives necessary to derive deep rewards from their home lives." In fact, his later reference to the work of Roebuck and Spray seems to deny the notion that extramarital sex (at least of the upper-middle-class cocktail lounge variety) has much if anything to do with home life. Thus, one of the questions unanswered by this paper has to do with the conditions under which men seek relationships with secretaries as a result of deficiencies in their home lives. As I have suggested elsewhere, extramarital sex of this variety may simply reflect cultural values in this society which emphasize newness, achievement, and agressiveness to gain ends of "success."[1] Certainly, success with the ladies is one of our achievement values in America; this may or may not have anything at all to do with the problems a man has at home.

Among the most valuable insights of the paper are those portions pointing up how male and female lives tend to become disparate entities instead of convergent unities. This may be considered among the real "pulling" forces that allow men to rationalize extramarital sex with secretaries or anyone else who is available or willing. Whether men in fact find themselves "pushed" by other forces, i.e., willing secretaries, is another problem.

There is little doubt that one consideration not mentioned by Dr. Peterson is responsible for what might be considered a chief restraining factor in developing sex relations among secretaries and their employers: the potential alteration of the relationship basis. If secretaries were to indulge in sex with their employers, there is a possibility that the disruption of business might ensue. There is no special natural reason for this to occur, but it is probably true that the altered definitions of the situations (once a boss has engaged his secretary sexually) would very much influence and change their relationship. It is no doubt the intuitive sense of this threatened alteration that prevents secretaries and bosses alike from expressing their feelings more openly and sexually. Were it not for this fear of altered status and perceptions of the work roles they play toward each other, there would probably be a great deal more sex play among office workers. It is, in short, the fear of operating in a context that has few or no guidelines tied to this altered status that precludes very much sexual interaction with secretaries—not the lack of desire or opportunity. There is also the problem of fear of detection by one's peers (more so than one's wife), for perceptive fellow employees are prone to note even superficial changes in male-female interaction, and to recast the office definitions of who stands where in relation to power and access to the right people in the office.

Quite simply put, once a man yields to the temptation to become overtly sexual with his secretary, the ability to control her (and treat her as a bureaucratic entity among a pool of well-defined types in terms of status) is very much threatened. Even if she claims no altered status, the fear of alteration may be a difficult problem for the man once he recognizes his increased involvement. In some cases, it may be as Dr. Peterson suggests—that some men are disinclined to seek extramarital interpersonal satisfactions as they become deeply involved with work; some men cannot tolerate emotional closeness from anyone, wife or secretary. This may also be one of the reasons executives seek the cocktail lounge variety of sex because it is not emotionally demanding but is usually ephemeral, body-centered, and casual in its chief orientations. With a secretary, it is more difficult to carry off a casual affair. At any rate, Dr. Peterson opens up the exploration of the "wifely" nature of secretarial work; this is an instructive lead that could be followed by more intensive study.

Perhaps the concept of office wives "winning" or not winning is an unfortunate choice of terms, betraying our American competitive stance and showing our limited conceptual abilities to perceive relating in another light. Perhaps many secretaries do "win" something by way of appreciation and loyalty of bosses and even love (albeit many times unexpressed because of the supposed threat) in a good number of cases. If the rewards are seen as fulfilling and adequate for everyone concerned and no one is manipulated, exploited, or otherwise toyed with, perhaps we should become a bit more honest as to what it is we are about when we interact with meaningful people not our spouses.

One of the really serious faults in our marital system as now constructed (and this point is made indirectly in the Peterson discussion) is duplicity, make-believe, and downright fraud. No husband in his right mind would believe it the "right" thing to go home and tell his wife how much he loves his secretary. As pointed out in this paper, all evidence is that people working for long periods of time on intensive projects, such as a secretary and a boss, will tend to become emotionally close. Why not call it what it is—love? Because we presume we can love only one person and that to admit love for another would be tantamount to starting the wheels of divorce in motion. Thus, our cultural pattern encourages duplicity and dishonesty, and the worst form is when we fail to recognize in ourselves the feelings of love and respect for those near us in the interest of family solidarity.

Another question arises, then—not why secretaries accept such relationships, or what motivates men to get sexually involved with secretaries, but rather, why is our culture so much involved in estranging us from our sense of "self-and other" development? Why is society so bent on *preventing* intimate relationships? It presumably lies in the interest of family solidarity, but this kind of solidarity is built on a dishonest foundation. The question then becomes, can we alter the norms so we can become honest in our interpersonal relations and still not totally disrupt family life? Increasing numbers of younger people, who are no longer willing to live lives in the shadow of self-deceit and dishonesty with mates whose total respect and love they cherish, are willing to take the risk. There will be more honesty about these feelings and sometimes more openness about the things we call "affairs" with secretaries and other significant people we love. If the trend becomes widespread, perhaps there is hope for the establishment of a more humanized and humanistically developed people yet.

References:

1. Whitehurst, R. N.: Extramarital sex: alienation or extension of normal behavior; in Neubeck, G. (ed.): Extramarital Relations (New York: Prentice-Hall, 1969), p. 129.

Comment by:
John Scanzoni
Evidently the chief catalyst to the emergence of the "office wife" pattern is the lack of dialogue about his job between the husband and his actual wife. To put the problem in perspective, we would note that studies show that blue-collar workers have greater difficulty in communicating with their wives regarding their jobs (and indeed about most things, including sex) than do white-collar workers. And in spite of the fact that few of them have secretaries, it is likely that some blue-collar workers do develop attachments which might be the equivalent of the white-collar worker's "office wife," or especially the "cocktail lounge model."

What procedures might stimulate greater dialogue about the husband's job between husbands and wives, thus reducing the gulf existing in some marriages between the domestic and occupational worlds? There are at least two such routes, the first of which might be labeled "manipulating the situation." Following this route, husbands and wives make themselves (and their mates) keenly aware of the potential of the ever widening gulf that could emerge owing to the "separateness" of the husband's job. Once aware, they simply take every step necessary to bridge the gulf. From the husband's standpoint, attempts are made to share the hopes, feelings, problems, difficulties, frustrations, etc., connected with his job. From the wife's side, efforts are made *not* to allow household distractions to keep her from understanding and sharing, as thoroughly as possible, all the many implications of her husband's job.

But manipulation of the situation is necessarily limited so long as the wife and husband define their roles in life in traditionally disparate fashion. Therefore, a second route is "changing the situation," especially husband-wife roles. This is, of course, one of the major goals of what might be termed "responsible feminists." These are women (and men who support them) who believe that women ought to be less directed toward submerging themselves in domestic duties, and ought to be more interested in varied types of extra-familial self-fulfillment, especially occupational careers. This would mean fewer children to distract husband and wife from each other's own interests. It would also mean less attention to ephemeral "busy-work" around the house. It could result in a more interesting companion for the husband —someone who is his equal—not just a "servant-girl housewife."

This "solution" has its pitfalls, too, in that each person could get so wrapped up in a separate career that not only would "office wives" emerge but so would "office husbands." However, those persons interested in the "liberation" of both sexes from stifling life-patterns could be expected to be aware of such possibilities and to try to guard against them.

Whichever solution is preferred, both are predicated on the notion that an "office-job gulf" need not be unbridgeable. Creative and determined persons should be able, and should at least try, to bridge it.

Comment by:
Martin Goldberg
This excellent paper suffers from one glaring fault, in my opinion: it is subtly but definitely male-oriented and male-biased. The focus is chiefly on the businessman, his marriage, his unmet needs, etc., and scant attention is paid to the secretary.

Perhaps because of this, a misleading implication is given: that all or most office wives are unmarried. In fact, a great many of them are married women whose emotional and sexual involvement at work reflects needs that are unfulfilled in their own marriages. Among these may be the need for recognition as an individual, for acknowledgement of personal competence, and for admiration, as well as physical and emotional needs for affection and sexual attention.

Dr. Peterson has traced the course of the businessman's marriage, with its problems and gradual deterioration. One could equally well trace the course of the secretary's marriage, which is often marked by increasing alienation from her husband, increasingly divergent interests, sparse and distorted communication, and gradual diminution of sexual activity and affection. The secretary with such a marriage not infrequently finds, in her employer, a man who can view her afresh and respond to her with appreciation and acceptance.

Thus, for both the executive (or lawyer, doctor, dentist, etc.) and his secretary, the office involvement is but another reflection of the difficulties most people encounter in attempting to maintain satisfactory marriages in our society today. As a psychiatrist, I see people involved in office affairs, generally when the liaison has become an unhappy one or has further complicated a difficult marriage. However, I am certain there are many other instances in which the office wife actually helps to maintain her employer's marriage, and/or *the employer's attentions serve to make life and marriage bearable for the secretary.* In the final analysis, generalizations and deductions are misleading, and only the persons directly involved in this form of relationship can fully know all of its meanings and implications.

Comment by:
Rebecca Liswood
In my experience, I find the "office wife" all too often becomes the real wife, while the women who has been married to the businessman or professional man for 10, 15, 20 years or more is completely rejected.

In the wife's involvement with the children and the home, she frequently neglects her own appearance and most definitely neglects her husband. She does not make her home a peaceful, attractive place for her "tired" husband to return to. She is quick to criticize him, indicates a complete lack of respect for him, and gets into violent arguments with him, for he is no angel, either. She complains in a nagging manner about her many problems with the household chores and the children, and is definitely resentful of the role she is placed in as "maid-housekeeper" in contrast to his "exciting life" in the outside world.

He begins to compare the placid behavior of the charming, well-groomed, slim seccretary to the ill-tempered, sharp, shrill behavior of his ill-dressed wife. Repeatedly, he suddenly finds he has important "business meetings" to go to—and so begins to draw away from his wife and home.

Sexually, his wife has begun to belittle her husband as a lover, telling him he has never given her an orgasm—she "gets nothing" out of sex, so why should she bother!

This young, "attractive, quiet, docile" girl is the one he loves and can have fun with—she makes him feel young and vital. He comes to feel he must marry her. He must divorce his wife, leaving untold tragic situations for the wife, the children, and even for himself and his beautiful secretary.

When he gets the divorce, he finds himself economically handicapped. He has visitation rights with the children, which his present wife resents. She is no longer that glamorous or gracious or even docile person, and he finds he has not benefited at all. He has exchanged one set of problems for another. In addition, he is now worried that this younger wife might be involved with some younger man she knew before she married him. He now regrets his involvement and may seek a second divorce.

PART IV

New Marital
Life Styles

17. Swinging: The Search For An Alternative

DUANE DENFELD

Just a few years ago if someone were to ask what is a swinger, most everyone would reply "a person who lives it up, has a good time, likes to party" or maybe a type of camera or even a model of a car. Few knew of swinging as an organized form of comarital sexual relations. In a few years, however, the term swinging or the sexual exchange of partners between couples has become part of our everyday vocabulary. In becoming so the term has become unfortunately ambiguous and misleading. Much of the ambiguity results from making definitional boundaries—who are considered swingers.

Swinging has been defined by Ramey as:

> two or more pair-bonded couples who mutually decide to switch sexual partners or engage in group sex. Singles may be included either through temporary coupling with another individual specifically for the purpose of swinging or as part of a triadic or larger group sexual experience.

This definition unlike many definitions of swinging includes singles. Many researchers have protrayed swinging as a married couples scene, which it predominantly is, but singles are an important ingredient especially for triadic relationships. As Ramey asserts, "some couples find it easier to relate to one person than to two. Some find it easier to locate one person who is compatible with both than to find another couple in which both the male and the female are compatible with both husband and wife." Gilmartin has noted that singles need to be included in the definition and analysis of swinging; in fact a sizable proportion of the swinging couples in his study claimed that they actually met their present spouse at "swinging-singles" gatherings.

Empirical research on swinging has produced compatible findings. The lack of disparity is quite surprising among the various researchers. Symonds (1967); Bartell (1970); Bell (1971); and Smith and Smith (1970) as well as other researchers found swingers to be generally middle-class couples who engage in typical middle-class political, domestic, and occupational behaviors. Their only deviance is in the area of sexual exchange of partners. The most remarkable feature to the social scientists studying the phenomenon has been the maintenance of highly conventional life styles by swingers except in the sexual area. Swingers "are not rebellious youth who have substituted a new value system, but rather people who grew up in the 1940s and 1950s, were exposed to the values of the time which included the importance of sexual fidelity and guilt following sexual infidelity." (Denfeld, 1974)

Where disparity of findings between researchers have emerged they are usually resolved by the use of typologies of swinging. This is to say that there are different types of swingers and each type is somewhat unique. Membership in the categories is not fixed. An individual who today might be classified as one type might be another tomorrow.

Carolyn Symonds in one typology divides swingers into two groups, "recreational" and "utopian." The recreational swinger is someone who uses swinging as a form of recreation or play; this person does not want to change the social order or to fight the establishment. Recreational swingers accept the current social order and are defenders of the status quo. The second group, utopian swingers, desire to build a new order through swinging. Swinging, for the Utopian, is part of a new life style that emphasizes communal living.

Another typology has been formulated by Varni. He found five types using degree of emotional involvement as the organizing criterion. "Generally speaking, movement along the continuum from 'hard-core' to 'communal' involves going from unstable to very stable group or couple affiliation . . ."

Varni's five types include:
Hard-core are swingers who want no emotional involvement and swing as often and with as many couples as possible.

Egotistical swingers want little emotional involvement, they swing to gratify their own needs and desires.

Recreational swingers view and use swinging as a form of play. Swinging for this group is entertainment.

Interpersonal swingers seek close emotional relationships with their partners. Swinging for them implies emotional as well as sexual exchange.

Communal swingers are similar to interpersonal except they propose group marriage as a new life style.

These two typologies and other typologies such as by Paulson and Paulson and Denfeld emphasize emotional aspects, and whether swinging is a recreational or also a political act.

A comparison of two studies suggests the influence of sampling techniques and the role of types in the description of swingers. Bartell's sample of 280 swingers appear to be drawn from the nonemotional end of Varni's continuum. Bartell describes swingers in his sample as people who even though they "think of themselves as liberated sexually, they are terrified of the idea that involvement might take place."

Varni on the other hand in the study from which his typology was developed found 12 of 32 swingers to be at the emotional rather than nonemotional end of the continuum. He did not find any hard core (nonemotional) swingers. The Paulsons similarly found their swingers to want emotional involvement. The nature of the subject matter has meant that researchers have had to use nonprobability samples and these were often organized groups of swingers with similar interests and attitudes. Groups tend to develop into populations of people who have shared norms and standards. Therefore the type of group that a researcher has access to will determine the type of swingers in his or her sample.

Theories and models of swinging

The remarkable lack of disparity in empirical research findings has not lead to a similar state with respect to theories or models of swinging. The main issues that the attempts at model or theory building have focused on are the source and ideologies of swingers. Models have been generated to account for the middle-class as a source for the swinging population and why the behavior becomes a "secret" exception to the straight life styles of the swingers. It should be pointed out that some communal or utopian swingers have an interest in not being secret swingers but obtain publicity for the new life style they advocate. However, the number of vocal swingers appears small compared to the other types.

The early theories of comarital sexual relationships fell within the general theoretical area of deviant behavior. One of the theories formulated by Denfeld and Gordon adopted the functional perspective of Davis and account for the existence of swinging within the monogamous family structure on the basis that such behavior is functionally integrated within the social system. Denfeld and Gordon assert that changes in role definitions for females along with changes in contraceptive techniques available to the female have set the stage for a sexual behavior pattern that relieves sexual monotony without undermining the marriage. Swinging revitalizes marriage but is not threatening when the participants follow certain rules. Among the rules that protect the monogamous or marital relationship are:

1. "Consensual adultery": the perception that sex is limited to the marital bond. Swingers have developed rules that serve to define the sexual relationship of marriage as one of love, of emotion. Some of the Smiths' respondents would answer "no" to questions pertaining to "extra-marital sexual experience," but would answer "yes" to questions pertaining to "mate-sharing or comarital relations" (J. and L. Smith, 1969). Sharing, for the swingers, means that the marriage partners are not "cheating." Swingers believe that the damaging aspect in extramarital sex is the lying and cheating, and if this is removed extramarital sex is beneficial to the marital bond. In other words, "those who swing together stay together." Swingers establish rules such as not allowing one of a couple to attend a group meeting without the other. Unmarried couples are kept out of some groups, because they "have less regard for the marital responsibilities" (W. and J. Breedlove, 1964). Guests who fail to conform to rules are asked "to leave a party when their behavior is not appropriate."

2. Swinging and Children. Swingers protect paternity by dropping out of swinging while the wife gets pregnant. The couple is assured that the husband is the father.

3. Discretion is the word among swingers. Swinging activities are kept secret from the "square" world. This secrecy assures maintenance of the couple's respectability in a given community.

4. Jealousy is reduced by giving the marriage complete loyalty, being open and honest with one's partner.

Walshok argues that the functionalist approach of Denfeld and Gordon "contributes less to our understanding of the etiology of this form of behavior than to an understanding of the maintenance and functional integration of a deviant commitment with a conventional life-style. Suggestive for an understanding of the etiology of comarital commitments is the concept of marginality and its consequences for the development of unconventional or nonconformist behavioral and attitudinal orientations."

Walshok suggests that swinging may be a result of the "marginal status" of individuals new to the middle-class, "which makes them more responsive to intense forms of experience." These individuals are susceptible to pressures to make contact with others to share a common experience, and swinging is one such experience.

Two more recent theories draw upon other theoretical frameworks. Ruppel analyzes comarital sex within the framework of the theory of anomie. He suggests that a shared cultural norm in North American society is that sex should be enjoyable and exciting for both partners. The monogamous marriage is the major institutionalized mechanism for achieving this goal. There are strains in terms of this goal and the means to achieve it and these strains encourage adaptation. One form of adaptation is innovation and comarital sex is one form of innovative response to strain in the marital system.

An attempt to test a set of propositions has been made by Gilmartin in a recent study. The study included one hundred swinging couples and one hundred nonswinging couples as a control group. Gilmartin suggested that the more tenuous or unsatisfied the ties to kin the more likely persons are to engage in and enjoy deviant behavior. On the basis of this "networks" theoretical framework Gilmartin derived three hypotheses: Relations with parents during the formative years were significantly less happy and emotionally gratifying for the swingers than they were for controls. Swingers interact with relatives and kin (other than spouse and children) significantly less frequently than do controls. Swingers view relatives and kin as being of significantly less importance to their personal life than do controls.

Swingers were found to come from less happy backgrounds, to have less kin contact, and, importantly, their parents failed to inspire the internalization of traditional norms and values which normally occurs in families.

Extent of swinging

All estimates of the extent of various non-normative sexual behavior must be considered rough. How one defines the behavior, for example, influences the estimate—this has been especially true with regard to estimates of the homosexual population. With respect to swinging, a similar definitional problem arises—are swingers anyone who has ever consensually exchanged partners, or those who do so with some sort of regularity?

There are two available estimates of the number of swinging couples. The Breedloves developed an estimate based upon a sample of 407 couples. They discovered that less than four percent of their sample had placed or replied to advertisements in swinging publications in a given year. In that year "almost 70,000 couples either replied to, or placed ads as swinging couples." They concluded, therefore, that two and one half million couples exchange partners on a somewhat regular basis (three or more times a year). Apart from criticisms that could be levelled at the Breedloves' sample representativeness, later studies challenge the four percent advertising and response figure. Bartell (1970) found that nearly all his sample of 280 swingers used the swinging publications.

Another problem with the Breedloves' formula is that the 70,000 total cited by them overstates the number of advertising or replying couples. Couples tend (according to the editor of a swingers' publication) to advertise in an average of 2.5 magazines and to reply to more than one ad. A figure of 70,000 ads and replies means far fewer actual swingers.

A more refined estimate was obtained by Spanier and Cole. They conducted their research "in a midwestern community of about 40,000 which included a university, its students, faculty and staff, light industry, and a large number of state employees." With the aid of the university statistical laboratory, a sample was carefully drawn. "A total of 500 households was selected, producing a theoretical maximum of 1,000 married people. A household was contacted a minimum of three times, and eliminated from the sample if no one was home on all occasions." A final response rate of 73% was obtained. In response to the question: "Have you or your spouse ever engaged in wife-swapping?" 10 respondents or 1.7% of the total sample indicated that they had participated on at least one occasion. If the percentages found in this midwestern city are representative of the nation, a nationwide estimate of 725,000-750,000 is in order. The two estimates differ dramatically—from a low of 725,000 to a high of two and one half million couples.

Discovery and origin

The origin of organized swinging (sexual exchange in groups) seems lost to history. William and Jerrye Breedlove in one of the early descriptions of swinging argue that in 1953 "the number of swap club members" was probably less than 2 percent of the married couples between the ages of 20 and 45 years. As indicated above, the Breed-loves' estimates of swingers may overstate the numbers but the date is worth noting. Other observers of the swinging scene when making reference to the origin of organized swinging refer to the early or mid 1950s. Evidence of organized swinging is the swingers' contact magazines. The first of these was La Plume which was established about 1955. It boasted for years that it was the first swingers magazine. During this period swingers also started to advertise in weekly na-tional tabloids. The best guess therefore as to origin or organized swinging is circa 1955.

Better guesses can be offered with respect to the discovery (and it may be as Oscar Wilde argues that nature imitates art) of swinging. Widespread coverage and knowledge of the swinging movement fol-lowed a 1957 article in *MR* magazine (a men's magazine). *MR* subsequently introduced a regular feature column of letters from mate-swapping readers. Each year since 1957 has witnessed greater coverage of comarital sex by the press. The role of coverage of the swinging scene in creating it is unknown.

Organization

Since most swingers are committed to a conventional life style they by necessity keep their swinging secret. They must then develop strategies, though not necessarily elaborate ones, that prevent their commitment to a conventional life style from being compromised. Swingers are thus faced with a rather interesting locating problem. How to contact couples with similar inclinations without running the danger of public exposure. Strategies have been developed by swin-gers and entrepreneurs to facilitate locating other swingers and at the same time minimizing the risks involved.

There are a number of strategies used by swingers in their locating activity. Bartell, based on his study of swingers, lists:

> four principle ways to acquire partners for sexual exchange. The first method is to place an advertisement in one of the swingers' publications. . . . The second method . . . is to visit a bar or club, set up exclusively for swingers. The third way of meeting couples is by personal reference from other swinging couples . . . The fourth choice . . . is personal recruitment. The advertisement method was almost universally used by our informants.

The swinging contact magazine because of its popularity among couples is of primary importance in the understanding of the locating strategies. In 1974 there were approximately one dozen contact publications that came out on a regular basis. These varied from mimeographed three page editions to glossy magazines.

Select stands apart from most contact publications in terms of its high quality printing and size. Issue No. 42 (1974) was 248 pages in length with over 6,000 ads in magazine format. A centerfold featuring a swinging couple gave the reader a break from the nearly 3,000 ads that precede it. The centerfold in this issue featured a southern Texas couple, or more accurately Laurie, the wife of the couple. Laurie adorned the centerfold and all the other photos except three photos in which Jerry is given what must be called a secondary place. The centerfold couple's coded number is provided so that interested couples could write them.

Select and the other swinging publications use a code system to insure secrecy. Replies to ads must be sent to the magazine and then forwarded to the advertiser for a fee of $1.00 per letter paid by the persons responding. Ads in *Select* are 10c per word per issue but new subscribers may place their personal ad free in one issue. This one-time rule is not consistently followed—advertisers often get a number of free placements. Photos with ads are free for women and couples but $5.00 for men.

Here are some representative examples of swingers ads:

Experienced young couple enjoy all adult fun & games . . . Have color home movies. Long lasting, gentle, considerate & good company. No weirdos please. Answer all letters immediately.

Attractive couple seek attractive females for 3somes, handsome couples to age 40 for adult fun . . . Photo requested and assures immediate reply.

Fun-loving couple wants to meet gals, couples, 21-40. We aren't interested in lengthy correspondence, but want meetings. We like photography, nudism, adult games.

Two really fun-loving people are we. She AC/DC. He just plain good. Both in our late 20s. All ads answered. Photo on request.

Swinging contact magazines include more than just advertisements. Many provide the reader with sexual advice columns, articles, letters from swingers, and news on the swinging scene.

An analysis of 2193 ads from three swinging publications demonstrate some of the types of persons (Table 1) or sexual encounters (Table 2) sought and characteristics of the advertisers (Table 3).

Swinging publications serve an important screening service. Advertising couples can set restrictions around whom should respond. The advertisers specify what their socio-sexual interests are

TABLE 1

Types of persons sought by advertisers

Other couple	1794
Female	1497
Female only	265
Males	970
White only	195
Blacks only	13
No racial barrier	197

TABLE 2

Sexual interests of advertisers[1]

B&D	
Yes	135
No	680
French	871
Greek	142
AC/DC	
Husband	223
Wife	399
Voyeur	44

[1] B&D refers to bondage (restraint) and discipline (i.e., flagellation). Other common terms are: French culture (Cunnilingus and fellatio), Greek (anal intercourse), AC-DC (bisexual), TV (transvestite).

TABLE 3

Physical characteristics of advertisers

Age stated	
Husband	1754
Wife	2086
"Well built"	
Husband	131
Wife	947

—enquirers with incompatible tastes need not apply. This delineation reduces unnecessary letter writing. Disappointment may arise, however, when products are falsely advertised. Couples may in their ad engage in claims that would have caused consternation among FTC lawyers if the advertisers were business firms. Couples frequently shave a few years off their age, a few pounds off their weight, a few inches off the waist, and add them to the bust of the woman or to the penis of the male. The inclusion of a photograph reduces, but does not erase, the chance of false advertising.

Swinging publications are effective in terms of secretly advertising for other partners but have one serious disadvantage. The time from placing an ad till results start coming in may be as long as six months. Delays in publication, time for mailing magazine, and then letter writing and forwarding make this a relatively slow locating technique.

Greater speed and efficiency in meeting other swingers has been accomplished through the development of swingers bars, socials and special events. There are about thirty bars that cater exclusively, at least one night a week, to swingers. Cities with bars that serve to bring together swingers include, Boston, New York City, Chicago, Miami, Kansas City, Mo., Westbury, L.I., New York and Vineland, New Jersey. Such bars provide the swinger with readily accessible contacts and a chance to directly see and converse with the other couple. Couples can meet other couples at these bars or just sit and talk about common interests or of previous good times. This social aspect of the swingers bar is very important, the bar provides not only contacts but is a place of social support and a community in which the swinger can be relatively free and open. It is very similar in function to the gay bar.

Swingers bars make very clear their purpose; to quote from a mailed advertisement of Noah's Ark of Boston:

"Noah's Ark is a swinging night club for couples only . . . to meet couples sharing similar interests."

Admission fee to Noah's Ark is $6.00 per couple or $35.00 for a three month membership. Swingers are offered for that fee, "admission, dancing, continuous free hot buffet, door prizes, and the pleasurable company of many swinging couples."

The swinging bar is careful to be sure that each couple that enters (only couples and single women allowed) knows that it is a swinging bar and once inside the hosts see to it that each couple meets other couples. Sexual exchanging does not take place in the bar but contact is made and parties often follow the closing hours of the bar.

Not all cities can financially support a swinging bar so for these areas the organized social is a way to find other swingers. Socials are one night affairs that offer for a $25.00 fee an evening of drinking, dancing, and socializing. Over a four week period of 1974 socials were held in the following cities: Meriden, Conn.; Cleveland, Ohio; Baltimore, Md.; Philadelphia, Pa. and Cincinnati, Ohio.

Swingers can also use exclusive swinging events such as cruises, or weekends at resorts, to find other swingers. One swinging resort that received national attention was the Sandstone retreat which has since been closed. E. Kronhausen (1973) described it for Playboy readers as "a sexual paradise . . . geographically ideal on a 15 acre site . . . overlooking the Pacific . . . beautiful grounds. A main house with teakwood floors and walls. A huge Oympic-sized indoor swimming pool." On weekends two to three hundred members would show up for sex and social exchange.

Probably the largest swinging get together was the National Swinging Convention for which Chicago was the three day host in August 1970.

> "The three exciting days of activities" included a get-acquainted dance, a bus tour of Chicago, a lingerie style show, hospitality rooms with unusual items on display, and the major event, a luau and grand ball. The convention was oversubscribed and couples had to be put up in Chicago area homes. (Denfeld, 1972)

The least popular method of finding other swingers is through couple to couple seduction (Bartell, 1971). This approach has dangers, for while another couple may talk about and be interested in mate swapping, when confronted with the opportunity to realize their fantasies become shocked and upset. The seductive couple may consequently be exposed or at least lose the couple as friends. The other locating schemes avoid this risky approach.

Swinging failures

A review of the literature on swinging suggests that swinging has positive contributions for the participants' marriages. This finding is surprising, considering the observation that swingers are likely drawn from middle-class populations in which there prevail norms of sexual fidelity and guilt following violation of these norms. This optimistic view of swinging may be partially a result of sample bias.

The secrecy involved in swinging makes it difficult if not impossible to gather representative samples. Researchers were forced to obtain their samples through contacts in or participation in swinging groups. Their final samples were frequently "snow-ball"—that is, one couple suggested for the study another couple and so on until the collection was large enough to meaningfully describe the behavior. This type of sample collection had the effect of excluding swingers who were failures at swinging. The swingers available for research were the successful ones.

Denfeld (1974) in an attempt to learn about the swinging dropouts contacted marriage counselors and asked if they had counseled swinging dropouts. Questionnaires were mailed to 2,147 marriage counselors listed in the directories of the American Association of Marriage and Family Counselors and the California Association of Marriage and Family Counselors—966 (45%) were returned.

Over fifty percent of the counselors had counseled at least one dropout couple. The total number of dropout couples was 1175—all of the dropout couples reported swinging related problems. It has been estimated that there are 50,000-75,000 persons (mental health offices, psychiatrists, general practitioners) counseling married couples. Extrapolating from the figures of the study of dropouts, a conservative estimate of swinging dropout couples is 75,000. One must also note that many dropouts with need of counseling do not show up at counseling offices.

The most common difficulties cited by the dropout couples are listed by order of frequency in Table 4.

TABLE 4

Reasons for Dropping out of Swinging

Problems
Jealousy
Guilt
Threatening marriage
Development of emotional attachment with other partners
Boredom/loss of interest
Disappointment
Divorce or separation
Wife's inability to "take it"
Fear of discovery
Impotence of husband

The problems listed suggest that for these couples at least the rules of swinging that serve to neutralize old values were not effective. Swinging dropouts were unable to avoid jealousy or guilt. The counselors responded that for these couples "the husband (or wife) could not handle the jealousy arising out of his (or her) mate having sex with another person." Husbands in greater frequency indicated jealous reactions.

> A number of husbands became quite concerned about their wives' popularity, their sexual performance (for example, endurance capabilities), or that their wives were having more fun than they were. When wives reported jealousy it was more likely related to fear of losing their mate. These findings suggest the influence of the double standard; the emphasis for the husband is on his pleasure and satisfaction as compared to his wife's pleasure and satisfaction, whereas the emphasis for the wife is on the mainte-nance of the marital unit. (Denfeld, 1974).

The remaining problems further demonstrate the failure of the swinging rules or maybe the failure of dropout couples to utilize them. Dropout couples replied that swinging weakened rather than rein-forced the marriage, that they became bored not excited by swinging, lost interest, and in a few cases the husband became impotent.

Wives more frequently initiated the dropping out, 54% compared to the husbands 34% and mutual decisions 12%. This evidence further questions earlier findings that swinging emphasizes sexual equality (Denfeld and Gordon) and that the wife often comes to enjoy swinging more than husbands. Henshel (1973) found that wives were less likely the initiators of swinging, Denfeld (1974) that wives were the most troubled by it, and the most likely partner to initiate dropping out.

The findings of the dropouts study do not allow us to reject the optimistic view of swinging. They do, however, raise some questions about the degree of positive outcomes and also document some of the problems associated with the consensual exchange of marriage part-ners. The problems of swinging have received little attention because successful swingers were more likely to be included in the various studies. Another possible explanation for the very positive portrayal of swinging may be that many swinging researchers are in fact "swin-gers" who, wittingly or unwittingly, play the role of advocate with a sometimes missionary zeal. (Denfeld, 1974).

Swinging, regardless of its success or failure, represents an effort at marital emancipation. The cultural ideology of monogamy and sexual values in North American society make difficult any attempts at sexual liberation. The continuing high rates of monogamous marriage failure will generate alternative patterns.

References

Bartell, G.D., 1970 "Group Sex Among Mid-Americans", Journal of Sex Research 6, no. 2, 113-130.

Bartell, G.D., 1971, Group Sex: A Scientist's Eyewitness Report on the American Way of Swinging. New York: Peter H. Wyden.

Bell, Robert, 1971, "Swinging—The Sexual Exchange of Married Persons" Sexual Behavior, May, 70-79.

Breedlove, William and Breedlove, Jerrye, 1964, Swap Clubs. Los Angeles: Sherbourne Press.

Denfeld, D. and Gordon, Michael "Sociology of Mate Swapping" Journal of Sex Research, 6, no. 2, pp. 85-100.

Denfeld, D. 1971 "Towards a Typology of Swinging" paper presented at Groves Conference, San Juan, Puerto Rico.

Denfeld, D., 1972, "How to Find a Swinger" Sexual Behavior. April.

Denfeld, D. 1974, "Dropouts From Swinging" Family Coordinator, Jan.

Gilmartin, Brian, 1974 "Sexual Deviance and Social Networks: A Study of Social Family, and Marital Interaction Patterns Among Co-Marital Sex Participants" in Smith, J.R. and Smith, Lynn, Beyond Monogamy, Baltimore: John Hopkins press.

Henshel, Anne-Marie, 1973 "Swinging: A Study of Decision Making in Marriage" American Journal of Sociology, Jan., 78-4, pp. 885-891.

Kronhausen, E. 1973, "Interview" Sept. Playboy.

Paulson, Charles and Paulson, Rebecca, 1972 "Swinging in Wedlock" Society, Vol. 9, no. 4, Feb., pp. 28-37.

Ramey, James W., 1974 "Emerging Patterns of Innovative Behavior in Marriage" in Smith, J. and Smith, L. Beyond Monogamy.

Ruppel, Howard, Jr., 1972 "A Theoretical Analysis of Co-Marital Sex" paper presented at meetings of the Midwestern Sociological Society, Kansas City, Mo., April.

Spanier, Graham and Cole, Charles, 1972 "Mate Swapping: Participation, Knowledge, and Values In a Midwestern Community" paper presented at meetings of the Midwestern Sociological Society, Kansas City, Mo., April.

Smith, James R. and Smith, Lynn G., 1970 "Co-Marital Sex and the Sexual Freedom Movement" Journal of Sex Research, 6, no. 2, pp. 131-142.

Symonds, Carolyn 1967, "Pilot Study of the Peripheral Behavior of Sexual Mate Swappers" Masters Thesis, University of California; Riverside.

Varni, Charles A., 1974, "An Exploratory Study of Spouse Swapping" in Smith and Smith Beyond Monogamy.

Walshok, Mary Lindenstein, 1971 "The Emergence of Middle-Class Deviant Subcultures: The Case of Swingers", Social Problems 18:4, pp. 488-495.

18. Can Group Marriage Work?

REESE DANLEY KILGO

Is group marriage an alternative to the existing family structure? This is a question of interest to increasing numbers of young people who are frustrated by what they see as the limitations of traditional one-to-one male-female relationships. Many of them see the traditional family as leading to monotony, to restrictiveness and possessiveness—even to sexual starvation and the demise of romantic love. Group marriage, these people feel, logically offers greater security (both material and psychological), wider sexual variety, greater potential for personal growth and individualism, the benefit to children of having more than two parents to love and care for them, and a broader economic base from which to operate a household.

As a marriage counselor and professor of Marriage and Family sociology courses, I have had contact with a few group marriages, usually on a counseling basis. I am also familiar with most of the literature on the subject—including such ingroup publications as *The Modern Utopian, The Harrad Newsletter,* and the reports of the Sexual Freedom League. From all this, I have been able to reach a number of conclusions about group marriages and just how much potential for success they really have. My prognosis? I am afraid it is not very optimistic.

The group marriage in its present form is a part of the so-called counterculture, the youthful rebellion against the "Establishment." It usually consists of a relatively small number of people, ideally equally balanced as to sexes, living together on a communal basis, sharing

231

work, money, home, children, love, and sexual intimacy. The United States and the Scandinavian nations are probably the leaders in this type of experimental activity, but there are reports of group marriage cropping in other countries as well, mainly in Europe.

Most (but not all) group marriages are comprised of young idealists. Usually the groups survive no more than a few years, and most have had a rather fluctuating membership, with some persons staying from only a few weeks to a few months. The more enduring communal "family" groups, whether or not they have practiced group marriage in the stricter sense, have generally had one or two very strong leaders, male or female, dedicated to the idea and willing to work for its continuation.

Most of the couples interested in group marriages are drawn to the idea from their enthusiasm and interest in all kinds of utopian schemes, their liberal or radical ideas of "alternatives" to contemporary social problems, and their disenchantment with monogamous marriage as they have experienced it.

But one couple I knew became interested in it because of a really close and loving relationship which they developed with another couple. The last I heard from them, however, the arrangement had failed. Now the wife in the first couple wants a divorce, claiming she never did love her husband. Although they had no history of marital discord prior to the group relationship, its failure prompted a disillusionment with marriage in general.

Another couple whom I know personally were motivated to enter a group marriage because they truly believed it to be a more satisfying arrangement than monogamy. They tried three-way households (once with an extra husband, and twice with additional wives) but none lasted. The extra people always left, although all remained friends. However, this couple is now having problems, and recently the wife almost decided to leave. She feels her husband imposes on her as far as housework and the care and attention of their two-year-old baby are concerned. I have worked with them on a more equitable division of household tasks and child care, and they seem happier about the marriage at the moment; but the future is still in doubt.

Group marriage, in many cases, evolves out of a good experience with "swinging." Couples who have engaged in this mate-swapping practice, or have otherwise had free-wheeling extramarital sexual experiences, tend to make these arrangements more permanent by joining together in a group marriage. Dub Blackwood, originator and leader of *Harrad West*, a long-lived and open group marriage in Berkeley, definitely recommends swinging before entering a group marriage.

People attracted to the group marriage concept usually begin encountering difficulties right from the beginning. One of the first problems, as one might imagine, is finding compatible persons who will go along with the idea. Most group marriages are begun by couples already married to each other, and it is naturally difficult to find another couple of whom both members are equally attractive to the original couple. But even when another interested couple or single person is found, there are difficulties of courtship and dating. A great degree of openness and honest expression of feeling is necessary in establishing and maintaining such a multilateral relationship. Where there are children involved, this increases the complexity of the relationships still further.

But suppose a group finally does get together? What problem then looms largest? Most people will immediately see the love-and-sex area as being the most difficult to work out satisfactorily, because of the human tendency toward jealousy and possessiveness. But strangely enough, this is not true. The reason is probably the extremely liberal attitudes toward sex held by the participants: sexual fidelity simply is not valued as it is in monogamous marriages. In fact, it is usually looked at as something to be overcome.

Sex relations are dealt with in varying ways. Some groups structure the process tightly, with a rotating system of who sleeps with whom. Others try to maintain some spontaneity and free choice. But regardless of the sex-style used—and many groups experiment with various styles, including "group sex" of the orgy type—the same sex problems occur among group marriages as crop up among the population at large—impotence, inadequate sexual response, inhibitions, etc.

Still, as I said, it is not within the area of sexual adjustment that the most discord seems to be generated. It has been my observation that most of the stress arises from the delegation of responsibilities, both within and without the home. Whose turn is it to clean the living room this week? Joe and Mary always leave dirty coffee cups in the sink. You were supposed to do the grocery shopping yesterday. Somebody used the desk and typewriter, and now I can't find my paper. One sociologist calls these the "tremendous trifles" of family living. And it is on such trifles that group marriages usually flounder.

Listen to the way one girl described it in *The Harrad Newsletter:*

"We lived in the city, so all of the men worked and some of the women did as well. There were three of us who stayed at home.

Everything went along for a while, until it became clear that Jill, Sarah, and I did all of the dinner cooking and cooked for each other during the day. None of the men ever did the dishes alone, and whenever the dishes were left it was—right!—Jill, or Sarah, or me who did them. We helped each other on things that seemed to get left, too, like straightening up and dusting. It wasn't much, and we thought a little talk would straighten things out. But it didn't. . . Finally we decided to see if the self-selection method would work. Unilaterally we stopped doing the things that were left. When the stink grew too awful to ignore, a couple of the men tackled part of it and called a group meeting to which all ten of us were invited. Now that it wasn't just three women bitching, it was a big deal. Everybody had to get everything 'up front.'

"We worked out our hassle, but it took abandoning the whole non-system thing. And if the place had ever had the chance of being more than a mixed dormitory, it was gone now. Our couple pairings reasserted themselves some, but they couldn't completely because some of us began to see that the Movement women were right. None of us had gotten into the Women's Liberation thing before, but now a few started to go to meetings. Funny thing, the first to go was Jill, and then me, and then Sarah."

Another problem that tears group marriages apart is financial affairs. By that I mean money management, not lack of money. In deciding on how to budget for various items such as clothing, personal spending money, and recreation, the more persons involved the more difficult it is to come to a satisfying arrangement. To try to be fair to all, to consider everyone's wishes and values, yet to keep the out-voted minority from feeling persecuted and ill-treated—these are the important issues. The cohesiveness of the group is dependent upon these issues being worked out satisfactorily. (Many groups attempt to sidestep this problem of money management by having each member remain relatively financially independent—but this destroys the group's cohesiveness.)

In the area of in-laws and friends, and in the area of children, there is a factor involved in group marriages not present in the traditional monogamous marriage. This is the factor of social unacceptability. Persons in group marriages usually live in a state of open rebellion against society in general and their parents in particular, causing either conflict or estrangement; or else they don't let others know of their unorthodox marital arrangements, which brings about problems caused by deception. From the children's viewpoint, if the child is of pre-school age the arrangement seems easily accepted and even enjoyed. But what of the older child who realizes the social disapproval he will encounter if his teachers or friends find out how his parents are living?

One case I know of serves as a pretty good illustration:

There were two couples involved. Each couple had three children—ages 3, 5, and 9 in one family, and ages 7, 9, and 16 in the other. They stayed together about five months, during which the younger children seemed very happy about the whole situation, probably not fully aware of what group marriage meant. But the teenager was resentful from the beginning. She resented the other family's "moving in," and she resented the "oddness" of her home life compared with that of her friends. Twice she ran away. She became depressed, repeatedly threatened suicide. It was mainly because of this child's problems that the "family" finally broke up, disillusioned and distrustful of their former "utopian ideas."

Still another problem present in group marriages not found in the one-to-one relationship of monogamy is that of "sensory overload," indicative of the intensity generated by the multiple emotional involvement. One group marriage participant described it as being "a marathon encounter group, but on a continuous basis." Periodic withdrawal into solitude and privacy may be necessary for emotional survival in such a situation. But this need itself presents some operational problems, such as who can have the privacy when, where one might go, and the arrangements necessary to carry out the plans.

Personal jealousies are certainly another strain in group marriages. Although many people claim to be "capable of loving more than one person," there seems to be a basic human need to be first with one other person—to feel that one is "truly loved best." Once this individualized feeling is removed it is very difficult for it to be replaced satisfactorily by a shared sense of cohesiveness or affection.

The entire idea of group marriage raises strong feelings among all who hear of it, contemplate it, attempt it, or study it. In most of the articles I have read—those by social scientists as well as those by popular journalists—one can usually detect a bias either "in favor of" or "definitely against." My personal feelings are that it is a fascinating social-psychological phenomenon to study; but as a marriage counselor I feel the problems encountered in group marriages are probably too great for most people to overcome. The more parties involved in a family, the more problems there are to cope with. Monogamous marriages usually suffer when the partners become disenchanted with each other's various quirks, eccentricities, and emotional demands. Imagine mutliplying all those annoyances by three, or even by five!

Perhaps the most accurate prediction for the future of group marriages was that quoted in *The Modern Utopian*, Communes, U.S.A.," by Dick Fairchild. The quote comes from a young man named Jim currently in the throes of trying to work out a group marriage:

"Considering how difficult this group living is, I think we are doing well. . . But I am beginning to think that a 90 to 95 percent failure rate for group marriages and a 50 to 75 percent turnover rate (per year) for communities might not be unrealistic."

He goes on to say that he still thinks this is better than what he imagines monogamous marriage would be like. But if stability is any criterion, it is pretty hard to agree with him.

Comment by:
Bob Rimmer
It amuses me that Dr. Kilgo is uncertain about the future of group marriage. Since the publication of my novel, *The Harrad Experiment* in 1967 and *Proposition 31* in 1968, I have received hundreds of letters from couples experimenting with various forms of group living from communes to two or three couple economic arrangements. Many of these letters come from the younger faculty members now teaching in various colleges and universities throughout the country and they tend to bear out my belief that emotionally sound group marriages can be a viable and life-expanding way of living. Interestingly, the experiments that are succeeding have three things in common. They are involvements of couples with a high educational level (hence the younger faculty interest). They are between couples who have been married five years or more and communicate reasonably well in their monogamous lives, and they avoid any publicity whatsoever of their group marital life. In fact, the general feelings about group marriage (in Dr. Kilgo's words, it "raises strong feelings among all who hear it, contemplate it, attempt it or study it") means that if an average suburban couple openly admit that they are sexually involved with another couple, they may well be creating a threat to their own economic existence. I know of at least five successful group relationships (they are going strong after three years) and any of them would think the idea of "being studied" or exposing themselves to marriage counselors would be the height of stupidity.

My feeling, reinforced by thousands of letters I have received, is that the true statistics of what is happening in alternate marriage forms (including very popular and long-lasting bigamous relationships) will never be revealed until society provides either a social or legal structure that condones group relationships. For example, if a Harrad-type undergraduate living arrangement was openly advocated by faculty members like Dr. Kilgo, and some university or college would offer such a structured form of premarital living, there would be absolutely no problem in obtaining the undergraduate enrollment. Thousands of youngsters and their parents would openly embrace a premarital exposure that ultimately would create a new style of young people who could easily handle the emotional and interpersonal relationships involved in the new kind of family life styles (including group marriages) that are inevitable in this society.

Many sociologists view the ferment in monogamous marriage styles from too narrow a perspective. My feeling is that the following peripheral forces now shaping the society will make structured group marriages a common experience in the next fifty years.

First, more than half the wives in families with incomes of $10,000 or more are working wives, and this percentage will increase rapidly. The female is not working only because of her own needs for self-determination. She is working because, economically, she has to, if her family is to enjoy a few of the materialistic joys in a society where real income will continue to lag far behind the inflationary forces of huge population.

Second, the process of working creates a new liberated female who is often contributing as much financially to a household as the male. This outgoing female inevitably will demand the joy of larger intimacies with members of the opposite sex, both as her natural right and her awareness that the one mate she is married to is no longer the unquestioned patriarch, but hopefully is a good friend. Men and women need intimate interaction with more than one other male or female if they are to grow continually and intellectually. Thousands of females are already demanding monogamous marriages that give them wider latitude without destroying the structure of their marriages.

Here is a quotation from a letter received today typical of hundreds I have received.

"For over a year an older man (36) and I have had a deep, loving relationship—complete with joyful sex. Only recently did I become open and honest enough to share the experience with my husband. Again thanks to you for showing me the way. While reading *You and I Searching for Tomorrow* I realized how typically old-fashioned my actions had been—shutting my husband out, telling him only half-truths, never being defenseless or allowing him to be defenseless. My decision to LIVE my new philosophy changes us both for the better. My husband proved to be more liberal than my lover (who can't quite accept the fact that my husband knows all about him). We are now working together in our marriage to realize our separate potentials."

Third, mushrooming senior citizen centers, thirty or forty years from now, will run smack into the present younger, numerically vast generation who one day will be in their sixties or seventies and will refuse out of hand to live age-segregated lives. Even if the present generation in their early twenties don't rebel against segregated living, economics will take over. It will be monetarily impossible for their children by the year 2000 to support a huge old age population living out their lives separated from the mainstream of society.

Fourth, both the problems of senior citizen centers and day care centers focus the problems of a society that has evolved no sound methods of rearing and caring for their young and aged.

In a sense, then, group marriage will become the counter-revolution, a way of living that will give the benefits of the extended family and the chance "to choose one's relatives." Group marriage could not only provide the group with larger material input (better homes and conveniences, less duplicate expenses like televisions and automobiles) but they could give the children and the adults deeper intimacies and make it much easier to preserve a family structure against the vicissitudes of time.

Finally, we are in a great new age where every man and every woman is seeking lives of greater meaning and greater potential for self-growth. The problems facing group marriage or open-end marriages are similar. They can be easily resolved not by the typical navel gazing of encounter or sensitivity training, but in the simple joy of living defenselessly, learning the art of self-disclosure and being able to give one's self and receive another's. Handling our reactions of jealousy or our sexual drives are things that can be learned, or for older people relearned, if they want to. Two couples to a maximum of three couples can make a group marriage work. But first they should have a "courtship" period to determine if they really dare to expand their lives.

Coming events cast their shadows before them. Just as the nuclear family in Suburbia was "created" by the post-World War II economics of low mortgage rates to veterans, and a sustained highway building program that changed the character and strength of our cities, so the sudden realization, with the energy crisis, that there are limitations to economic growth will eventually force people to surrender some of their "privatism." In a novel I have just completed called *The Premar*

Challenge, I have explored a new style cooperative pooling of some family resources, especially the portion of income devoted to food and shelter.

In a Confamiliaum—the name I have given to family groups of up to 48 families, sexual exchange would not be the keynote of these family clusters. But the environment would create group friendships, and as Confamiliaums developed these friendships would encompass sexual exchange between specific couples without destroying the original marriage. Whether it's called group marriage or corporate marriage, or it simply becomes a way of life, we are moving toward a world that will accept comarital relationships as normal behavior.

Comment by:
Larry L. and Joan M. Constantine
It may well be that all attempts to dispel general ignorance and misunderstanding on alternative sexual and marital life styles are doomed at the outset. Let us face it: we, the people, *want* to hear that the prognosis for group marriage is not good. As a people we have a vested interest in our monogamous norm, a monolithic code that penalizes any deviation from the norm. It is one of the curses of our time that the clinical demonstration (even one based on a few cases) has functionally replaced moral dictum in the control of deviation. "Unhealthy" or "unworkable" has replaced "immoral" as the justification for social and legal sanctions. We are not putting the onus on the writer to assure against insidious misuse of information. However, an awareness of this common potential *is* a factor in our own previous avoidance of popularization and in these comments.

The danger, as we see it, is not so much from a dearth of information (or words) on group marriage, not so much from distortion or bias (though this is common, as Dr. Kilgo herself has stated), but from incomplete, fragmentary pictures. Dr. Kilgo's "findings" are, of course, based on a clinical sample, that is on groups who have sought her out as a counselor. Clinical samples, even when large (and her's is very small) severely limit generalizations. In the same vein, after a couple of years of practice, a marriage counselor seeing couples with serious problems might conclude: "Marriage: the prognosis is not good." We have no reason to doubt that her summary is an accurate distillation of what she sees of group marriage from the vantage point of her office in the heart of Dixie. What we see from three years of longitudinal research involving groups across the entire country is quite different in most respects.

The emphasis on youth, rebellion (against parents and society), and counterculture is entirely misrepresentative of the larger picture. The median age of participants in our study is 30; half are "over the hill" in the vernacular. Few are idealistic utopians. As a group they are nowhere near as conventional or middle class as swingers (sexual mateswappers), but most have various ties into the community, including ordinary jobs. Indeed, part of Dr. Kilgo's prognosis may derive from her proximity to college people, for we find some relationship between ability to function in a multilateral situation and prior formation of a lasting two-person relationship.

The observation that sex is not the problem, though it may be hard for many to believe, is borne out in our study. If anything, multiple sexual involvement may be one benign bonus in otherwise difficult times, and it greatly enhances a good relationship. While life style conflicts (the "tremendous trifles") are factors in the complexity of group marriage, they are totally overshadowed by more fundamental issues of personal compatibility. Money management, for example, has proven to be an issue only in the formative stages; once policies —any policies, including completely separate finances—are negotiated, money ceases to be an issue in all but rare cases. There is no pattern relating financial structure and cohesiveness.

It is easy to excuse some confusion of group marriage with communes, since the confusion is nearly universal. The distinction is real and important, however, exactly as real and important as for a man to know the difference between his wife and his neighbor. While some communes include group marriages (even as some include conventional ones), they tend to be larger, undergo "turnover" of membership (unknown in group marriage), and often depend for cohesiveness on function or on a charismatic leader.

Our own detailed study (with Angela Hunt) of children in group marriages shows that a few children do have trouble with their parents' relationship but that most, regardless of age, do not. Older children are more likely to suffer from being replaced as the center of attention and a few voice concern over being different, but the latter ceases to be important as the relationship lasts. As for very young children, we find most of them adapting well and being fully aware of what the group marriage means.

America has a preoccupation with success and failure and carries this preoccupation over into marriage. What is success? Is it only longevity? What does a 95 percent "failure" rate for group marriage really mean? It is true that the majority of group marriages we have located have dissolved (though the median for such dissolved groups is 16 months). It is also true that the overwhelming majority of participants valued their experience in a positive sense, felt that they had grown, and would—with the right people—probably try again. The relationship was a success even if not "stable." The fact is that group marriage as a sociological phenomenon only dates back to the mid-sixties. For some of the oldest groups, together now for seven or more . . . the prognosis is excellent.

People who enter group marriage generally do so with high expectations, with a goal of a level of intimacy and honesty beyond that in most conventional marriages. Against this they are confronted by no social or legal barriers to separation. Even without greater difficulties one would expect shorter duration. The pattern is similar to that of young people simply living together.

For a picture to be complete it would have to make note of the benefits of group marriage and similar altered marital forms. Not the theoretical utopian benefits, but the ones actually accrued by people who have lived—are living—this life style. We would have to mention substantial personal growth and enhanced self-concept of many participants, especially the women. Or the benefit to a couple's relationship from outgrowing the need to possess each other. Or the enhanced interpersonal skills in sharing feedback, in consensual decision making, and in conflict-resolution. Or simply, the warm joy of being genuinely loved "by so many people, at once, right now," even if it may not last forever.

Even with our much more comprehensive data, we are hesitant to give a prognosis for group marriage. For specific marriages, yes: some we are quite certain will not last the year; others we give at least as good a chance as any other marriage to last a lifetime. Maybe a little better. Whatever the prognosis, we as a people have an obligation to permit, even encourage these and other experiments. If it is not enough that our laws and extra-legal sanctions glaringly contradict basic principles of human freedom, then from a selfish standpoint we need new marital forms for it is entirely likely that we could learn how to make marriages—even very conventional ones—more fulfilling.

Bibliography

1. Constantine, L. L. and Constantine, J. M.: Group Marriage: A Study of Contemporary Multilateral Marriage (N.Y. Macmillan, 1973)
2. Group and multilateral marriage: definitional notes, glossary, and annotated bibliography. Family Process, 10, No. 2, pp. 157-176, June, 1971.
3. —: Pragmatics of Group Marriage. The Modern Utopian Vol. 4, No. 3/4. Summer/Fall, 1971.
4. —: Sexual aspects of multilateral relations. J. Sex Research 7, No. 3, pp. 204-255, Aug., 1971.

Comment by:
George R. Bach

I am sympathetic with the longing on the part of the television-raised (and now hopefully television-satiated) young people to reduce the poisonous effects of media-spewed smog, the implication being that what is good for ABC/CBS/NBC is good for them. Simply insulating themselves within utopian multiple-family units is, however, a limited approach. Most of these utopians are too passive and too unskilled in politically effective action to competently participate in a fundamental overhauling of our society by replacing the dehumanizing money and power interests with values which reinforce spiritually and emotionally meaningful joyful human experience. The ESTABLISHMENT SOCIETY looms too powerful!

The enormous popularity and current growth of the "human potential movement," encounter groups, and sensitivity training are major expressions of man's longing to form little societies which promote humanistic values and stress growth-relevant patterns of interaction, productive of warm, joyful, fulfilling, authentic, hearty, nonsymbolic, nonmanipulative, nonalienating experiences for their members. The participants in these programs have a reprieve, however fleeting, from the materialistic value-smog which pollutes the interactions of regular work, social, family, and sex life.

The social experiments in the development and maintenance of utopian multi-family communes can be viewed as an extension of the encounter group culture. Commune members are trying to make the temporary reprieve from value pollution offered by encounter programs a more permanent life style. I hope that more and more of these groups working for new psychologically meaningful life styles will succeed. I believe they will succeed if they become sophisticated and competent in group dynamics. They must become organizationally realistic and learn from the mistakes of the unsuccessful, sloppy, romantic utopian group marriages whose failures to survive are described by Dr. Kilgo. Without this sophistication these groups merely become insulated fertile ground for other forms of value pollution.

As more thousands, soon millions, of intelligent, young Americans, Europeans, Asians, Israelis, etc., wake up and actively protect themselves and their families from further ethnic-smog and antihumanistic attitudes and values, they will seek, find, and create so many humanistically oriented little societies that eventually "establishment society" must join them or perish. (For a thorough discussion see: Bach, G. and Goldberg, H., *Creative Aggression*, Doubleday, New York, 1974.)

Comment by:
Herbert L. Smith

Dr. Kilgo indicated that it was not the love and sex relationships that provided the source of tension for the membership of those groups with which she had contact. This adds further to our understanding that it may well be true that it is easier to find individuals with whom one can engage in sexual relations and find satisfaction than it is to work out a satisfactory living arrangement which has to do with the "routine chores" of housekeeping and the making of decisions as to the allocation of resources. It may be that many men and women today are more capable of engaging in sexual relations with others, singly or multilaterally, than they are capable of dealing successfully with the problems that would permit such sexual arrangements to continue through time.

Another question has to do with the sensory overload. If the dyadic relationship creates strains and works at cross-pressures with individual development, how much greater is the possibility of a given person being subjected to the pressures of the other group members to give in to the needs of the larger group? In short, does group marriage really provide greater opportunity for individual development, or do just one or two develop at the expense of the others? This is an important question in that crosscultural data indicate that in those societies where polygyny is practiced or where the extended family is well developed, individualism is achieved only at great costs to both the actor and the family. It may well be that one of the real costs of the security of group marriage is a denial of one's individualism and the opportunities for growth and development to say nothing of privacy. We need to know more about the personalities of those entering group marriage arrangements, and more about the factors in the breakup of such units. It could well be that, for some at least, their very makeup in terms of experiences and temperament mediate against achieving the goals they seek upon entering group marriage. Those entering group marriage arrangements indicate by their behavior, if not verbally, that monogamy is less desirable than group marriages and that the latter holds more promise of fulfilling those needs they find unmet or inadequately satisfied in conventional living arrangements. It is also possible that they become part of multilateral units for the thrill or prospect of finding new satisfaction. But if one surveys the current empirical data (of which there is little at present) and combines this with the personal experiences of those who have in some way had contact with group marriage participants, there is little support for the assumption that it provides the members with what they were desiring. The facts of the matter may change with new data. This remains to be seen. Certainly their short life-span indicates the many groups are unable to meet their problems adequately for survival. It may be no surprise, upon further examination, to find that many persons enter group marriages to compensate for their lack of development and feelings of alienation from others, rather than as the expression of concern for the well-being and development of the lives of the other members within the group. It may be that what is desired through group marriage is frustrated by the naivete, inexperience, lack of discipline, or intrapersonal deficiences of the membership.

Comment by:
David Smith
At the Haight-Ashbury Free Medical Clinic, we have had experience with a wide variety of communes including those of the group marriage type described by Dr. Kilgo.

Our experience with this alternative life style, however, differs somewhat from Dr. Kilgo's observations. For example, many participants of group marriage communes in our area are not married in the legal sense, and in fact actively resist or renounce "certification." Many are not balanced sexually, but have an excess of females with one central charismatic male figure who provides a sustaining ideology for the group. Often male jealousies develop as to who the central male figure is (although that figure may vehemently deny that he exercises such control) and there is often a status hierarchy amongst the females depending on who is "closest" to the head man. The most extreme example of this system that I have seen was the Manson family commune[1] whom we studied in 1968 while they were part of the Haight-Ashbury scene and several months before their trip south and subsequent well-publicized violence.

I agree with Dr. Kilgo's broader interpretations of the group marriage commune, however, for its instability is second only to the chaotic "crashpad" commune in my experience.

But to stop here does the counter-culture life style a disservice, for as the commune dweller matures he moves toward the family-style commune and gravitates toward monogamous sexual relationships. Certainly most group marriage communes fail, but many individuals involved contine to seek intentional communities as a preferable alternative to "straight" society and the monogamous nuclear family.

Reference
1. **Our findings are described in:** *The Group Marriage Commune: a Case Study.* Journal of Psychedelic Drugs, Volume III, Issue I, 1970.

19. Age-Discrepant Marriages

JOHN F. CUBER

About twenty years ago, a brilliant and popular "fortyish" bachelor announced his marriage to a coed "young enough to be his daughter." As would be anticipated, news of this marriage brought forth an inordinate amount of speculation, interpretation, and negative prognostication. In spite of the wagers and mildly obscene imagery of colleagues and "friends," the children of this marriage are now in college, the husband is still a vigorous and capable professional, the wife an attractive late-thirties suburbanite.

There are many marriages in which the partners span a generation or more. Life styles which are unusual, especially in marriage, tend to be negatively appraised because they seem to flout standards of behavior which are rooted in tradition and rationalized by seemingly impressive logic. Yet despite the negative judgments, there are people, often of marked intelligence and accomplishment, who choose the May-September mode of pairing, not out of impulse as a rule but after rather careful analysis.

It is my observation that May-September marriages are not distributed randomly in the population; they are most frequent in what could loosely be called the upper-middle class. The reasons are, to put the matter quite simply, that the life circumstances of people in this position make this life style both possible and appealing. This class is less dominated by traditional thinking about manners and morals and these people, through education, travel, and career style, are more exposed to alternatives of many sorts. It is my view also that we may expect more May-September marriages in the future than we are now accustomed to. We are living in a period when the traditional rigidities about what is "proper" are breaking at every turn, and the current philosophies of life are much more present-oriented than future-oriented. This is the psychological stuff out of which "unthinkable" modes of life are invented.

For a variety of reasons the marriage of the older man to the younger woman is far more prevalent than the reverse. While I am familiar with numerous marriages of younger men to older women, I know of very few where there is a *marked* age differential. Also, the rationales for the two appear to be markedly different. Because of the prevalence of the older man-younger woman form, this paper will discuss primarily this arrangement.

As a backdrop for examining the May-Septmeber marriage, it may be instructive to examine the conventional wisdom of the subject. This kind of marriage is said to be very precarious for the man psychologically, particularly when his sexual powers or interests begin to flag. This occurs, of course, at very different ages for different men, but it is a risk which is very difficult to anticipate accurately even if one is quite well informed on the subject. Our folklore has it that when this occurs the marriage is severely threatened, and no matter what kind of adjustment is made both parties will "surely suffer." The woman, it is said, has a choice between adulterous relationships of one sort or another, or sublimation. Either way the man suffers. He is either sexually upstaged or he lives with a resentful woman who takes out on him her sexual frustrations.

Another caution light in the conventional wisdom is the view that the woman is likely to be exploiting the man. She is thought to be "after his money," his "good name," or his life insurance.

The conventional wisdom has another interpretation. In short the May-September marriage is a "sick" arrangement and "they are more to be pitied than censured." The man is supposedly reaching frantically for a spur to his waning sexuality; he wants to flatter his ego and is afraid of getting old. This kind of marriage gives the illusion of a second and more youthful life. The woman too is said to be sick. She may have a "father fixation" and cannot relate emotionally to a man her own age. Or the unhappy creature has been rejected by her own age group. And so she has to settle for the less desirable, older man.

I would not deny fully that any or all of the above may be accurate in selected cases, nor that they are logical on the face of it. The more measured judgment, however, seems that these statements exaggerate and overly generalize so as to derogate the May-September marriage. Conventional wisdom overlooks the fact that these perils are also perils in age-peer marriages. Any marriage has a potential for exploitation and psychological aberrations of a wide variety.

It is well, however, not to underestimate the negative influence of the conventional wisdom upon May-September loves. I have known numerous instances in which potentially good marriages were not undertaken because purveyors of conventional wisdom shook the faith of one or both of the partners in their ability to pull it off. Possibly even more serious are the resulting exaggerated doubts and hyperconsciousness about risks even though one decided to defy the conventional wisdom. Then there are also the unending major and minor cruelties from the remarks, sometimes quite subtle, of other people. The May-September marriage, like any other kind of unconventional life style, is threatened psychologically both from within and from without by the persistent intrusion of conventional wisdom. An important factor giving cohesiveness to *any* relationship is the reinforcement from knowing that one is "normal" and that he is thought to be doing well by other people of sound mind and values. These couples lack such reinforcement from the outside. If there is an infidelity in an age-peer marriage, there are various ways of interpreting it and handling it. If it occurs in a May-September marriage, the conventional wisdom says, "Well, what did he expect?"

For a May-September marriage to succeed (however one chooses to define success) requires a somewhat different kind of personality structure than does the conventional age-peer marriage. At the outset, the ability even to contemplate seriously an unconventional marriage calls for a level of emancipation and of self-confidence which many persons simply do not have. The very ability to perceive a man old enough to be one's father as a lover, or a woman young enough to be one's daughter as a spouse, is an uncommon capability. Then to act on such an insight requires equally uncommon independence and confidence. On the other hand, perhaps it merely calls for a naivete in anticipating life problems—a naivete which would function to give a green light, where a more thoughtful and cautious person would see a red light—or at least an amber one. At any rate, the woman in a May-September marriage obviously takes a quite different view of the future than is conventional. She needs to be more present-oriented. "I'd rather have ten years with this man than forty years with anybody else I've ever known."

Voluntary relationships of all sorts come into being because they fulfill some kind of conscious or unconscious purposes for the people involved. This is not to imply that relationships are necessarily exploitative, that one does not enjoy giving satisfaction as well as receiving it. It is simply a blunt way of acknowledging that people seek self-fulfillment through relationships with other people. Marriage is no exception, despite the fact that we have an elaborate etiquette which often pretends something else. A woman who is attracted to a man who is affluent and who can give her status and possessions which she has never had before is much more likely to tell him and others that she just "loves him for himself," rather than the whole truth which may include the fact that she loves him *because* he has provided her with this affluence. The situation can be reversed where the man appreciates his wife primarily because she is an excellent mother and homemaker. He too simply says that he loves her and leaves it at that.

"What's in it" for the partners involved?

It may be instructive, then, to examine May-September marriages from a point of view of "what's in it" for the man and for the woman which is different from the age-peer marriage. We shall then look at the May-September marriage in terms of the risks invovled for the woman and for the man.

What's in it, then, for the man? As everyone knows, our is a youth-centered society. The "attractive" man is relatively young, well-muscled, quick of step. The attractive woman is likewise young, somewhat sensual, and vivacious. An endless amount of energy, especially among women, goes into trying to look young longer or trying to look younger than they are. To accomplish this is a great triumph. Men may be a little less frantic about it, but they do much the same, because both tacitly recognize that there is some special virtue in looking young. This is reflected in age differentials in marriage and especially in *re*marriages. The May-September marriage appeals to the man typically because he has the outward status to attract the more valued young woman and the inner gratification of having access to youth again. This is not a matter of mere physical beauty; it involves the whole spectrum of the generally presumed superiority of the young over the not-so-young. One of the worst tribulations of the middle-aged divorcee or widow, if she wishes to remarry, is that she is unavoidably in competition with younger women and she feels (and is) discriminated against in the competition.

In other instances the man has come to this point in life as a "refugee" from a disappointing age-peer marriage. With divorce becoming more and more prevalent among middle-aged couples, there is a considerable number of men who are disillusioned because the conventional marriage has not afforded the satisfactions he had hoped for. He doesn't want children again. He doesn't want the struggle nor the dull routine of the usual life. He doesn't so much want a second chance as he wants a *different kind* of marital life style, and the younger woman is that promise.

Some older men prefer young women because they believe that they can fashion them more in accord with their own image of what a woman should be. The age-equal is more rigid, if for no other reason because her habits are more entrenched. The younger woman is more awed by the confidence and seeming wisdom of the older man and seems less resistant to his kind of intention and it works as intended in some instances. But it entails certain risks. Without carrying the imagery too far, one is reminded of Shaw's *Pygmalion* and *My Fair Lady*. It worked for Professor Higgins and Liza—for a while.

Vivacity of young women

More important than any of the above, in my view, is the need among some older men for a high degree of *joie de vivre* in their intimate lives. By the time they reach their forties, the partners in a large proportion of marriages are bored by the humdrum, monotonous, listless, dull nature of the man-woman relationship. Many couples accept this with resignation and some even prefer life this way, but there is a minority of both men and women who feel seriously disenchanted with their spouses because they would like a more exciting, emotionally charged relationship. This is not uncommon as an underlying cause of middle-aged divorce.

However, whether divorced, widowed, or never married, the promise of finding a vivacious life mated to a younger woman may become an almost compelling urge. A disproportionate number of women in May-September marriages, in my experience, have personalities which could aptly be termed vivacious. There is a *joie* which seems to permeate their activities, their conversation, their outlooks. To a degree, the conventional wisdom is partly right; the older man who wants to live vigorously needs a younger woman because she provides the stimulation to invigorate him, and she is more likely to want and be able to "keep up" with him. To the extent that she can and does, she can be the joy of his life.

"Instant status" for the woman

But what's in it for the woman? First of all, there is "instant status." "I'm Mrs. Somebody who amounts to something—right away. He opened up a world overnight which it would have taken any of my boyfriends twenty years to put together. No years of grubby poverty for me—I don't just mean money and possessions. I mean having to wait to find out where I am in the scheme of things." This woman is almost the stereotype of the conventional wisdom, but she does dramatize the woman's satisfaction. In most instances, however, the woman sees the advantages and expresses them much less baldly. She really loves the man, and a significant ingredient of the love is her and others' admiration for what he has become. This she is privileged to share immediately. Even a respected name, apart from material affluence, can be a source of satisfaction. The older man is likely to have superior status in his occupation. There is a kind of reflected glory for the younger woman in being his partner and sharing this. She enjoys the places she goes and the people she meets. A young man can almost never provide this kind of instant status.

This is one of the reasons why I anticipate an increase in May-September marriages in the immediate future. Many of the "now" generation of young people are less inclined to wait for the things they want, whether material or psychological, in the way in which past generations were willing to. I have spoken with numerous college girls and women graduate students who frankly say that one of the reasons why they are quite willing to become involved either in liaisons or marriages with older men is that the instant status and associated comforts appeal to them.

Benefits of a sexually experienced man

There is also a certain sexual attraction for the woman, particularly since she is typically somewhat sexually experienced and somewhat sophisticated. The older man can often provide a higher standard of living sexually, not because he's a sexual athlete but because he is more experienced. As one man put it, "you have to be damn near 50 before you've really learned how to treat a woman." You would seldom be able to convince a 20- or 30-year-old man of this, but many a 20- or 30-year-old woman will attest to it. "I had an awful lot of sex in college and just after, but I didn't begin to realize my sex potential until a 50-year-old man made love to me." In this generation of premarital sexual freedom, there are considerable numbers of college age girls who know this. Of course, they will not all marry older men. Many won't get the chance, even if they want it. But the knowledge is there just the same and so they are potential candidates. They say, "He (an older man) makes me feel more appreciated and that goes a long way." Or, "He makes me feel more like a woman in bed."

Women needn't fear aging

One of the psychological factors which reinforces the May-September marriage for the woman is again related to the social attitudes toward aging which characterize our society. Says one woman, "As men age they get some status out of it; a woman just gets older." Some women find the terror of aging much easier when the edge is taken off by a May-September marriage. "A 50-year-old woman can still look good to a 70-year-old man but to a 50-year-old man she's showing her age." It is unlikely that this is a motivation on the wedding day, but as the marriage matures it becomes, for some, a very sustaining comfort.

Hazards vs. advantages

The people in the May-September marriages, of course, take risks. But everybody in a marriage takes a risk. Whenever one commits himself to someone else in marriage, he assumes a battery of risks whether or not he knows it. Comparing May-September marriages and age-peer marriages reveals similarities as well as differences. Some risks are common to both groups. There is competition from others. There is the chance of psychological incompatibility. There are serious intrusions from persons outside. There is disillusionment. Some of these risks, to be sure, are worse for the May-September marriages. Some, however, are less. Marriages for example, run potential risks which devolve from the immaturity of one or the other of the spouses. In this respect the May-September marriage is sometimes more secure. As one woman said, "If both of them are young and childlike, forget it! But if one is more mature, he may be able to carry the other one along." He may be. But not necessarily.

All marriages run the risk of intrusion by third parties. As the conventional wisdom maintains, the May-September marriage is, on the average, more vulnerable. An attractive, relatively young woman whose husband is recovering from a coronary may quite understandably be more vulnerable to an advance at the office party than she would have been at another time, even though she still loves her husband.

On the other hand, there are some standard risks of marriages among age-peers from which the May-September marriages may not be immune, but are certainly somewhat protected. The conventional marriage suffers the unavoidable consequences of intrusions from children, financial insecurity, and the other familiar struggles with the hard facts of life. As a rule, the May-September marriage, because the husband's position in life is so much more secure, tends to avoid these things. He doesn't have to worry when he comes home from the office party somewhat invigorated sexually that he will face a dishevelled wife staggering under the burden of diapers, dishes, and a fever or two. Instead, he comes home to something as good or better than even his bolder fantasies at the office party!

Special risks for men

More systematically we turn to the risks involved in the May-September marriage—first for the man.

Competition, real or imagined, sooner or later, cannot realistically be ruled out. And the competition is not from equals. It is from those with the natural advantage: they are younger. This typically does not occur at first, but later. One does not wish to keep his young wife in a cell. She is unavoidably exposed, whether at the cocktail party, the office, or the resort to younger, exciting, and seemingly more virile men. This does not matter at first, when the man is revelling in his sexual prowess with his delectable and grateful "young thing." But later on, when perhaps the conventional wisdom begins to haunt, the pressure starts to build. The tragic part of all this is that the competition often is not real. She may not be enticed. But he can't quite believe that she isn't. "He can't believe that I'm faithful—he thinks that I'm just too clever to get caught."

The problem here is not narrowly sexual. It takes more subtle forms, like animated conversation at the cocktail party with another man. Or a slackening in the vigor of the recreational pace. Or even bona fide health problems for her, which, once he is suspicious, can easily be interpreted as a desire to avoid intimacy. The consequent jealousy is a subtle as well as a devastating backdrop. No one is ever completely free of it, but the older man, when he realizes his position in the life cycle, is particularly adept at self-torture. All this is not totally in the imagination. The younger woman married to an older man *is* frequently vulnerable if her husband is sexually apathetic or inept.

A second risk for the man is even more subtle. The conventional wisdom, as expressed and reinforced by other people such as children from an earlier marriage, ever reminds him that perhaps he is being exploited. Here the conventional wisdom often hammers hard. There may even be some objective truth in the case. Not that it was her intention at first, but that unconsciously, when other rewards were not realized, she became a little more conscious of the relationship in terms of what it could materially bring to her. And even if *she* didn't think so, *he* may.

The facts of life expectancy being what they are, the odds are high that he will ultimately become her "patient." She may not be as good a nurse and companion as she was a lover, and yet it may be precisely her competency as a nurse which spells the difference between a few dismal years and some reasonably comfortable ones.

Since the man in the May-September marriage is likely to have been married before, he probably has children from the earlier marriage—children of about the same age as his present wife. Sometimes, contrary to popular stereotypes, this presents no serious problem. I have known instances of children and wives who are age-peers who have developed gratifying and mutually enforcing relationships with each other. They present no threat or problem to the husband. But this is not necessarily the situation. One cannot really know, where remarriage is involved, how over a period of time one's children will define their parent's new life. Some of these ultimate evaluations may be exceedingly negative. The older man may know that his wife is really a devoted, cooperative, and empathic mate, but his children think she is "just after his money." The fact that he knows better is small comfort. He has to deal in some way with their views. At 65 this can be hard to manage.

Sometimes the practical aspects can be more important even than the psychological tensions. Any probate judge can attest to the entanglements and fights between a man's children and his subsequent wife over inheritance. What the court records do not show may be most important: his prior agonies trying to work things out reasonably and equitably.

Risks for the woman

While the woman shares most of her husband's problems, if she is empathic, she has some additional ones which are uniquely her own—not always but often enough to consider. The potential is almost always there.

One of these risks is sexual. It is my observation that women who become the younger partners in the May-September marriages are generally sexually aggrandizing people. Part of the initial attraction is sexual. At the beginning of the relationship the man is sexually vigorous, perhaps innately so and perhaps because of the stimulation resulting from the newness of the experience. However, he has taken on a risk not merely for himself but also for his young wife. His potency may not have the longevity he intends. Normally, high sexual ability at 40 or 50 continues relatively late in life, so there may be no problem. But not necessarily so. Termination or drastic reduction of potency and sexual interest may be drastic and swift for some men, and even though he may be able to take the change gracefully (which is doubt-ful), she may not be able to. A man 65 with a wife of 40 may be able to make the transition from overt coital sex to more gentle, diffused, and less localized affection without serious psychological threat. But can she? For age peers this may, of course, be a problem too, but typically for them it occurs more gradually and is more readily adjusted to.

It is a very short step from sexual frustration to conscious, and especially unconscious, touchiness on the subject, bickering about it, and sooner or later conflict. What may be the saddest irony of all is that this comes to them against the backdrop of what was earlier a magnifi-cent experience. One can only fully appreciate a deprivation if he has previously known fulfillment.

It was indicated earlier that one of the rewards for a woman in this kind of marriage is that she, earlier than her age-peer friends, moves into a higher status position, with all its attendant rewards and com-forts. True enough, but affluence is a vulnerable condition. Fortunes may not last; she may then find herself with a seriously atrophied standard of living, possibly having to become a breadwinner again, or even for the first time. All it may take to make the sharp transition is a coronary—not a particularly unusual experience—or any of a dozen other vulnerabilities for an older man. Because the relationship has been based on empathy and sharing, in the initial stages she may take on the new life style with grace, but in the longer pull the contrast between present circumstances and past satisfactions can easily be-come an obsession. This is especially true if she has not had previous work experience, or even worse if because of her good position in the meantime she has become somewhat disdainful of "women who have to support their husbands."

Aside from the economic aspects of prolonged illness there is also the reality of the caring and feeding of a semi-invalid—"I didn't marry him to become his nurse." The woman who said this was not speaking out of bitterness but out of simple candor. Ten or fifteen years ago he was an older but dapper man of accomplishment. She reveled in his reflected glory. But now he's sick—chronically or terminally. This can, of course, happen in any marriage, but with an age discrepancy of 20 or 30 years the odds are heavily in favor of this kind of outcome for many May-September marriages. This is hard on the man too, of course. But the wife often bears the brunt of it.

While the clear tendency is for the May-September marriages to be childless, by no means all of them are. Childrearing is never easy, even though rewarding. Child adoption agencies have a general rule of thumb to the effect that if either of the parents desiring adoption is over

40, placement is ill-advised, even though sometimes permitted. The rationale behind this policy is that childrearing is a demanding and sometimes nerve-wracking occupation, an enterprise which more flexible, healthy, and energetic younger people are somehow able to manage, but older ones find difficult. In the May-September marriages the new father is very likely to be in his late 40's, 50's, or even older. If the couple has children at, say, 50, these children are in college when the husband is 70. The flexibility necessary for the parent of a late adolescent or early adult child taxes the ingenuity of even the younger parent.

It is interesting to note that at least two professional researchers in recent years have shown that even parents who have children at conventional ages, and want them, find that children constitute a threat to the spousal relationship. If this is true for people in the relatively flexible and healthy years, it seems reasonable to assume that it will be even more so in the advanced ones.

If the couple does not have children, there may be second thoughts—and they may be hurtful. Sometimes the young wife would like to have children, but he has already had his and wants "no more of the diapers and dishes routine." Or again, the stark facts of infertility in their middle age and beyond may preclude paternity even if she wants it. This leaves the young wife, if she desires children, in a serious predicament; she cannot have children in the present marriage and she will be too old to have them in any future marriage.

Women in May-September marriages frequently complain about the irrational and unjustified insecurity and jealousy of their aging husbands. "I need to be a psychiatrist to handle the way he feels about himself and about me. If I assure him that I have no designs on another man, he counters that it will just be a question of time. After all, a sexual tigress like me can't long be sustained by the moderate sexual outlets we have. How can you handle that? *I* can't."

It is irrelevant to point out that this man's jealousy is irrational, that his insecurity is falsely based. He *feels* insecure, upstaged by some other man or men out there somewhere. He is not altogether irrational either, because there *are* instances in which younger women with older husbands have affairs and are mistresses to other men. This is her problem as much as his because, whether the accusation is correct or not, she carries the burden of his suffering and her own agony which results from it.

The final and in some ways most summary problem for the young wife grows out of the hard facts of demography. A woman not only lives on the average several years longer than a man but in the May-

September marriage the husband is already 20 or 30 years older. Thus, even under the most optimistic circumstances, if she is at all rational she must realize that she is in for an eventual widowhood, quite likely at a point in her life when she is still relatively young. There is, of course, the chance of remarriage. But again, the statistics are hurtful. The chances of remarriage for a widow of 40 or 50 are decidedly not good, particularly in her case because she is likely to have a level of expectation well above the average. In a sense she is in the same kind of spot as the mistress who gets "dumped." The "best years of her life" are past and, however delightful they may have been, she is now faced with a far more austere future.

Overall appraisal

While it is true that all of these risks are accentuated in the May-September marriages, it is wise not to overestimate them. As we have said, the age-peer marriage has many of the same risks. Some marriages are essentially sexless at 40. Some men and women are irrationally jealous; others are jealous with reason. There are always competitions from outside the pair, whether recognized or not. Age-peers may exploit their spouses. A young man may become an invalid. Status aspirations may be shattered at any age for a variety of reasons. Children can and do severely compromise spousal fulfillments. Any one may lose a spouse by death or divorce. Remarriage can be a problem at any age.

So we have said that there is something special in the May-September marriage for men and for women, and also that there are some risks for men and others for women. What is the balance of risks and fulfillments? Can any sensible kind of determination be made which might permit a judgment as to the advisability of this kind of marriage? My answer is "no." Not because we know so little but because we know enough not to generalize. All marriages work themselves out amidst an admixture of sunshine and shadow. Can one draw a balance sheet? Even if one if fully rational—and few of us in this aspect of life really are—one really cannot.

Fortunately, or otherwise, relatively few people have to face the decision. The overwhelming majority don't because they marry age-peers. It is conventional to say this is their choice. The society is set up in such a way that we are exposed to each other in a variety of situations which result in a decision to marry age-peers. Many who may be tempted to step out of the age-peer pattern do so only briefly, then they become seduced by the conventional wisdom and abandon the impulse. "It wouldn't work," they say. And they render the hard decision, often out of deep empathy for the loved one as well as concern for themselves. But ultimately there are those, I think a growing number, who do make the opposite choice. Looking at it from their point of view, it may be well to examine the decision-making process as they experience it.

As we have said earlier, persons who venture this kind of life pattern perceive themselves and life management differently from the conventional ones. I think a psychiatric interpretation of why they do might be an appropriate inquiry, but at this point suffice it to say that "somehow" some people seriously consider getting into a May-September marriage. What are they like? What distinguishes them from the general run of people? First, they seem to be more venturesome. Somehow this kind of person judges that the risks, as "everyone knows them," are worth taking and that somewhere out there are some rewards worth seeking. I strongly suspect that if we were to make some kind of psychological test of these people we would find that they are more present-oriented than future-oriented.

Then there is *"love."* However defined, and the schoolish semantics aside, there is some sort of psychic alchemy which closely binds some particular man to some particular woman at a particular time. Folklore has it both ways, of course. Love is on the one hand blind, and on the other hand the highest and noblest state of being. But folklore isn't supposed to be consistent, and maybe it shouldn't be.Persons of different persuasions however, can, I think, agree that love exists, is real, that it motivates people to take risks in order to achieve some indescribable kind of fulfillment and that it tends to persist despite impediments. It may sound a little sophomoric to say that the people who enter into May-September marriages are simply people who fall in love, as in age-peer marriages. Yet conversations with and observations of these people strongly hint, at least to me, that love is often influenced by other kinds of considerations—such as those which we have attempted to focus on here.

People in May-September marriages seem different from others in that they seem to have faith, whether rational or not, that they can "beat the system" or at least that they can successfully ignore it. They know that the system is blueprinted by the conventional wisdom and, in my experience at least, they are quite aware of the risks. But they think they can pull it off. As in other aspects of life, of course, such choices are only to a limited degree rational. The realistic total assessment must always include the nonrational dimensions.

Some people in May-September marriages feel that the world is against them—at least when they are encountering problems—and to a degree it is. In my view, one of the most difficult aspects of conventional wisdom is that it is not merely present in other people but sometimes also in themselves. The May-September couple is not something apart from the larger society. They were reared in it; they live in it as do their friends and their children; and even though they have made the decision to go a somewhat separate way in finding their own marital fulfillment, they can never be quite unaware of the fact that they are different and that they are thought to be different. The outside judgments about them often bear little resemblance to their experiences inside the marriage. What looks like a "father fixation" to others may be a true and devoted love. Under such circumstances it is to be expected that there would be a considerable amount of ambivalence for the partners in the May-September marriage. Whether or not the resulting lurking doubts become a problem cannot be generalized because to some the fulfillments are just too overwhelming to worry about the risks. Others have a different experience and a different judgment.

Now to come back to the May-September marital couple with which this discussion began. It is now 20 years later. Nothing really dramatic or tragic has happened to this pair, at least nothing which is publicly known. The children are not particularly close to their parents, but this is hardly unique in these times. The husband and wife largely go their own separate way, he with his professional activities and she with her community ones. A kind of apathy has settled on the intimate relationship, much as it does on any 20-year-old marriage. They maintain a beautiful and comfortable home in the best part of town; his career is flourishing; she is prominent on the society page. All of this could be said for countless people in their own community who have age-peer marriages. As far as their personal satisfactions and fulfillments at this point in time, who can say that it was a mistake for them to marry—or that it was a wise thing for them to marry. Who can say that he would have been happier with another woman for the last 20 years, or that she would have been better off with a younger man? Perhaps they, themselves, would be unable to say what the true balance of risks and fulfillments has been.

20. *How men really feel about Women's Lib*

A discussion led by WARREN FARRELL

The pseudonyms of the participants are:

Jim—a professor of psychology, married, with two children and living in a communal arrangement with another family.

Mike—a magazine writer who has one child, a daughter, and whose wife is an editor of arts and crafts books.

Steve—a college teacher of history, father of a son, whose wife takes care of the home and does some voluntary fund raising work in connection with their child's school.

Bill—a labor organizer, married for thirty years, father of a grown daughter, and whose wife is a book editor on an executive level.

Gil—a divorced Wall Street stock analyst; he is an ardent sports enthusiast.

Larry—a commercial artist, father of a preschool age boy and girl, whose wife stays home with them.

Harold—a college English teacher, whose wife recently stopped teaching and is now pregnant with their first child.

LARRY: As I understand it, we're to discuss the various gripes of Women's Liberation groups, our attitudes toward women and ways that we act which might offend them.

JIM: I don't think we're just reacting to Women's Liberation; we're adjusting to a reformation of the whole sexual scene.

WARREN: Jim and I are members of a men's consciousness-raising group. When we really started raising our consciousness about sex roles, we saw that men had as many problems as women. We were always interrupting each other, constantly being aggressive. Each of us operates on the assumption that we alone have the right thing to say. We couldn't listen to men and we couldn't listen to women. That creates part of the women's problem too—they learn to be dependent on men for solutions and men have to prove that they have them.

MIKE: But a group of women together would have the same kind of interrupting and aggressiveness and interaction, wouldn't they?

WARREN: No, it's a very male trait. We met with a group from the National Organization for Women. Fourteen of us, seven men and seven women, were sitting around in a circle and a woman posed a serious employment problem she had. *Every one* of the men in the group told her how to handle the problem, constantly interrupting the other in the process of "solving" her problem. It was a woman asking for help—all the men had ready solutions and not one woman said anything about it for twenty solid minutes. When we realized this we backtracked and systematically asked for the women's opinions. They gave a whole lot of good suggestions then, but felt in the heat of the conversation that the men knew best. I'll give you another example. When I used to do work for a certain company, we used to sit around at the table and there would be five or six men, you know, big corporate types, and they were trying to make decisions and there would be one or two women on the same executive level.

Almost automatically the women would be looked at to take notes. Since they were taking notes, they could no longer contribute actively. They were back in the passive role.

LARRY: You mean the women automatically assumed an inferior intellectual role. Well, maybe this stems from something many women's Lib people have been condemning—the male-imposed beauty standard. The women are tutored to be passive and look attractive—all the important things in a woman's life, whether she will successfully marry, and thus be able to have children, and even whether she will have a choice of lovers, depends so much on her appearance.

WARREN: Actually, this is what I call "the sex object trap." For example, a man walks into a party, looks around and selects the woman who is most sexually attractive to him that he thinks he can get.

He might spend the entire four or five hours at the party catering to her, building himself up, so that eventually he can take her to bed.

When he's satisfied sexually he starts looking at her for other things. It's only a coincidence if he gets them—the intelligent woman probably went home alone. He finds himself emotionally involved (the woman has "given" him something) and he's in the first stage of a sex object trap with a woman whom he really doesn't respect intellectually. He can't deal with her as an equal, he hasn't learned to listen to her and they each start manipulating each other from their own vantage point. A lot of men dislike or disrespect women in general because they have always been in the position of having to manipulate women in order to be accepted or to have sexual relations. They get themselves into a trap because of the beauty standard that they follow.

STEVE: I can certainly see myself acting that way with my own wife, as much as I try not to. But, can't we turn a person into an object a little bit? I mean, is that so wrong? I like nice vases, okay? And I like to have nice things around the house, okay?

JIM: Try to talk politics with vases.

STEVE: I don't have to. You would be surprised at the kind of relationships you can have with objects. Keats tells you that in the "Ode to a Grecian Urn."

LARRY: Wait, wait, that was an orgy on the Grecian urn! It was just another sex object. (Laughter)

BILL: How can you deal with humans the way you deal with a—a Grecian urn—man, this is ridiculous.

HAROLD: Visual perception of beauty is not such a bad starting point. After all, it entails all of your intellectual and emotional capacities. One man's visual perception is very different from another's. And a person's character and other qualities are revealed in their appearance.

WARREN: Harold, you are intellectualizing.

JIM: Yes, but a woman straps herself in, paints her lips, paints her eyes, rubies her cheeks, dyes her hair, curls it, puts holes in her ears, straps herself up in the most ungodly garments, sticks her breasts out so they are on her shoulders instead of where they are supposed to be—

HAROLD: The braless look is sexier!

JIM: —straps her belly in, wears high-heeled shoes, immobilizes herself, wears dresses so that she is half exposed half of the time. Why?—so that you will come over and talk to her.

Do men do that? No, because men are in the power position. She is on the market and you are there to buy whatever particular product looks the best: the ripest cantaloupe, the best ear of corn.

HAROLD: *I* dress in a way that expresses my inner self in the hope that it will attract other people.

JIM: You don't subject yourself to physical pain. You don't distort your body.

HAROLD: I wear a tie.

JIM: I don't.

LARRY: Women went through this torture of looking beautiful to attract guys, but we suffered the torture of being horny because they would not satisfy us sexually. They make themselves tantalizing but don't deliver on the lust they arouse. I'd say the beauty standard often works to their advantage.

When I was in college, I worked in resort hotels whose customers tended to be hard-headed businessmen. To me, the most striking thing about them was that each seemed to believe he had a wife who was a little bit more attractive than he deserved—sort of imitation Liz Taylors—and each of these tough buys was servile toward and fearful of his wife. This is only speculation, but I'd bet these wives doled out sex like it was water in the Sahara and kept these men dancing through hoops in the hope of being granted sexual "favors." This is an exaggerated case, but in most marriages the woman looks like a pretty shiny apple at first and this motivates the man to be permanently indentured to support her.

WARREN: This is why Women's Liberation will also mean men's liberation.

LARRY: But men are also controlled by the beauty standard—*because of women.* When we were young men we were obsessed with sex because we couldn't have any. Our fantasies and lust were fed by the movie screen. We wished for the girl who looked like Marilyn Monroe, and girls adopted sweaters and hairdos to imitate Marilyn and Liz in order to turn us on—yet seldom parted with the precious nectar we craved.

BILL: Well, who set up those fantasies?

LARRY: But who should a man desire as a wife or sexual partner? Someone who *doesn't* attract him?

BILL: You'll find who you wish in life. You look for the things that you need: somebody who needs you. That's the way it works out. This business of you marrying an ugly woman out of a sense of democracy is just plain ridiculous. That's not the way it happens. But if you're going to be a slave to the Hollywood standard, you'll be in worse shape yet.

LARRY: How do you change this? Can women who think of themselves as outcasts because they don't look beautiful be made happier and share in more of life's joys?

BILL: I don't think that a lot of women consider themselves outcasts any more. A great many of them are convinced that there is to be a change in their roles in this society and probably every society.

WARREN: How do you select a woman at parties, Gil?

GIL: Completely on looks. Of course, if she opens up her mouth and something like "Ken I have a cuppa black cawfee" comes out, then I leave.

BILL: She could also say something very interesting that would really make you feel that you would want to know her better.

MIKE: Actually, the most beautiful woman is sometimes left completely alone because men are too inhibited to go to her. They feel too insecure about her.

WARREN: I can remember saying to myself when I was at a party: I'm good enough for this level of beauty; the ones above that are too good for me; the ones below that, well, I can do better.

MIKE: That's exactly how I behave.

WARREN: This whole sex objectivism is a matter of degree. You can measure it by looking at the amount of time that a woman spends and the amount of money that a woman spends to make herself beautiful. Until recently that has been phenomenally more than the amount of money that a man spends.

The beauty obsession begins with the little girl in a baby carriage. You walk up to her, pinch her cheek and say, "Oh, how pretty she is." If it is a boy in the baby carriage, you give a gentle little punch or something that is masculine and say, "Boy, now there's a future President!"

STEVE: I'd like to testify to the truth of what you are saying. You know, I teach at a college and I have a lot of women in my class; eighteen to nineteen years old. I know that in 1967 or 1968 I was grading those girls in large part on their looks. I'm only becoming aware of it now.

WARREN: I have been studying this for a year, and when I see a little girl, I still say, gee, she's pretty.

HAROLD: What else should you say to a cute little girl? That's the quality that strikes you right off the bat, isn't it?

JIM: You've been conditioned to say that. A friend of ours just had twins, a boy and a girl—they were about two weeks old, just home from the hospital, and their uncle was visiting. He picked up the boy and he threw him in the air and he bounced him around and said, "what a great kid." Then he laid him back down again and walked away.

The mother said: "What about the little girl?"

He said, "Oh, no, girls are much too delicate. I'd be afraid to touch her."

That's where it starts. A woman can't visualize herself in terms of her intelligence or her ability. All she can do is visualize herself in terms of her looks.

MIKE: In connection with an article I am writing, I interviewed a bunch of teenage girls the other day. Almost as a body they complained that their fathers looked at them as pretty little girls and encouraged them to be smart but not too smart, and to get married. They complained that the fathers thought they were pretty, and this was the major concern of their fathers.

GIL: Were they pretty?

MIKE: Not one. (Laughter)

GIL: It's pretty obvious they don't want to be judged on the one quality they don't have.

LARRY: Do you think boys and girls should be treated the same?

GIL: That's impossible. I don't believe in the equality of women. I think it is self-evidently not true.

BILL: Any man who wants any kind of relationship with his daughter is going to have to be a very different kind of a human being than you are.

LARRY: I think that many of these real crazy Women's Lib advocates, the ones who jump down your throat if you call them "baby" or some other term of endearment, are lesbians. They claim to want all the male prerogatives when they really want the males' women. It's to their advantage in the sexual competition to paint men as oppressors and clods. They're outside the system and want to break it down.

WARREN: Just for argument's sake let's say these name-callers are right. Let's take the lesbian. She is the first woman that is able to get the insight into the fact that women in general are being treated as sexual objects, because she has nothing to gain by it. She can't get married and get the "free ride" which is really very costly. So, having nothing to gain by it, she's the first to object to society's forcing the sexual standard on women.

The second to notice it is the less attractive woman who realizes that she has little to gain by the sexual standard. And what these women are saying to us is, why should society be allowed to force one standard of what is attractive about a woman down everybody's throat? And force that standard down everybody's throat to such an extent that the unattractive woman is held up to ridicule.

MIKE: Even if the leaders of Women's Lib are aggressive, even if they are lesbians, they are getting response. If they didn't, the movement would die. And this movement is accelerating.

LARRY: But the fact is that according to polls most women think that there is something odd about Women's Liberation.

BILL: Sure, because they watch television.

LARRY: What is happening in the marriages of women who are trying to rethink their whole situation and take offense at things men are accustomed to saying and doing?

BILL: I'll tell you what's happening in my marriage. I guess the story has been enacted a million times. My wife and I were married thirty years ago. She had three years of college when she met me. The day we were married she stopped going to college because I needed her to take care of the house. She accepted that. Thinking back, even that long ago there was a resentment on her part. I didn't want her to work. I come from a milieu where a woman worked only when her husband was a drunkard, a gambler, played the horses, and didn't have any money. It was a disgrace. So, in my marriage there was no value in my wife's going to college, because I never intended that my wife should work. She gave up her education and then we had two children. Throughout all these years she serviced my needs. Someone is servicing your needs now, if you are married. Then my wife became involved in Women's Liberation, and I am being made to understand now for the first time in thirty years that I am dealing with another human being—and it is a very painful thing. It has been slow for me, but there is no way out of it where my marriage is concerned.

WARREN: Can you tell us some of the things that have been happening in your family situation?

BILL: Well, my daughter is very conscious of this whole thing too. I used the word "chick," and I didn't think there is anything derogatory about it, but my daughter and my wife felt very strongly about people using that term with women. I've begun to think more carefully about what I say about women.

LARRY: My wife is a college graduate and very bright. Before we got married she was never really happy at jobs she had. The people at work always got her down. I'm pleased that she's home. I think it would be unfair to send her into the work world that I'm in because it's so unpleasant.

BILL: You are not supposed to be *sending* anybody. Just think about what you just said!

WARREN: I've found that I'm free to do the writing and the working that I am doing in part because my wife decided she would pursue a career and do the things that she really wanted to do. I'm a more liberated person as a result of her decision to liberate herself.

LARRY: But what do you think the Women's Liberation movement is going to mean in bed? Will it change what people want from sex? Will it make woman more often the aggressor? I don't see any better way of my ego being satisfied than if a woman is aggressive, moving around freely and happily. If she is free to be active, that to me is very sexually gratifying.

HAROLD: I agree, but is that happening?

MIKE: It is happening, but sometimes it's a problem. I do a lot of work in the area of marital problems in my writing, so I talk to a lot of marriage counselors and therapists. Many come to them and complain: "My wife is too aggressive." Men haven't been conditioned to this. They feel threatened by it.

JIM: Aggressive is the wrong word; it implies that a woman is taking over. These men who complain are missing the point. There's nothing aggressive about a woman suddenly coming to recognize her own sexuality and becoming strong enough as an individual to express that.

MIKE: The fact is men are still hung up about it.

BILL: On the contrary, what is bugging most guys is that women are totally passive. They'd be happy if they found a partner in bed who really began to assert herself.

LARRY: Is Women's Lib going to make a woman so demanding of orgasm that no man will be able to please her? Is she going to adopt the male standard of saying, well, if I am not getting any good sex in this marriage I am going to go outside and get it?

JIM: That's entirely possible.

HAROLD: Women can cut out now, and do cut out now without permission of their husbands, in order to find extra sex.

LARRY: But will Women's Lib encourage that by telling women that sexual pleasure is their birthright?

BILL: Is sexual pleasure your birthright?

LARRY: No, but I am going to get it.

BILL: So, why shouldn't your wife have it?

LARRY: Because it may hurt me.

BILL: It's not going to hurt you. It's only going to hurt you if you maintain that sexual pleasure is your prerogative and not hers.

LARRY: Well, what about the male reaction? I pay her bills and she is beholden to me to a considerable degree. I'm not saying it's fair, but if she depends on me it's inevitable that I'll use her dependency for leverage, to satisfy my ego needs and other needs such as doing my laundry. That's the way the world works. That's what my boss does to me and it's what his customers do to him.

WARREN: That's called prostitution.

STEVE: Prostitution happens to the guy, too, in all kinds of subtle ways. But sexually, once you have her trapped, then you are trapped. So, if she has a very nice looking girl friend, you cannot make it with the girl friend. Right? Because you're trapped into not making it. You have to go oustide and hustle around and look for it when she's not around. It's awful.

HAROLD: Let's take this thing one step further about aggressiveness in bed. What kind of sexual responsibility has Women's Lib placed on men? After all, a man will probably have an orgasm first, prior to his woman, and it places a great deal of responsibility on the man to have to wait for her.

MIKE: There are a few answers to that. If you have a loving relationship it's not a matter of responsibility. It's a matter of wanting to satisfy the other person.

LARRY: What about the myth that the vaginal orgasm is the only mature womanly orgasm?

WARREN: Well, it's been a real contribution of Women's Lib to publicize this as wrong. Vaginal orgasm is set up to please the man. The clitoris is very sensitive—the equivalent of the penis—which means that women can have endless orgasms without men to help them.

BILL: Germaine Greer said that even if she has a clitoral orgasm she feels much better when there is a penis in her vagina. I think what she is saying has a lot of meaning.

LARRY: Women can live sexually without men, but I don't think many would want to. Men can masturbate, too. But who prefers that?

WARREN: We have to stop being so afraid of a woman having sex without us, or being afraid of a woman having sex with another man.

GIL: I don't feel insecure about my girlfriend having sex by herself or with somebody else. It doesn't cross my mind.

LARRY: Let me raise something here, it has to do with sexual roles. A girl who is working for me asked for a raise—

JIM: Excuse me, how old is she?

LARRY: About twenty-four.

JIM: Why do you call her a girl?

LARRY: I would call her a girl if she were forty.

JIM: If a forty-year-old person with a penis came in would you call him a boy?

LARRY: No.

JIM: I think that it would help vastly if you would refer to them as women in your mind. Call them women and react to them as women. It helps. It's the same thing with blacks years ago; you called them boys and it kept them at a lower level.

GIL: I think it's a great compliment if they are over thirty five and we call them girls.

BILL: Not anymore it isn't.

LARRY: Well, she wanted a raise and I gave her a raise, but she wasn't happy with it. The thing that was on her mind most was that if she were a guy she would be making more money.

WARREN: Is it true?

LARRY: She wouldn't be typing bills if she were a man.

WARREN: Would you hire me to type letters? Seriously, if I came into your office and showed my resume, my college degree and all, what would you say?

LARRY: I'd say, well look, Warren, do you intend to get pregnant? (Laughter)

JIM: The probability that a woman will leave her job within the first five years is less than it is for men. Employers say we cannot hire her because she is going to get married and pregnant and leave. In fact, the probability is higher that the man you hire is going to leave.

GIL: Let's talk about women wanting equal jobs for equal qualifications. I don't think they really have equal qualifications. I'll give you an example. I was at Amherst and this girl I knew was at Mt. Holyoke. We were both in the same astronomy course, same professor, I in the men's section, she in the women's. Their book, their test for the entire semester was a book that we men were assigned to do in three days. That was the difference. She showed me her final exam. One of the questions was to name the planets in descending order away from the sun. While I sweated my tail off on chemical makeups and supernovi and things like that, she was writing "First comes Mercury, then comes Venus." So as far as hiring women college graduates to type, I would check if they could really type first.

WARREN: Obviously Gil disagrees with the whole premise of Women's Lib, with which most of us agree somewhat—that is, that men and women can successfully change roles.

LARRY: My point is that the Women's Lib movement has turned a lot of women into soreheads and gripe artists. They go around searching for insults, looking for injustices being done to women, yet at the same time want every one of the privileges and protections the despised "chivalry" gives to women!

JIM: Let me give you some evidence about how the inequality of women develops. Look at the education of boys and girls, starting with grade one. There are very, very few differences between them. The level of accomplishment across all fields, mathematics, science, as well as literature, is about the same. Slightly higher for the girls actually. They have higher grades in certain types of IQ tests.

It is not clear whether girls are really superior or just conform better to the educational system's image of a good student, because they sit quietly with their hands folded while boys run around the room and tend to be more rambunctious and aggressive.

WARREN: Is this an education feedback, that women learn to obey more effectively at a young age?

JIM: Most teachers will tell you this. What they want more than anything else is decorum.

GIL: Could that be that most of the teachers at the grade level are women?

JIM: Most of them are women, but I don't understand what bearing that has.

GIL: Well, Steve said he graded people for looks; maybe women teachers grade people on sex too, at least in terms of behavior.

JIM: Perhaps they do. But, the point is, early in this training you find relative equality with perhaps the girls having the slight advantage. But around puberty, when sex becomes terribly important, you find a dramatic shift in the opposite direction. The girls drop off precipitously in their abilities in the things that are called abstract, like mathematics and physics and chemistry and biology, and they continue at a fairly comparable level on the verbal.

The college board scores have different scales for determining percentile scores. If a boy gets 700 on the verbal, it is worth maybe the 85th percentile. For a woman, it is only worth the 80th percentile, because she is supposed to be better in the verbal area. But 700 mathematical might be worth 95 percentile for a woman, but only 85 percentile for a man, because by and large the whole scale for women is shifted downwards in those categories. It is clearly a cultural thing. It can't be biology.

BILL: So people become what they are supposed to become.

JIM: That's right. I was trying to give you some evidence for strong cultural conditioning.

GIL: The reason that I hold women in contempt is, for whatever reason, they have turned out deserving of it. I'm not saying that if you didn't raise women in a different way they wouldn't be different. However conditioned she is, a woman chooses certain goals, and if she succeeds in achieving them and is happy I don't see what the hassle is. If a woman, for example, has rationally decided that she wants to marry a guy with a lot of money or who has a Ph.D. or for whatever reasons, and she does it and is happy, then I'm delighted.

WARREN: But that's like saying: "I programmed this card a certain way, put it through the computer, took it out and, gee whiz! fantastic! It wants to be the way it was programmed!" That's ridiculous, Gil.

LARRY: Warren, you are asking us to upset an order that has worked terrifically for us, to satisfy some extremist rhetoric.

WARREN: Oh yeah, real terrifically. Almost every man and woman end up hating each other. The incidence of divorce rises phenomenally as soon as the children grow up. Housewives attempt suicide at an atrocious rate.

GIL: This is a comment about the institution of marriage.

WARREN: The institution of marriage is made up of what we do with the sex roles in marriage. And what we do with the sex roles in marriage is tell the man to achieve, achieve, achieve, and we push him until he is sick and tired of achieving but is caught for the rest of his life in the endless task of proving his masculinity. Meanwhile, we are doing the same type of thing to women in the opposite direction. We are keeping the women in the home where they get sick and tired of the children. They can't get out of their role. Both are reaching the point of diminishing returns in opposite directions—they're driven apart, from themselves and their partners.

LARRY: The simple fact is that this world doesn't function on fairness. My boss doesn't give me his wealth and his job because I'm deserving of it—because I'm smarter than he is and work harder. By the same token, I'm not voluntarily trading places with my secretary simply because I think she deserves it. Nor am I going to keep house for my family. It gets on my nerves, and I'll do everything I can to avoid it. So even if I agree with the issues raised by Women's Lib, and even if most men do, you can expect only minimal voluntary concessions. I can't help but feel that you fellows are trying to ingratiate yourself to women because their militant rhetoric has you afraid they are about to take over. I think you guys have psychological fears that you're cloaking in pious rhetoric.

WARREN: No, Larry—it's the secure man who does not have to worry about a woman being aggressive in bed, or what other people think if he stays home for a year to take care of the children. It's the secure man who doesn't worry about what he looks like doing the dishes or dusting. It's the guy who does have psychological fears that has to have all these artificial ego supports like kow-towing women and beauty symbols to keep his penis alive.

LARRY: You're going to have problems if the children don't have a mother around.

WARREN: You're going to have problems if the man is off proving himself as the best traveling salesman, or golfer, or what have you, and he isn't around. Children need a balanced relationship in the home. All the men who give lip service to "I love my children, they need a good mother" better start asking themselves why, if they love their children, they aren't willing to spend a couple of years with them?

HAROLD: How do we break these role habits that are so stifling?

BILL: One way is to let your wife get out of the bag that she's in, and maybe you can help each other so that neither of you has to be a slave. Men have got to control this whole male aggressive feeling that you've got to go out and provide, and you have got to destroy everybody that ever gets in your way, and you want to go up to some height because someone has told you that's where you belong.

This whole endless routine, which goes through our whole society, brings us into situations like Viet Nam. That may sound funny to you, but I believe one of the reasons we couldn't get out of that place is that it is not manly to admit that you've been defeated. It's not manly to admit you have tenderness. Mussolini once made a statement that what maternity does for women, war does for men. In Nazi Germany they made women into breeding machines. The only difference is the way we apply it here. See?

LARRY: Do women have the education and training to find alternatives to domesticity?

JIM: No, they do not.

BILL: My wife is working for a publisher. She has a very responsible job. Next to her they've got this guy who runs the whole department. And that's it. No matter how good she is or how much they depend on her, she can go no further. It's easy for us to turn our backs on it and deal with it in the male, trivial, superficial way. But, for these women whose lives are being affected by that injustice, it can't be dismissed that easily. And I'm beginning to see that I don't want to dismiss it that easily either.

LARRY: How can Women's Lib relieve a man from being an economic slave?

STEVE: It has changed attitudes. First of all my wife no longer expects me to go out and sell myself just to make more money. Her own frustrations have lessened, so she isn't driving me so hard any more. When a man has a frustrated wife at home, what does he do? He says, money will solve the problem. Okay? All right, money does solve problems, but it's not the answer to *that* problem.

JIM: Because it becomes a dual burden for him. It's not only a burden to succeed for himself. He also has to succeed for her and for the kids and for his mother and his cousins and aunts and uncles and everyone else.

LARRY: Since one of the gripes of Women's Lib is that their potential is not realized, but rather stifled, what steps do you take to redefine roles? Do you think the dating system must change?

WARREN: Oh yes, the dating scene expresses the very essence of male chauvinism. We want a woman to be independent, and a liberated man goes ahead and says that, while at the same time he is driving the car on the date, paying the bill, has control over the whole situation. She can veto, but she can't initiate.

JIM: A woman, who went through a whole bad marriage scene with kids and everything, and is now free and enjoying her sexuality, was relating this bizarre thing to me about dating.

She was just starting to feel sexy so she went down to a bar and met this really cool guy. She just really wanted to hop in the hay with him. But, she had to play the moronic game and it drove her crazy. You know forty-five minutes of the most boring conversation—it was just awful—until she could finally work it around until everything just naturally led to the sack, which is what she wanted in the first place.

GIL: You are not suggesting that you go up to someone and say let's go to bed?

JIM: There are individuals I think with whom that might be a perfectly acceptable response.

GIL: I was married once and I was constantly trying to keep my wife from showing what an ass she was, at least what I thought she was. Particularly, when you got onto stuff like political science or economics and she would stick her foot into it. And I would say, oh, my God, and look around for forgiveness for having brought this person along.

WARREN: What you are saying now is the perfect example of what I call the sex object trap. The man has selected, and he is stuck.

GIL: I got into the sex trap, then the ego involvement trap, and then I was damned if anyone else was going to lay her, so I married her to keep it from happening.

WARREN: Yes, right.

GIL: And when that need is satisfied, then you start looking for other things and you say, holy smokes, what have I done?

JIM: You're really going to turn into one of the best liberated people around. You're really ready for it.

WARREN: That's for sure. More than anyone, you've been caught by this role stereotyping and magnifying of differences.

LARRY: To what extent do we *need* roles; to what extent do roles solve a lot of communication problems and make for a certain economy in dealing with each other?

JIM: Part of the problem is that we tend to make role and identity synonymous. They should be kept apart, separate. You can have your identity and you can have male identity or female identity, but this shouldn't prescribe for you certain roles. It's perfectly reasonable to be a male and to be soft, be gentle and to cry, to want to take care of children and still be a male, still be a father and a husband. Similarly, it's possible to be a woman and to be female and to be aggressive and forthright and to want to be on top and strive for success and still be a mother and a wife. You have to separate identity from role.

WARREN: Roles don't determine identity. True identity is self-determined.

LARRY: If we don't have these roles that accompany physical gender, are we going to have more homosexuality as a result?

WARREN: A lot less homosexuality coming from the wrong reasons, like a boy who is rejected because his father is never at home.

JIM: I think you will have a lot more homosexuality. I'm pretty much convinced now that biologically we are intrinsically bisexual. If we do away with this role differentiation, and if you do away with society's restrictions in this way, you are going to get more bisexuality.

LARRY: But why should a guy go home to his wife if he has access to all kinds of fancy lovemaking?

JIM: You have access to a library and yet you go home and read. You have access to television in the bar but you go home to watch TV. You have access to liquor but you go home to drink. The trouble is, we take the sex thing and put it in a little compartment over here. We say, this is special.

LARRY: But the stability of the home and the care of the children are integrated with this sexual thing.

MIKE: You have in your mind the traditional model of marriage, and I think that is going to change radically in the future.

STEVE: That's true. Every one of my close friends is engaging in one form or another form of what we might call communal living.

WARREN: How old are you?

STEVE: I'm going to be thirty.

WARREN: And your friends are in communal arrangements broad enough to be open to bisexuality?

STEVE: Right. Everything is open. If a friend is engaging in bisexuality, nobody says anything, nobody cares. And about children: the first to benefit from this kind of breakdown are children, because what you have is a home where the father is gone most of the time and the male image is gone. That extra guy who is around all the time can play another kind of a role with the child. The child is incredibly enhanced. He gets much more security, I think, than he would from a limited familial relationship.

JIM: My family and I just moved into a commune last month. Well, not in the sense that most of the hippie communes are. It's two families. We moved in together. We each have two children. And, yes, we are beginning to see some of these things happening. For example if a kid falls down, skins his knee, he doesn't have to go to his father or mother. He can go to the other adults for comfort.

MIKE: You were asking before, is the Women's Lib movement having an effect? I don't think you can gauge it by how many women belong to cells. A lot of this is a subtle thing which is going on, when your thinking changes and you don't realize it. But, I think it is making a profound impact.

21. *The Invisible American Father*

HENRY B. BILLER, and DENNIS L. MEREDITH

The modern father has been relegated to a second-class role in the family. His importance has been ignored, not only by society but until recently by the social scientist. Thus, the contemporary father, often uneasy with his role, ignorant of its importance, and subject to profound social pressures, has resorted to the accumulation of material goods, lessened involvement at home, and often abandonment of his family.

Father-absence in America is a wide-spread and profound problem—over 10 percent of the children in this country live in fatherless homes. In some ghettoes the figure is as high as 50 percent. These statistics give some indication of the scope of the problem, but they fail to spell out the serious consequences of the paternal deprivation found in even many so-called "father-present" American families. Research and clinical work with both intact and "broken" families have revealed a wide-spread lack of the father-involvement necessary for the optimal personality development of children.

In order to understand the father's role in the family, it is helpful to clarify the concept of sex-role—a person's masculinity or feminity. There seem to be at least three basic and interacting components to this important facet of personality: sex-role orientation, the self-concept a person holds about his masculinity or feminity; sex-role preference, the way a person evaluates certain socially sex-typed activities, such as games and toys; and sex-role adoption, the success with which a person takes on an appropriate sex-typed role in interactions with his physical and social environment.

But what of the relationship between masculinity and feminity? To use a simplistic analogy, if the psychologies of the sexes can be represented by two spheres, the "natural" relationship of these spheres is overlapped, like two bubbles linked. Thus a man may have some traits that are "feminine" and a woman some that are "masculine." We should emphasize that definitions of appropriate sex role behavior are heavily influenced by cultural values and vary somewhat from society to society. In our society, the person with the best chance of vocational and interpersonal fulfillment is one who can comfortably possess traditionally feminine traits such as nurturance and sensitivity, as well as traditionally masculine traits such as assertiveness and independence. We should stress, though, that there appear to be constitutionally predisposed sex differences, and these differences cannot be ignored or expected to take a psychological "back seat." For instance, scientists studying infants have found that even before socialization males are usually more physically active and more muscular, while females are usually more sensitive to environmental stimuli and more responsive to affection.

Unfortunately a sex-role segregation is present in most societies, and it has contributed greatly to the father alienation which we shall discuss. There seems to be the idea that the spheres of sexuality are to be separated, and any crossing over should be socially forbidden. For instance, the American male is often afraid to express physical affection for his son. This polarized male-female view overemphasizes the separateness of the sexes, disregarding the simple fact that being human is more important than being male or female.

Another dangerous stereotype is that the sexes represent psychological opposites. "Unmasculinity" is not the same as "femininity," and vice versa. Unmasculine or unfeminine behavior, rather, may indicate an insecure person whose sex role does not occupy a firm, satisfying place in his self-concept. This insecurity, as we shall see can be the result as well as the cause of a father deprived upbringing.

Father's role in the family

Recent research has revealed the father's significant influence on the sex-role development of both his male and female offspring. He tends to differentiate considerably more than the mother between his sons and daughters and rewards his children's sex-appropriate behavior more than she does. The father thus helps to delineate his child's sex-role and reward his child's positive evaluation of his or her maleness or femaleness.

A boy's adequate sex-role development hinges on a warm relationship with a father or father-figure who is himself masculine. Generally, boys who have passive, ineffectual fathers are less masculine and less well-adjusted than boys who have interested fathers who play a decisive role in the family. The father provides his son with an important model of masculinity in action. This model not only affects the boy's feeling about himself, but his ability to interact with children and adults of both sexes.

The father's influence on his daughter is also very substantial. The father-daughter relationship not only provides the female child a model for interaction between the sexes, but by valuing her individuality he fosters development of a positive feminine self-concept. Of course, the father can also contribute to the development of maladaptive behaviors in his children. An example is a father who has a very rigid and negative view of femininity and encourages his daughter to conform to his stereotype. Unfortunately, in Western society, femininity is often associated with passivity, dependency, and timidity. Feminine patterns of behavior which are best fostered by both father and mother include expressiveness of warmth, sensitivity to the needs of others, and pride in being a female. Ideally the father encourages warmth and sensitivity in his sons as well as his daughters.

Another important role for the father is that of helping to set long-range goals for the family. The father's competency can complement that of the mother in coping with family problems and developing meaningful goals. Because he is usually the chief dealer with institutions outside the family, the father also influences much of the social and intellectual development of his children. Father-deprivation, as we shall see, can have long-lasting adverse effects on a child's intellectual, as well as interpersonal functioning.

The invisibility of the American father is very much connected to the recent history of Western society. Industrialization had profound effects on the family, particularly in the late 1800s, taking the father away from home more extensively than ever before. The relative unavailability of the father seemed to force him into a more peripheral family role. In some segments of American society the father has been, thus, psychologically disenfranchised. And this devaluation of his paternal role often passes from father to son, generation to generation, like a family curse.

He has often been left out in the cold by the social scientist.

Surveys of the literature reveal that less than 10 percent of the studies on parent-child relationships take into account the father's role. This ratio exists in spite of the statistics—not completely facetious—that 50 percent of all parents are fathers. Many times the father seems to be included in family studies only as an afterthought.

Disregard of the father could be due to a reluctance by social scientists to examine what seems to be a secondary role of the male. While motherhood is traditionally strongly associated with femininity, fatherhood in our society is not usually considered an essential dimension of masculinity. Many researchers have observed that social scientists tend to neglect roles that persons play with detachment, shame, or resentment. The role of father might indeed have become one of these.

By spot-lighting the mother's importance, social scientists inspire even more mother-oriented research. This vicious cycle has produced a badly lopsided view of the family.

Although far from complete, research done on the father's role in the family has produced results consistent enough to indicate serious problems related to father deprivation.

Effects of father-deprivation

Ironically it may be better for a child to have no father at all than one living with him but uninvolved in his upbringing. While the father-absent child may find an adequate father-substitute in a friend, relative or other male, the child with an uninvolved father may be "stuck" with his natural and inadequate predecessor. An inadequate father may lead the child toward a negative stereotyped view of adult males, short-circuiting his search for a masculine model.

The effects of father-absence are most felt in the preschool years, when the child is developing what appears to be the foundation for his later sex-role development. Without a father the male child has little opportunity to interact with and imitate males in positions of competence. Girls in the same situation have difficulty developing a positive concept of masculinity and how it complements their femininity.

Father-deprived individuals are more likely to have problems in their relationships with the opposite sex, stemming from a lack of a secure sex-role orientation and a low level of self-confidence. Studies of the family backgrounds of both male and female homosexuals reveal a very high incidence of father-deprivation.

Sexual problems often arise in father-deprived children because of an overly intense relationship with the mother and from lack of opportunity to observe appropriate male-female relationships. For example, researchers have found that homosexuals of both sexes frequently characterize their fathers as weak and incompetent. Also, maladjusted behavior in dating and marriage relationships often appears linked with inadequate fathering.

We should stress that the quality of the father-daughter or father-son relationship is more important than the absolute amount of time the father spends at home. Some of the most confused children have been produced by families in which the father spent a considerable amount of time at home, but did not develop an affectionate and meaningful relationship with his child. The father who is dynamic and active with his friends and at work, yet follows the nap-on-the-couch, newspaper-reading, television-watching route at home may create a fatherless atmosphere just as surely as if he were not there.

The relationship between parents also determines to a great extent the father's influence on the personality development of the child. In one study by Biller a thorough evaluation of the aspects of sex-role —orientation, preference, and adoption—was done on 186 kindergarten boys. It was observed how the children drew figures of people and participated in imagining situations, what games and toys they preferred, and how their teachers rated them on typical male traits. The children were also interviewed to assess their concept of their parents' influence in the family (e.g., "Who's boss at home? Who in your family knows the most about animals? Who tells you when to go to bed at night?"). Finally the parents' relationship was determined by observing how the parents changed or modified their individual opinions when they were together.

A consistent relationship was found between the degree of importance the boys attached to their fathers and the boys' masculinity. The degree to which sons perceived their fathers as having an influential family role was positively related to the boys' masculinity of sex-role orientation, preference, and adoption.

This does not mean that the father demands submission from the mother, but that he is secure and effective in his role in the family. In a well-functioning family there is a mutual relationship between parents in decision-making—with both parents effective and involved. A dominating, restrictive father can injure a child's sex-role development. Several unmasculine boys had fathers who were very influential in father-mother interaction but who were also controlling and restrictive of their sons' activities. This type of father—the male counterpart of the domineering, overprotective mother—seemed to punish his son for functioning independently or disagreeing with him.

It is clear that the child's sex role development seems to be most facilitated when both parents warmly accept the child and encourage exploration and mastery of the environment.

A child's personality development is greatly fostered by an affectionate relationship with a father who encourages initiative and independence. A child who has been distant from his father may show anxiety and discomfort in his relations with others. Many studies have shown that boys with active, involved loving fathers are more popular, friendly, and take more initiative than their paternally deprived child counterparts. The father-deprived child is often not secure in·the presence of males. He has had limited, often negative experience with them, so he is not sure how they will react to him.

A growing body of scientific evidence indicates an association between father deprivation and a variety of different types of psychopathology. These disturbances are frequently linked to inadequate sex-role development. Both paternally deprived males and females have been found to have a greater chance of becoming neurotic or schizophrenic. Many father-deprived children show an inability to control their impulses or to plan ahead. They have not developed the feeling of confidence or efficacy in controlling their environment that an involved father would help them to develop.

The upbringing of a child in a fatherless household is very much affected by the mother's reaction to her predicament. She may feel abandoned by her husband and as a result develop negative attitudes about males that affect her child-raising. This negative outlook may cause her to devalue her sons and discourage both her sons and daughters from interacting with males. Many studies of father-absent children have shown that the mother often does not encourage masculinity in her male children or show her female children the value of masculinity to an extent necessary for their balanced development. Other studies have suggested that among middle-class mothers, those who are husband-absent are more protective and restrictive of their children's activities than those whose husbands are present.

The absence of inadequacy of the father is not invariably associated with negative consequences for the child. For example, having a father absent but a warm meaningful relationship with the mother is better than growing up in a family in which there is constant mother-father conflict. Researchers have paid far too little attention to variations among father-mother and father-child relationships when they have compared father-present and father-absent children. Many variables must be considered if one is to clearly understand the effects of father absence. These variables include the reason for and timing of the absence, the family's sociocultural background, the child's sex and developmental level, the quality of the mother-child relationship, and the availability (and adequacy) of surrogate models including siblings.

Father-absence or father-deprivation can also affect the intellectual development of a child.

A study by Robert Blanchard and Biller reveals the effects of inadequate fathering on academic functioning. Third-grade boys were separated into the following groups: (1) early father-absence (before age five); (2) late father-absence (beginning after age five); (3) low father-presence (less than six hours per week); (4) high father-presence (more than two hours per day of father-child interaction). Their achievement test scores and their grades were compared. The high father-present group demonstrated a much higher level of academic performance compared to the other three groups. They consistently received superior grades and performed above grade level on the indexes of academic achievement. The late father-absent and low father-present group generally functioned slightly below grade level, and the early father-absent group generally functioned a year below grade level.

These results dramatize both the negative effects of early father-absence on a boy's intellectual development, and the equally clear positive effect of high father-involvement.

The children in the Blanchard and Biller study were from predominantly working-class backgrounds. There is evidence that inadequately fathered middle-class children are not as handicapped in their verbal functioning but they, too, often seem to be somewhat hampered on tasks requiring analytical and quantitative skills. Again, the behavior of the mother and the sociocultural background of the family must be taken into account in determining the specific effects of paternal deprivation.

Social consequences

If the psychological impact of the ineffectual father is serious for the individual child, the social consequences of widespread father-deprivation are even more profound.

Father-absent or paternally deprived teenagers are generally found to be more often delinquent than those who are adequately fathered. The father-deprived male often lacks a model of self-control and competence in coping with his environment. This, along with the absence of a basis for dealing with authority figures and an over-compensation for a feeling of unmasculinity can predispose him toward antisocial behavior.

Assessing the damage caused to a family by father-deprivation is difficult because father-deprivation is also associated with economic deprivation, which also has profound effects. Available data, however, suggest that the negative effects of paternal deprivation of families exacerbate those created by economic deprivation. It appears children's personality development can weather economic storms much better if a father is present and actively involved. In fact, father-deprivation may be a contributing factor to economic deprivation. Studies of father-deprived individuals indicate they are more likely to be unemployed; this cannot be attributed directly to, but is probably aggravated by, father-deprivation.

Fathers as well as their children suffer the consequences of father-deprivation. The child-deprived father misses out on the gratifying experience of contributing to his child's development into a successful adult. Thus, he loses a unique opportunity to learn to deal sensitively and meaningfully with human problems.

This is a contributing factor to the so-called generation gap. The wide-spread father alienation in Western society has contributed to the production of large numbers of socially insensitive men in police work, school administration, and other positions involving dealings with the young. Their alienation as fathers has damaged their ability to interact successfully with others. The result is friction, misunderstanding, sometimes tragedy.

Perhaps it might be possible to alleviate some of these strains on our society and help develop in our authority figures a better feeling and understanding of others by bringing more women into these highly interpersonal jobs. For instance, many of the frictions of the ghetto, the university, and even the average city street might be overcome if 50 percent of our officers were women. Women in our sexually polarized society bear much of the family responsibility for handling interpersonal relationships, yet in many roles which depend extensively on skills in dealing with people, they are often conspicuously absent.

A more natural partnership than two male policemen on a beat might be a policeman and a policewoman, each personality complementing the other—a sort of "family" approach to law enforcement. Such a partnership would not only improve the image of authority figures, but would provide useful role models of successful interaction of the sexes.

An obvious objection to this scheme would be that women could not handle some of the brutalities encountered in law enforcement. But on closer examination might not this objection be another example of the traditional view of women as passive and helpless?

Ironically, the hard-hat mentality and the bomb-throwing radical outlook may both have the same roots—a family in which the father is alienated from the job of raising his offspring. A man in such a family, divorced from the father role, may lack the deep feeling for others that an involved fatherhood would instill in him. The child of such a family might easily develop a lessened sense of discipline and security—a child whose frustration and feeling of inefficacy might engender violent or antisocial behavior.

The Women's Liberation movement is very much concerned with the lack of responsibility of men in the child-rearing process. Women have a very legitimate grievance in their treatment at the hands of a polarized male society. But perhaps most germane to this discussion are their valid assertions that heaped on them is an unfair portion of child-raising.

Less valid is the implication on the part of some liberationists that females should occupy exactly the same sociological and psychological niche as males. Job restrictions on women are intolerable, but also intolerable are assertions that women must be just like men in their psychological functions and aspirations.

Equally intolerable is the idea that "men are men and women are women and never the twain shall meet"—that they are separate, opposite personalities. Ideally we should recognize that although biopsychological differences in the sexes do exist, and these differences do affect behavior, that the sexes more importantly are two facets of the same human species.

Remedies

The basic antidote for the alienation that has taken the American male out of family life is improved appreciation of the value of active fathering. A widespread campaign should be mounted to convince males, both young and old, of their "father-power." Using our educational system and mass media we should emphasize the active part a father must play in the family to insure his children's development into mature, well-adjusted adults.

It is interesting to observe that in the many years television has been a force in our society, there has been an almost total lack of programs (with exceptions such as "Father Knows Best," and more recently "The Smith Family" and "Apple's Way") which portray an active and effective father. In fact programs such as "The Courtship of Eddie's Father," "To Rome with Love," "Family Affair," and until recently "My Three Sons," have depicted active fathering as aberrant behavior occurring only in the absence of a mother.

The dangers of the "elusive" father and the inequity of expecting the woman to bear the burden of child-rearing should also be stressed in this campaign. With more understanding and confidence in his potential importance the American father might reemerge from the woodwork.

Greater emphasis and support must be given to father-surrogate programs, such as Big Brother, which is geared to older children, and to the development of similar programs for both boys and girls under age five. The first few years of a child's life are particularly crucial in establishing his sex-role orientation, interpersonal skills, and intellectual values.

We must also deal with the paucity of male teachers in the lower elementary school grades, nursery schools, and kindergartens. This lack of masculine models greatly decreases both boys' and girls' chances to observe competent males. The unavailability of male teachers also leads many children to view intellectual pursuits as feminine, rather than a legitimate function of both sexes. Many father-deprived boys overcompensate for their lack of masculine security, adopt a "tough guy" attitude, and reject education as unmasculine.

Female teachers often stifle assertiveness, initiative, and independence—appropriate characteristics of both boys and girls, but ones which the tradition-oriented female teacher may not value. Additionally, female teachers usually respond more favorably to girls than to boys.

The paucity of male teachers can also compound the effects of paternal deprivation at home. The male child, seeing a large incongruency between the values of his peer group and the overwhelming female establishment, may become conflicted and rigid in his behavior. This rigidity may take the form of either an overcompensating hypermasculinity or hyperfemininity.

Another way of alleviating the lack of masculine influence in schools would be to relocate existing male teachers into the lower grades. A system of teacher rotation might further spread the male teacher's influence, so that all students would have some access to a competent male model. Perhaps retired men, older boys, and other male volunteers could be brought into classroom or playground situations, giving children a chance to observe males, not only engaged in intellectual pursuits, but successfully coping with other issues in their environment.

The problem of father-deprivation transcends social and economic class boundaries. The father is an important part of the complex series of interrelationships that constitute the family, and both males and females must come to realize this if the family is to remain an effective social institution.

Bibliography

1. Biller, H.B.: Father, Child, and Sex Role; Paternal Determinants of Personality Development (Lexington, Mass.: Heath-Lexington Books, Heath & Company, 1971).
2. Biller, H.B., and Weiss, S.D.: The father-daughter relationship and the personality development of the female. J. Genet. Psychol. 116:79, 1970.
3. Biller, H.B.: Father absence and the personality development of the male child. Devel. Psychol. 2:181, 1970.
4. Biller, H.B.: Father dominance and sex-role development in kindergarten-age boys. Devel. Psychol. 1:291, 1969.
5. Biller, H.B.: The mother-child relationship and the father-absent boy's personality development. Merrill-Palmer Quart. 17:227, 1971.
6. Blanchard, R.W., and Biller, H.B.: Father availability and academic performance among third grade boys. Devel. Psychol. 4:301, 1971.

Comment by:
Irving Bieber

Recognition of the central importance of the father's role in personality development and in serious emotional disorders has not been sudden. In 1962, my colleagues and I published a long-term investigation comparing two groups of men, one homosexual, the other heterosexual.[1] The study documented paternal influence in engendering homosexual problems in a son; in fact, we found that the father's role was at least as important as the mother's. I have repeatedly emphasized that when a father is warmly and affectionately related to his son, though the mother may be attempting a silver cord relationship, the boy does not become homosexual. Furthermore, a father who is constructive to his son will not stand by and permit his wife to take over and relate to the boy in inappropriate ways; such a father protects his son from being infantalized and sissified.

We hear a great deal these days about the deleterious effects of a "weak" father. Whatever that term means precisely, it does not in itself engender homosexuality. If a father is a loving one and wishes his son well, paternal strength or weakness is not decisive. Many fathers have difficulties coping with people and other life situations, yet they are able to raise strongly assertive, effective children who are comparatively free of sexual difficulties, provided love and understanding are there.

The question of absent fathers, however, must be viewed somewhat differently. In these situations, the child rearing responsibility falls entirely upon the mother. Where a mother is psychologically unable to form a stable relationship with a suitable man, her difficulties in this area will negatively influence a child's development. But if a mother is unable to remarry for realistic reasons yet relates well to men, it would be unlikely that such a woman would adversely affect her child. Or, where a father is compelled to be away from home as happens in a war situation, and the mother preserves a positive image of him, the child is not then psychologically fatherless.

The absence of a father or suitable father surrogate may produce deleterious effects in the development of girls as well as boys. In a study that compared wed and unwed mothers, Toby Bieber found that most of the women who were pregnant out of wedlock came from a fatherless home; some had never even had a meaningful relationship with a significant older male figure.[2]

Recent observations also underscore the father's role in producing schizophrenia in children. For many years it had been assumed that schizophrenia resulted primarily from defective mothering. We now know that when a father has serious emotional problems, his effect on his children is never benign and for some conditions, is more decisive than the mother's influence.

References

1. Bieber, I., et al.: Homosexuality—A Psychoanalytic Study of Male Homosexuals (New York: Basic Books, 1962).
2. Bieber, T.B.: A comparison study of Negro wed and unwed mothers. Unpublished doctoral dissertation (Columbia University, 1963).

Comment by:
Leo Davids

Neglect of the father and of his contribution to socialization is indeed a major problem in social science literature as well as the real world. The authors' contention that research has not included the father for such reasons as the shame or embarrassment with which many fathers carry out their roles has considerable merit, but one must add a very simple factor: if researchers work a normal nine-to-five day, they will be able to speak with very few fathers. Research on fathers requires interviewing at night or on weekends, when those precious beings have the time to discuss non-economic activities and concerns.

It is not entirely clear in my mind whether father lack is most severely felt when the boy is a pre-schooler, rather than when he is at the threshold of adolescence. Perhaps father absence or deprivation is psychologically most damaging for pre-school children, but reaches its peak in other ways when the child is going through pubescence and the adjustment of the early teenage years. Increasingly, the father's contribution to "launching" his child into the outside world is being substituted by social and educational agencies which can counsel young people preparing to leave their families, provide loans or other financial assistance, and generally do the things which until about twenty years ago were done by middle-class fathers.

Many of the suggestions for supplementing or increasing fathers' influence, which Biller and Meredith make, are valuable. One of the things that is occasionally mentioned by thinkers on this subject is "paternity leave," which differs from maternity leave (time off work when the biological event of birth makes work extremely difficult or hazardous for mothers) in that it need not be restricted to the neonatal period. Paternity leave might be granted to men by an income-supplement scheme which makes it possible for them, say, to work part-time for several years, so that they can spend more hours together with their pre-adolescent children. It may be that severe behavior disturbances in school would stimulate society to demand that fathers should spend more time with such children, as an alternative to this child launching himself into a delinquent career and ultimately requiring help from social service agencies or institutions.

Bibliography

1. Tasch, R.J.: The role of the father in the family. J. Exper. Educ. 20, No. 4, June, 1952.
2. Benson, L.: Fatherhood—A Sociological Perspective (New York: Random House, 1968).
3. Tavuchis, N.: The analysis of family roles; in Elliott, K. (ed.): The family and Its Future (London: Longman Group, 1970).
4. Davids, L.: Foster fatherhood: the untapped resource. Family Coordinator 20:49, 1971.
5. LeMasters, E.E.: Parents in Modern America (Homewood, Ill.: Dorsey Press, 1970).